Date

# Projects in Oral Interpretation

# PROJECTS IN
# *Oral*
# *Interpretation*

GLADYS E. LYNCH

Late of the State University of Iowa

AND

HAROLD C. CRAIN

San Jose State College

**A Holt-Dryden Book**

HENRY HOLT AND COMPANY · NEW YORK

# PREFACE

THIS BOOK DEALS WITH THE FUNDAMENTAL ASPECTS OF INTERPRETATION and has been written to assist the beginning student to understand the bases of his art and develop skills in its performance. Breaking up a complex art form into its component parts in order that each principle and each skill can be grasped and mastered by the student is the aim of every teacher. A second essential objective is the classification and arrangement of principles and skills in an orderly progression. This book grew out of the effort to achieve these goals.

It is also the result of an effort to design a course for the student whose interest in interpretation may lead him in any of several directions—the study of literature, acting, platform reading, radio and television performance, story-telling, impersonation, or any other of the related arts. The desire was to extract and present those principles common and fundamental to all areas that could be taught in a first course, either serving as a foundation for more specialized and advanced work or complete in itself.

A further consideration was the need for a flexible book useful in different kinds of teaching situations. The teacher may want to omit some projects and assign only the study of theory in others. Such an adjustment may be desirable in a one-semester course. Some instructors may not want to use all the voice and diction material. The authors have believed fully in the need to integrate all the materials included in this book when teaching interpretation. But the teacher will permit emphasis and proportion in choice of materials to be determined by the situation in which he finds himself.

Dr. Lynch's death leaves me with a deep sense of loss. She was a woman of high courage, a friend valued by many of us who knew her. She was a teacher devoted to the highest artistic development of her students and persistent in searching for the most effective means of accomplishing her goals. To work with her in planning and refining the course out of which this book grew was a valued privilege. To complete the book at her request was an honor and a responsibility I have approached humbly. For the errors to be found I take full blame. To Dr. Lynch we owe the vision of the basic approach to teaching interpretation reflected here. To the many students of both of us is owed the opportunity to test these projects.

My thanks are due the many people—librarians, colleagues, typists—who have assisted in the preparation and criticism of this manuscript. I am especially grateful to Professor Ward Rasmus for his precious vacation days devoted to reading and checking the pages of this book.

H.C.

*San Jose, California*
*January 1959*

# Acknowledgments

Thanks are tendered to the following for permission to reproduce the cited passages. Page references are to this book.

GEORGE ALLEN AND UNWIN LTD.: Excerpt from *Playboy of the Western World* by J. M. Synge (copyright 1935) (pp. 217 ff.).

CURTIS BROWN, LTD.: Excerpt from *Mr. Pim Passes By* from *Second Plays* by A. A. Milne (p. 270). Reprinted by permission of the author's estate. Copyright © 1921–1948 by A. A. Milne.

JONATHAN CAPE LIMITED: Excerpts from *Anna Christie* from *Pulitzer Prize Plays 1918–1934*, edited by Kathryn Coe and William H. Cordell (copyright 1935) (pp. 270, 272 f., 273) and from *The Emperor Jones*, by Eugene O'Neill (pp. 274 f., 275). Excerpts from "Mending Wall" (p. 28) and "To Earthward" (pp. 73, 76) from *Complete Poems of Robert Frost* (copyright 1930, 1949). Excerpts from "Is My Team Ploughing" (p. 85) and "When I Was One-and-Twenty" (p. 74) from *Collected Poems of A. E. Housman* (copyright 1940).

COWARD-MCCANN, INC.: Excerpt from *Our Town* by Thornton Wilder (copyright 1938) (p. 7).

E. E. CUMMINGS: Excerpt from "nobody loses all the time" from *Poems 1923–1954* (Harcourt, Brace and Company, Inc.; copyright 1926, 1954 by E. E. Cummings) (p. 68).

DOUBLEDAY AND COMPANY: Excerpt from "Recessional" from *The Five Nations* by Rudyard Kipling (copyright 1903 by Rudyard Kipling) (pp. 95 f.).

GERALD DUCKWORTH AND CO., LTD.: Excerpt from *Strife* by John Galsworthy (p. 279). Excerpt from "Trio for Two Cats and a Trombone" from *The Collected Poems of Edith Sitwell* (copyright 1930) (pp. 74 f.).

FABER AND FABER LIMITED: Excerpts from "Preludes" I and II from *Collected Poems 1909–1935* by T. S. Eliot (pp. 74 f.).

HARCOURT, BRACE AND COMPANY, INC.: Excerpts from "Preludes" I and II from *Collected Poems 1909–1935* by T. S. Eliot (copyright 1936) (pp. 74 f.).

HARPER & BROTHERS: Excerpt from *Voice and Articulation Drillbook* by Grant Fairbanks (copyright 1940) (pp. 256 f.).

WILLIAM HEINEMANN LTD.: Excerpt from *The Grapes of Wrath* by John Steinbeck (copyright 1939) (pp. 284 f.). Excerpts from *The Weavers* by Gerhart Hauptmann (pp. 270, 275 f.).

HENRY HOLT AND COMPANY, INC.: Excerpts from "Is My Team Ploughing" (p. 85), "Shot? So Quick, So Clean an Ending" (p. 285), and "When I was One-and-Twenty" (p. 74) from *Collected Poems of A. E. Housman* (copyright 1940). Excerpts from "Mending Wall" (p. 28) and "To Earthward" (pp. 73, 76) from *Complete Poems of Robert Frost* (copyright 1930, 1949). Excerpts from "Chicago" (p. 66) and "The Pasture" (p. 18), and "Fog" (p. 84) from *Chicago Poems* by Carl Sandburg (copyright 1916).

HOUGHTON MIFFLIN COMPANY: Excerpt from "A Lady" from *Sword Blades and Poppy Seeds* by Amy Lowell (copyright 1914) (p. 70).

ALFRED A. KNOPF, INCORPORATED: "Mother to Son" from *The Dream Keeper* by Langston Hughes (copyright 1945) (p. 71).

THE MACMILLAN COMPANY: "Waiting Both" from *Collected Poems of Thomas Hardy* (copyright 1940) (pp. 92 f.) and "The Leaden Eyed" from *Collected Poems of Vachel Lindsay* (copyright 1941) pp. 93 f.).

THE ESTATE OF FERENC MOLNAR, Lili Darvas Molnar, Executor: Excerpt from *Liliom* (pp. 245 f.).

G. P. Putnam's Sons: Excerpt from *Teahouse of the August Moon* by John Patrick (copyright 1952) (pp. 262 f.).

RANDOM HOUSE, INC.: Excerpts from *Anna Christie* by Eugene O'Neill from *Pulitzer Prize Plays 1918–1934*, ed. by Kathryn Coe and William H. Cordell (copyright 1935) (pp. 270, 272 f., 273). Excerpt from *Playboy of the Western World* from *The Complete Works of John M. Synge* (copyright 1907 and renewed 1934 by the Executors of the Author's Estate) (pp. 217 ff.). Excerpt from "The Trap" from *Selected Poetry of Robinson Jeffers* (copyright 1935 by The Modern Library, Inc.) (p. 78) and from "Night" from *The Roan Stallion, Tamar, and Other Poems* by Robinson Jeffers (copyright 1925) (p. 64).

RINEHART & COMPANY, INCORPORATED: Excerpt from *The Green Pastures* by Marc Connelly (copyright 1930) (p. 252).

MRS. LEO SARETT: "Weeng" from *Slow Smoke* by Lew Sarett (copyright 1925 by Henry Holt and Company; 1948 by Lew Sarett) (pp. 246 f.).

CHARLES SCRIBNER'S SONS: Excerpt from "Miniver Cheevy" from *Collected Poems of Edwin Arlington Robinson* (copyright 1952) (p. 28). Excerpt from *The Silver Cord* by Sidney Howard (copyright 1927 by Sidney Howard; renewal copyright 1955 by Leopoldine B. D. Howard) (pp. 250 f.). Excerpt from "Fog's Thickening, Sir" by Morgan Farrell, from *A Quarto of Modern Literature*, ed. by Leonard Brown and Porter G. Perrin (copyright 1935, 1940) (p. 67). Excerpt from *Strife* by John Galsworthy (copyright 1901 by John Galsworthy; renewal copyright 1936 by Ada Galsworthy) (p. 279).

SIMON AND SCHUSTER, INC.: Excerpt from *With Malice Toward Some* by Margaret Halsey (copyright 1938) (p. 99).

EDITH SITWELL: Excerpt from "Trio for Two Cats and a Trombone" from *The Collected Poems of Edith Sitwell* (copyright 1930) (pp. 74 f.).

THE PUBLIC TRUSTEE AND THE SOCIETY OF AUTHORS, LONDON: Excerpts from *Candida* (pp. 212 f.) and from *Man and Superman* (pp. 211 f.) by George Bernard Shaw.

THE SOCIETY OF AUTHORS, LONDON: Excerpts from "Is My Team Ploughing" (p. 85), "Shot? So Quick, So Clean an Ending" (p. 285), and "When I Was One-and-Twenty" (p. 74) from *Collected Poems by A. E. Housman* (copyright 1940).

THE VIKING PRESS, INC.: Excerpt from *The Grapes of Wrath* by John Steinbeck (pp. 284 f.). Copyright 1939 by John Steinbeck. Permission granted by the Viking Press, Inc., N.Y.28 for class use only;

no public reading or any other use without formal authorization from the publishers.

JAMES THURBER: "The Unicorn in the Garden" (© 1939 The New Yorker Magazine) (pp. 259 f.). Excerpt from "University Days" from *My Life and Hard Times* (© 1933 The New Yorker Magazine) (pp. 260 ff.).

A. P. WATT AND SON, MRS. GEORGE BAMBRIDGE, THE MACMILLAN CO. OF CANADA, MESSRS. METHUEN, AND MESSRS. TAUCHNITZ: Excerpt from "Recessional" from *The Five Nations* by Rudyard Kipling (copyright 1903 by Rudyard Kipling) (pp. 95 f.).

# CONTENTS

# Projects in Oral Interpretation

# *I*

# AN APPROACH TO THE STUDY
# OF ORAL INTERPRETATION

THE HUMAN RACE HAS DEVELOPED ITS LANGUAGE AND MEANS OF communication through speech to such a degree of complexity, flexibility, and expressiveness that many years of study and practice are required to achieve mastery of the communicative arts. Nevertheless, these arts are recognized as being so important to the well-being of the individual and of society as a whole that, in spite of the many demands made upon us for our time and energies, we make their study a required part of the education of the young. All through elementary and secondary school attention is given to the mastery of language and the arts of communicating with it by nearly every teacher with whom the child has contact. In many schools specialists attend to his needs if his speech is not up to normal standards. In many high schools the student enrolls for a semester or two in a course which gives full attention to developing his oral communicative skills. In college and university curricula we reserve an important place for advanced study in the speech arts. This study has been organized in many different ways, but usually the division falls roughly into three major areas: constructive speech, interpretative speech, and speech re-education.

All these areas center around the spoken word. Constructive speech is that area of study which involves the organization, reinforcement, and phrasing of the speaker's own ideas and convictions. Speech re-education is the area of study concerned with improvement to a normal standard and the correction of errors and defects in the process of producing sound and articulating words. In interpretative speech the student is concerned with re-creation of the ideas, convictions, and emotions, the characters and actions, the experiences set down by an author. Each area of study deals with a different aspect of oral communication, but the purpose of each is increased effectiveness in human communication, human sharing of experience, and the interplay of human influence through the spoken word. In each area the instrument of communication is the human being, his voice and body. His media of communication are light and sound waves.

The student of constructive speech studies rhetoric, public speaking, debate, discussion, and the many applications of principle involved. The student of speech re-education studies the physics of sound, anatomy, phonetics, psychology, and all the principles to be applied in re-educating faulty speech or improving barely adequate speech. Since the distinguishing characteristic of interpretative speech is the act of re-creation of experience as set down by an author, study in this field includes analysis of literature, the processes of assimilating the experience of others into one's own, the techniques of body and voice which project meaning and experience to an audience, and the facts of human thought and feeling, which affect the audience reaction. The objective of this communicative process is an interactivity between the speaker and his audience in which the speaker shares his thoughts, feelings, and experiences with the audience whose own thoughts and feelings are affected in the process, who react to this experience, and, who in turn, affect the speaker through their response.

The human being finds that this interacting process of communication is of the utmost importance to him. We are constantly being reminded by our experience that we live essentially in isolation in that no feeling, no sensation can be communicated directly or fully to any other person. No one can ever perceive or experience anything quite as we do. Yet—and perhaps because of this fact—to communicate is one of our strongest urges and most intensively pursued goals. We are hungry to know how experience feels to other people. We recognize that some people are more skillful than others in manipulating language so that it permits us to catch vivid glimpses of their feelings. We recognize, too, that the experiences of some people have been richer, more varied than our own. When these people record their feelings and thoughts and experiences in poetry, novels, plays, or other literary forms we are eager to share with them. This sharing is not always easy, however, for the written words are at best a poor guide to the whole content. The words communicate much more to us when they come directly from a human being who can clothe them in emotional tones, in all the symbolism of melody, rhythm, loudness changes, bodily action, and facial expression which human beings have developed to give meaning to their oral discourse. And so we turn to the interpreter to help us—the platform reader, the storyteller, the actor, the mother reading to her child, the minister reading the Scriptures, the announcer, the salesman on radio and television, the teacher reading to her class. All these people employ their skills to help us experience the thoughts, feelings, actions, and reactions that lie within recorded material.

There are, of course, many kinds of material the interpreter can use. It may be primarily factual, expository in purpose, instructive in intent. It may be persuasive, as is usually the case of the radio and television "commercial" performer's material. It may be imaginary or real, lyrical, narrative or dramatic. But as long as the function of the person who presents it is to re-create for an audience an experience of what he finds on the page, he is performing as an interpreter.

Great differences exist between interpreters, differences so great that practitioners of one branch of the art often disclaim kinship with the others. There are ministers who see little relation between their art as readers of the Scriptures and that of the actor playing villain roles in the television Western drama. There are actors who claim little or no kinship with the radio or television announcer or pitch man. There are platform readers who see little relationship between their art and that of the actor on the stage. Differentiations between the platform reader, the impersonator, and the actor have long troubled many people.

The manners in which these interpreters present their materials vary so much as to call attention to their differences. The minister in the pulpit, surrounded by the symbols of his faith and the dignity of the occasion, reads with considerable restraint of physical action and always in the character of a minister of God. The platform reader usually retains his own identity yet tries to minimize his own personality so that he does not himself intrude upon the scene he is creating for his audience. Through suggestion he creates an illusion of physical action. The impersonator, however, intrudes his own person, usually costumed and made up to represent the character he is presenting, as a part of the experience he is bringing to his audience. His presentation is more literal than the platform reader's, more dramatic in form, and at the same time more limited in range of materials to be chosen. The actor is even further removed from the platform reader in that he does not present the whole piece the author has written. He interprets only his part. Like the impersonator he wears costume and make-up to give the illusion that he *is* the character, but he becomes even more a part of a whole by moving within a setting, making entrances and exits, talking directly with other characters, working as one member of a team whose total effort results in an "interpretation" of the author's work.

One difference among the various branches of the interpretative arts, then, is mobility upon the stage. The actor is permitted total mobility by his role, even to the extent of leaving the stage entirely for periods of time. The impersonator is almost as free in motion, although he rarely does more than suggest entrances and exits. The platform reader normally remains very much in one position. A second difference lies in the form of the material. The actor presents only a component part of a work that has been designed for presentation by several participants. The impersonator works with material that usually requires only one character. The reader takes all parts and presents material with many points of view. The actor and impersonator limit themselves to character portrayals; the reader ranges over all literature for his materials. A third difference is the degree to which the interpreter seems to lose his own identity in the act of re-creating his material. The platform reader suggests by voice and gesture, the impersonator is more literal, and the actor is completely literal in his presentation of the character—in appearance, dress, actions, voice, and dialect. The reader usually maintains his identity in the consciousness of the audience. The actor tries to give an illusion of another identity.

The major differences all boil down, then, primarily to a difference in degree of literalness or of suggestion. This difference can be demonstrated in principle if a person grasps the edges of a heavy table and says, with determination, "I am going to lift this!" Let him then move away from the actual table, grasp the edges of an imaginary table, and lift this imagined weight while he says the same words. Now let him feel all the tensions of lifting without lifting anything, and we have suggestion. Within himself the individual feels very much the same in all of these situations, but the externals are different.

The externals, the differences, are very important to each interpreter's art. The actor spends months and even years perfecting his powers of concentration on one character, his pantomimic skills, his techniques of character building, the arts of ensemble playing, his use of costume, make-up, and stage space. The mother reading to her child pays attention to the setting in which she reads, the place of the child by her, the pictures in the book which help to create the mental pictures for the child. The platform reader pays attention to his reading stand, the way in which he handles his book, the lighting, the clothes he wears. All of these details are important enough to warrant special, and in many cases prolonged, training.

The arts of all these various kinds of interpreters, different as they are, spring nevertheless from certain basic and fundamental processes common to each of them. All work with materials already written and all function to re-create the experience in the materials for an audience. Each interpreter is thus faced with the problem of finding the meaning in his materials, of searching them for every shade of logical thought, every nuance of feeling, expressed or unexpressed. He must not only understand the meaning, but also assimilate it into his own thought and feeling processes so thoroughly that it no longer seems to have been someone else's experience and has come to feel like his own. Not until the experience (and a thought is an experience) seems like his own can he re-create it for an audience. Then, in order to re-create it, he must communicate the meaning through the instrument of his own body and voice, using all the techniques of bodily action and control, articulation, and voice production which signify to his audience the meaning he intends and, in addition, cause the audience to attain a similar experience. These three processes—finding meaning, assimilating meaning, and communicating meaning—are the foundations upon which all the interpreters build their work. The principles and the methods which apply to each of these processes are the same whether the final product is a platform reading, a role in a play, an impersonation, a story read to a group of children in a classroom, or any other of the final forms which the interpreter's art may take. The basic preparations are the same for all of these people. The instruments and tools of body and voice, of articulation and pronunciation, of thought and emotion are the same for each one.

At first glance, the principles to be learned and the disciplines to be imposed along the road to artistry in interpretation have an appearance of such simplicity that they would seem too easy to warrant spending much time in learning them. Many, if not all, may even have the ring of familiarity about them. The serious student soon realizes, however, that the simplicity is deceiving and the ring of familiarity represents only a brush with the principles or a gesture in the direction of the discipline, half learned, if at all. Our techniques of reading, especially where we want to achieve total understanding and total assimilation, are never developed so far as we would wish. Most of the time we read quickly and try only for an outline of the content or an impression. But the interpreter must be thorough and methodical. He cannot afford to miss anything. And in his attempt to glean all the meaning he usually discovers he only half knew the principles of reading for meaning. The student usually discovers that the ability to assimilate meaning grows with practice and that his own capacity for receptivity develops as he makes demands upon it. The astonishing and delightful fact is that the more you practice and learn, the more you find to learn and to practice; the richer your experience, the richer it can become. As in all the arts, the more we approach perfection, the further our concept of it grows and the more distant becomes the goal.

Even if one had no intention of becoming an interpreter in one or other form of the art, several important reasons make time spent in the study of the principles and processes involved well worth the student's while. His habits and powers of observation are sharpened. His sensitivity to experience and to the experience of other people— intellectual, emotional, and sensory—becomes keener and makes him more aware of himself and his fellow human beings. As Emily Webb says near the end of *Our Town*

*Oh! Oh. It [life] goes so fast. We don't have time to look at one another . . . . clocks ticking . . . and Mama's sunflowers. And food and coffee. And new-ironed dresses and hot baths . . . and sleeping and waking. Oh, earth, you're too wonderful for anyone to realize you.*

Study in interpretation encourages mastery of the techniques of analysis—reading through the printed words to the nature, mood, and intent of the writer, finding implications of meaning in the words the writer chooses, discovering the function of organization in determining the whole meaning, noting the means by which points are made—these and many other techniques contribute to the general competence of everyone in reading and to his especial pleasure in literature of every kind. Mastering the techniques of interpretation results in greater physical and vocal effectiveness in all communication. The authoritativeness of presentation developed by the skilled interpreter commands attention in almost any situation. He has developed clarity and force in articulation and pronunciation. He has developed a voice fully flexible in pitch, quality, loudness, and timing so that it expresses meaning and feeling. He has disciplined his body to reinforce the expression of his whole thought. And finally, he has become so thoroughly familiar with the literature he has presented that it has made an intimate and forceful contribution to his own life of thought and feeling. These are all important aspects of the liberal education and life enrichment of any man or woman.

There are several reasons behind the design for the chapters which follow and the order in which various topics are studied. Knowing the meaning does not necessarily mean that the interpreter can assimilate meaning or make it his own, especially when he gets ready to communicate. It is perfectly possible to answer any number of questions regarding the meaning of a selection without re-experiencing that meaning at all. During the rehearsals for a play a director occasionally finds an actor who, though highly intelligent and perfectly cast so far as voice and body are concerned, simply cannot act the role. Conferences show that the actor knows all about his character. He could psychoanalyze his character, but he cannot be his character. He cannot make the meaning his thought and feeling. He cannot assimilate. Since more and better assimilation is a continuing goal in oral interpretation, it is studied first. It is assumed that the college student is able to get some meaning from the materials he is given or that he chooses to present. The second unit of study, analysis of material, is presented so that meanings may be more accurate, deeper, and of more importance to the interpreter, and so that he may explore the implications of his material. Finally, communication techniques are analyzed and studied.

Part of a liberal education is the exploration of men's thinking as they have set it down in print. The oral interpreter, especially, needs to become acquainted with the literature of his time and of all time. No anthology could be extensive enough to give the reader the background he should have. Therefore, though authors and specific works will be suggested, every reader will be encouraged to find his own selections to read aloud. In doing so, it is hoped that he will look for material that touches his own experiences and that can be expected to touch the experiences of his audiences. The reader should take note of materials that delight or move him. He will often find that simple things are more universal in their appeal than the bizarre. It is hoped that each reader will consider the tastes of his audience, and will neither offend them with sophisticated innuendo nor insult them with the mediocre. The goals of universality of appeal, individuality of style, and stimulation to further thought and feeling should always be kept in mind.

Historically, a nice balance between the importance of artistic conception and skillful communication to listeners has been difficult to maintain. There is evidence that during the eighteenth and nineteenth centuries the technique of communication was overemphasized, and we had the various so-called "mechanical" schools of speech. The ways in which voice and body communicate meaning were emphasized in great detail. Then came the naturalistic schools of the nineteenth and twentieth centuries, with the theory that if an interpreter knew and felt his meaning he would have no trouble communicating it. More recently, both meaning and technique for communicating meaning have been stressed and eclecticism has been the aim. If the interpreter can think of technique as the manner of artistic performance (the first definition in Funk and Wagnall's *New Standard Dictionary*), he will realize that every performer has technique of some sort—good, mediocre, or bad—and that part of his work as an interpreter is to improve his manner of artistic performance: he needs to learn ways of improving both physical and vocal expressiveness. Since the voice is the most obvious conveyor of meaning in oral interpretation, vocal techniques are stressed more than physical techniques in the projects that follow. Since in acting physical responses are fuller and more obvious than they are in oral interpretation, they will receive more complete consideration in acting courses.

A reader learns much by simply reading aloud to an audience as often as possible. He gradually becomes more aware of his audience instead of being solely aware of his own reactions. In the performances of others he can see techniques that are successful as well as those that exhibit lack of mastery. He can see his own strengths and weaknesses in others and may even find inspiration for renewed work and study when he sees what a delight oral interpretation can be for both reader and audience. Most teachers of oral interpretation therefore prefer to spend class time in hearing the performances of their students. This poses a problem. Even when a short selection is used, time is necessary to present techniques, to hear readings and to criticize them, and students sometimes do not get enough practice before an audience. For that reason, an attempt has been made in the projects that follow to present goals and techniques very simply so that several readings may be heard consecutively. Then all of them may be criticized to see which has been most successful in accomplishing the goals set up.

No student should feel, when the class has finished working on a project, that the goals are accomplished and that he does not need to think about these projects again. The better an interpreter becomes, the harder he will work on assimilation, analysis, and communication of meaning. There is no ceiling on artistic performance. Since, as we noted earlier, perfection recedes as one approaches it, the elusiveness of it makes artistic performance a constant challenge.

Oral interpretation is not a course in the art of imitation. Though Charles Laughton's readings may delight us, we do not try to imitate Charles Laughton. Neither do we imitate each other. In the process of interpreting printed symbols into vivid experience, we must use our own voices and bodies and our own experiences, real and vicarious. One reader may see implications in a selection that have never occurred to another reader, and one reader may have better techniques of communication than another. It is an excellent practice to listen to many readings, both good and bad. But this listening should be done, not to imitate, but to note techniques of communication and to appreciate the fuller meanings that are found.

Many students are concerned about whether they should read from manuscript or work from memory. Some readers find that they have memorized their materials when the selections are fully assimilated and that holding a manuscript distracts them. Others find that, even though they have memorized, they feel far more comfortable and secure if they have a manuscript in hand. Still others are so appalled by the idea of trying to memorize and so fearful that they might forget lines memorized that their reading is very bad. An interpretation should never be judged by whether or not it is memorized. It should be judged by the fullness of meaning, the completeness of assimilation, and the communicativeness of the reader.

There are many reasons for studying oral interpretation, but prominent among them are a desire for greater poise and less stage fright in speaking, and a feeling that the course should be fun and not much work. Let us consider the first reason. Appearing often before any group should develop poise, especially when communicativeness is established. But sooner or later one learns that if a communicative situation is important to him, whether it be reading to an audience, an interview for a job, or an important date, he is going to be anxious about the outcome. It would be a matter of concern if he were not. To keep such anxiety from being paralyzing one must be so sure of *what* he intends to do and *how* he intends to do it that there is no room for a question, expressed or unexpressed, such as "How am I doing?" The reader himself can be very sure of how he is doing by his audience response. All performers experience nervousness or "stage fright" before they perform. But all good performers lose this feeling just as soon as they begin to perform, because they have practiced enough to know exactly what they mean to do and how they mean to do it. They concentrate fully on communicating with the audience and forget to worry about how they look and feel.

The second reason often given for taking an oral interpretation course—that it should be fun and not much work—is half true. It should be fun and satisfying, but satisfaction results from work and self-discipline. Just as attendance at laboratory sections of a laboratory course is required, music students must sign up for a practice room and practice hours at a time, a specific number of pages must be studied for a reading course, and actors must give up some four hours a day for supervised practice for six weeks before they appear in a play—so also must oral interpreters impose vigorous discipline upon themselves. They must find material to interpret early enough so that there is sufficient time for analysis and outloud practice of the selection chosen. They must find a place to practice every day, and realize that two short periods of practice daily are more profitable than one longer period. They should find a person or persons to whom to read the finished product in order to get a degree of audience reaction, but they must learn that the average audience is more critical than a roommate or friend. None of this preparation can be put off because of the pressure of other courses or events. This requires a degree of planning on the part of students that is complex and meticulous. Without such self-discipline a course in oral interpretation can be the dullest in the curriculum; with it, the study of oral interpretation can yield the highest kind of satisfaction.

## Additional Readings

Crocker, Lionel, and Louis M. Eich, *Oral Reading* (ed. 2). New York: Prentice-Hall, Inc., 1955, pp. 1-20; 50-59.

Cunningham, Cornelius C., *Literature as a Fine Art.* New York: Thomas Nelson & Sons, 1941, pp. 259-283.

Johnson, Gertrude E. (ed.), *Studies in the Art of Interpretation.* New York: D. Appleton-Century Company (Appleton-Century-Crofts, Inc.), 1940, pp. 3-76; 79-161.

Lee, Charlotte I., *Oral Interpretation.* Boston: Houghton Mifflin Co., 1952, pp. 3-12; 573-580.

Lowrey, Sara, and Gertrude E. Johnson, *Interpretative Reading: Techniques and Selections* (rev. ed.). New York: Appleton-Century-Crofts, Inc., 1953, pp. 13-25.

McLean, Margaret Prendergast, *Oral Interpretation of Forms of Literature.* New York: E. P. Dutton & Co., Inc., 1942, pp. 9-14.

Parrish, Wayland Maxfield, *Reading Aloud* (ed. 3). New York: The Ronald Press Company, 1953, pp. 3-17.

Robb, Mary Margaret, *Oral Interpretation of Literature in American Colleges and Universities.* New York: H. W. Wilson Co., 1941, pp. 189-213.

Woolbert, Charles H., and Severina E. Nelson, *The Art of Interpretative Speech* (ed. 4). New York: Appleton-Century-Crofts, Inc., 1956, pp. 3-30.

# 2

# PROJECTS IN
# Assimilation

# The Experience of Assimilating

AMONG THE SKILLS ESSENTIAL TO THE ORAL INTERPRETER IS AN ABILITY to make the ideas, emotions, and words of a writer seem to himself and his listeners to emanate, not from an absent author, not from the pages of a book, nor even from somewhere back in memory, but from him, at this moment, as he appears before them. The actor or the reader who is obviously recalling memorized material, whether haltingly or fluently, fails to invest the experience with directness and vitality. The one who mechanically articulates words he sees on the page, like a child parroting the words of his school program "piece," is perhaps even less successful. The reader who keeps the listener conscious of an absent author whose experience this is rather than his own, has failed to succeed. Interpretation is a living, immediate experience, and what takes place between the interpreter and his audience is personal. It is made personal in large part by the interpreter's presentation of the material out of himself. The result of this skill is variously described as *believability, convincingness, reliving, feeling,* and *thinking the thought.* The process involved we call assimilation.

Much as food is digested and made a part of a person, so the writer's materials are assimilated into the interpreter's thinking and experience. He must think the thoughts of the material, see and feel its images for himself until the mood, the structure and content, the very manner of expressing the thought feel like his own, fresh and new at the moment.

If what the interpreter had to say were the spontaneous expression of what he was doing and feeling as he stood before his audience there would be no problem to face and no skill to master. But he goes before his audience to present some other person's words which convey thoughts and experiences far removed from what he is doing and feeling (unless he directs his acts and his responses). When he expresses himself spontaneously in words the speaker responds to his body feelings, his conscious thought, the welter of stimuli which assault him both from within and from without. Almost without his choosing them the words tumble out, and as they do they tend to have their effect on his responses to the stimuli, reforming the sensations of the whole experience. The words reflect the whole experience and at the same time become an experience.

If he were a writer he would put his words on paper, alter and rework them, reshaping as he did so the quality and nature of the whole experience they reflect. The words are a sort of distillation of the whole process. Although they have played their role in forming the feelings and thoughts of the writer, now, frozen on the page, they exist as a pattern of symbols whose function is to serve as a guide to the original experience.

At this point the interpreter enters the picture to become the medium of re-creating for an audience the whole experience the words stand for. He will present the material orally. He will speak the words. But since the words are a distillation, an abbreviation, of the whole complex reaction and formulation they represent, the interpreter must fill in, with voice and body, to complete the communication. Repeating the words through the mechanical process of recognition through the eye and reformulation through the speech mechanism obviously leaves out much. An idea, clearly, is more than words. It must exist as a response of a whole person. Just as it did when it was being written down, it must again exist in the reader's consciousness, in his muscles, his nerves which sense his physical conditions, his chemistry, his very pose.

By directing his thoughts, willing his feelings, concentrating on mental pictures, by giving his whole person over to the process of "having" the thoughts of the selection in himself, of reformulating the whole complex of action and reaction, of sensation, judgment and idea, the interpreter attempts to re-create the poem or story or play in the full sense of its creator. At the moment this is his experience, created by him—guided, defined, and shaped by the original, but none the less being experienced in a very real sense by the interpreter. He has assimilated his material.

The student is reminded that the interpreter *willed* the process, he *directed* his thoughts, and he *gave* his person over to the reformulation. Assimilating material is nothing unusual or out of the ordinary. Everyone employs these processes of the human mind. We use our imaginations constantly in understanding the feelings and thoughts of other people, in inventing things and processes to make life more pleasing. We can daydream when we please, and we can "turn it off" when we please. For the interpreter this principle of willing the re-creation of the experience is important because it takes several tries to make the assimilation complete. The experience grows as one repeats it, exploring further the mental and emotional and physical dimensions of the experience with each repetition. In turn these feelings have a direct effect upon voice and body as they communicate the words to an audience. All those elements of voice and body that carry meaning—pitch, loudness, quality and timing of voice, gestures, stance, and muscular tensions of body—reflect the inner feelings, mental images, and thoughts of a speaker. The fact that the speaker does feel is reflected in voice and body. What he feels is reflected in voice and body. If, then, he feels what the selection directs him to feel, his utterances come out spontaneously, freshly, and—all other elements being under control—accurately. Even before his audience he re-creates the experience of his selection in his whole person, because he must use the feelings to create the vocal and physical effects he wants. He wills yet another repetition, now grown easier through practice, of the entire experience.

Assimilation is not simply an intellectual understanding of ideas. A reader, conceivably, could pass a comprehensive examination on the content of a selection without having assimilated it. Nor is assimilation a critical evaluation. One could discuss the style of an author or the quality of his writing at length without making it one's own. The reader needs not only to have an intellectual understanding and, perhaps, to develop a critical evaluation of a selection, but he also needs an intimate experience with it.

The difference in manner of reading materials the interpreter has thoroughly assimilated and those he has only partially made his own may be demonstrated by comparing spontaneous utterance with reading the same words immediately afterward. Ask a friend to assist you in the demonstration of those differences. Look around the room or out the window and state, in a complete sentence, one thing you see. Ask your friend to write down what you say as you say it. (The demonstration would be even clearer if the friend could write down one of your spontaneous statements when you do not know which one it will be). Now read the written sentence and answer the following questions:

1. Does my reading sound the same to me as my spontaneous statement did?
2. Does my mind work the same in reading and in spontaneous speech?
3. Is my feeling tone the same in speaking and in reading?
4. Do I actually form the idea or the mental image before I begin to speak?
5. When does the idea begin to form and to be important?
6. Does my voice sound different in pitch? In loudness? In timing? In quality?
7. Does my emphasis seem the same in reading and in spontaneous speech?

You may demonstrate to yourself the contrast between the feeling of not having assimilated material and of having made it your own in another way. Read aloud a poem with which you are unfamiliar. Now read aloud a poem you have yourself written or one that has long been a meaningful favorite of yours. Notice the differences in the sound of your voice. Notice the differences in your way of forming mental images. Notice how with the familiar material your whole body is involved in feeling the selection. Note also differences in how you form the ideas and when you form them.

## EXERCISES

1. Some people feel that it is very important that an image be formed in their minds before they begin to speak. Others need to reproduce the whole complex background from which the original statement came. Still others find that they cannot re-experience easily

while looking at the printed page. Read and re-read the experimental sentence copied by your friend to decide what you must do to make it seem and sound as if the sentence were uttered spontaneously. Try a new observation and sentence to test your theories and then write a paragraph summarizing your results.

2. The following poem is so simply phrased that anyone might use these words. Can you read it so that it seems to be your spontaneous statement?

> *I'm going out to clean the pasture spring;*
> *I'll only stop to rake the leaves away*
> *(And wait to watch the water clear, I may):*
> *I sha'n't be gone long.—You come too.*
>
> *I'm going out to fetch the little calf*
> *That's standing by the mother. It's so young,*
> *It totters when she licks it with her tongue.*
> *I sha'n't be gone long.—You come too.*
>
> "The Pasture," ROBERT FROST

As each person reads, let the class rate his degree of assimilation on a scale of one to five, with one being high and five being low. In order to get a clear-cut judgment of relative success in the project, each class member must so spread his ratings that at least one reader is rated one and at least one reader is rated five.

3. Can you give yourself so completely to Lincoln's thought that you forget the following lines are Lincoln's and that they come from his Gettysburg Address? Can you assimilate them to the degree that it seems to you thinking and speaking these thoughts? If you do not already know the passage, you may find it helpful to memorize it.

*But, in a larger sense, we cannot dedicate—we cannot consecrate—we cannot hallow—this ground. The brave men, living and dead, who struggled here, have consecrated it, far above our poor power to add or detract. The world will little note, nor long remember what we say here, but it can never forget what they did here.*

Try to imagine Lincoln's thoughts as he wrote the passage. Try to imagine his memories. Then try to think those thoughts yourself and to remember those same feelings, reactions, and ideas.

## Additional Readings

Aggertt, Otis J., and Elbert R. Bowen, *Communicative Reading.* New York: The Macmillan Co., 1956, pp. 341-364.

Bassett, Lee Emerson, *Handbook of Oral Reading.* Boston: Houghton Mifflin Co., 1917, pp. 15-23.

Chekhov, Michael, *To the Actor.* New York: Harper & Brothers, 1953, pp. 21-34.

Cunningham, Cornelius C., *Making Words Come Alive.* Dubuque, Iowa: William C. Brown Company, 1951, pp. 110-142.

Daniels, Earl, *The Art of Reading Poetry.* New York: Farrar and Rinehart, Inc., 1941, pp. 50-70.

Dolman, John, *The Art of Acting.* New York: Harper & Brothers, 1949, pp. 54-62.

Lowrey, Sara, and Gertrude E. Johnson, *Interpretative Reading: Techniques and Selections* (rev. ed.). New York: Appleton-Century-Crofts, Inc., 1953, pp. 30-32.

# Imagery as an Aid to Assimilation

POEMS, NOVELS AND PLAYS, ADVERTISING COPY, MAGAZINE ARTICLES, and speeches are all full of images which carry within them vital parts of the total experience the author has written into his work. These elements lend color and feeling, breathe life and vigor into the writing. They give the thought a vivid relation to reality.

Webster's *New International Dictionary* gives several definitions of the word *image*. One of them is as follows: "A mental representation of anything not actually present to the senses; a revival or imitation of sensible experience, or of sensible experience together with accompanying feelings." It is in this sense that we shall use the term in our efforts to recreate experiences as they are set down in literature.

The experiences of the senses are popularly considered to be sight, sound, taste, smell, and touch (though touch is a combination of such senses as pressure, temperature, pain, etc.). Actually there are in the human body many more sensory nerve endings which produce sensations than those external receptors which produce the five senses. There are nerve endings in the walls of the body, in the muscles, the joints, and the tendons, as well as nerve endings within the body (the alimentary system, for instance). There are nerve endings in the semicircular canals of the ears, which help give us a sense of equilibrium. These nerve endings transfer our direct experiences, the impressions of the world, to our conscious minds. There they are interpreted as sensations or feelings of sight and sound, of stomach aches and tingling scalps, of sticky days and yellow dresses.

But not all experience comes to us directly. As we read we find symbols or words which stand for, or substitute for, or refer to experience. We read of the sighing wind, the bleak cold of the November afternoon, the sickening pain, the smell of the lavender and the rosemary in the northwest corner of the garden on a warm July afternoon.

These words stand for sense impressions that the author had in mind, and the author hopes through the imagery of these words to stimulate the reader to experience the same feelings and sensations as he had. These are not experience, of course. But the words are intended to make the reader share indirectly the experience of the author.

Matthew Arnold's story of "The Forsaken Merman" begins with the merman and his children calling one last time to Margaret, the mother who has deserted her lover and her children to return to the world, leaving her lonely loved ones in their sea caves. The world of the merman is an imagined one, but Arnold makes it possible to capture the feeling of his character through the familiar imagery:

> *Children dear, was it yesterday*
> *(Call yet once) that she went away?*
> *Once she sate with you and me,*
> *On a red gold throne in the heart of the sea,*
> *And the youngest sate on her knee.*
> *She combed its bright hair and she tended it well,*
> *When down swung the sound of a far-off bell.*
> *She sighed, she looked up through the clear green sea;*
> *She said, "I must go, for my kinsfolk pray*
> *In the little gray church on the shore today . . ."*

The image of the father asking his children if it was yesterday that their mother went away fills us with pain and hurt and longing when we put ourselves in his place. We recall the feelings of being separated from someone we loved very dearly, whose footsteps in another room once caused a pang in the heart, whose voice was a fondly remembered sound. When we add to these feelings the premonition that the loved one is forever lost to us and we recall our own starts of panic when these thoughts occurred, we have begun to make the merman's feelings our own. The pathetic "Call yet once" only serves to heighten the lost and lonely feeling. Then our memories travel with the merman's back to scenes of women sitting with children on their knees, combing their hair. We recall the deep sense of peace, of love, of security the scene held for us. The sudden realization that the scene is gone now, the mother has left her child and her lover, sharpens even more the pain of the first two lines.

If we stop to analyze what is happening, we note that our feelings and mental processes have become exactly like those we imagine the merman's to be; we can hardly distinguish one from the other. Out of our experience we have created his and at the same time created our own. Not before had there been quite this combination of feelings, ideas, and reactions in our lives, but now we have so assimilated the material that the poem is as much ours as it was Arnold's. Had we not put our own feelings and experience into the poem, it could only have remained a distant and impersonal story. The casual reader may merely comprehend the presence of the images, vaguely aware that they refer to experiences of the senses, but the thorough reader will re-create them, relive them in all the rich detail and intensity common to his own direct experiences. For the interpreter, of course, mere comprehension is never sufficient. He finds it essential to be a thorough reader, to re-create the sensory experience referred to by the writer in order to complete his identification with the selection. To grasp the full function and all the implications of the image to the whole piece, he must, in his mind, hear the sighing wind, feel the cold, sense the pain, and smell the herbs.

Anyone who would develop skill in interpreting the writings of others must cultivate and develop skill in creating and re-creating images. He must be able to remember experiences. At will he must be able to call them up into consciousness and to re-experience them in something approaching their original sharpness of detail and intensity of feeling.

The ability to recall and to re-create sensory experience can be improved with effort and careful practice. Generally speaking, people find it easiest to recall or re-create sensory images that involve sight, sound, taste, smell, and touch. Images of muscle tensions and body positions, or images from the receptors in the body walls are probably next in ease of recall. Internal images are hard to recall, and for most people, fortunately, pain is difficult to remember.

Sensations seldom occur singly. A mental image of steak on a platter is usually a combination of the sight, sound, and smell of the steak plus the feel of the flow of saliva, and the feeling of reaction toward steak—pleasurable, repulsive, or neutral.

To make recall of images sharper and more vivid, a number of suggestions may be offered.

1. Re-experience! If you cannot recall what tweedy texture of cloth feels like, feel a piece of tweedy cloth. Then try to re-experience the feel without actually touching the cloth.

2. Go through the motions of feeling, tasting, smelling, etc., as you try to recall an experience.

3. Make a habit of savoring experience, pleasant or unpleasant. As you walk to classes, be aware of your reaction to budding trees, pounding rain, or hurrying people.

4. Become aware of empathic response. Empathy is a sort of natural imitative response. Our muscles tend to "feel into" that which has our attention. We tend to push forward with the football player, to want to feel our muscles doing the walk of the fat man just ahead of us; we feel ourselves and our muscles reaching up to follow the lines of a Gothic arch, or flatten down as we observe a low, flat structure; youngsters watching racing horses feel themselves riding horseback and actually bounce; our muscles want to assume the same expressions as the pictures of grief or horror or pain that have our attention. Be aware of empathic experiences. Encourage and savor them.

5. Make a business of observing. When they listen to a lecture what do people do with their feet? Their hands? How do their faces look when they listen? Do they watch the speaker or look out of the window or into space?

## EXERCISES

1. To practice recall of images, try the following:

a. Recall a visual image of your home, of your best friend at college, or the teacher of your next class.

b. Recall the sound of a fire siren, of a locomotive rushing by, of the babble of many voices in a large assembly before it is called to order, of the sound of a meadow lark.

    c. Recall the taste of your favorite dessert, of aspirin, or your favorite meat, of a lemon.

    d. Recall the smell of onions cooking, of a rose, of the dustiest part of the library, of coffee percolating.

    e. Recall the feeling of deep-piled fur, of rough wood, of well-groomed hair, of warm water.

    f. Recall the feeling of your muscles when you were frightened, angry, amused, utterly tranquil, very cold and shivering.

    g. Try to recall the feeling within you when you were suddenly and extremely frightened, when you were angry and dared not show it outwardly, when you wanted to laugh and could not without offending someone, when you lost your balance or when you were falling, when you have had stage fright.

    h. Recall the feeling of a burn, of a cut finger, of a bad headache.

2. Having practiced enough so that you can come to a reasonably valid conclusion, arrange the sensations in the order of their ease of recall for you, and practice further on those most difficult for you.

3. The following "Preludes" by T. S. Eliot contain many images. Underline the image-carrying words, and try to read the passages so that you and the audience savor the images. Those in the audience should rate each individual's ability to make them feel the image with him on a scale of 1 to 5, with 1 high and 5 low. (Each rater should have at least one 1 and one 5 in the group.)

*I.*

*The winter evening settles down*
*With smell of steaks in passageways.*
*Six o'clock.*
*The burnt-out ends of smoky days*
*And now a gusty shower wraps*
*The grimy scraps*
*Of withered leaves about your feet*
*And newspapers from vacant lots;*
*The showers beat*
*On broken blinds and chimney-pots,*
*And at the corner of the street*

A lonely cab-horse steams and stamps.
And then the lighting of the lamps.

## II.

The morning comes to consciousness
Of faint stale smells of beer
From the sawdust-trampled street
With all its muddy feet that press
To early coffee stands.
With the other masquerades
That time resumes,
One thinks of all the hands
That are raising dingy shades
In a thousand furnished rooms.

## Additional Readings

Boardman, Gail, *Oral Communication of Literature*. New York: Prentice-Hall, Inc., 1952, pp. 32-80.

Crocker, Lionel, and Louis M. Eich, *Oral Reading* (ed. 2). New York: Prentice-Hall, Inc., 1955, pp. 85-91.

Cunningham, Cornelius C., *Making Words Come Alive*. Dubuque, Iowa: William C. Brown Company, 1951, pp. 25-109.

Daniels, Earl, *The Art of Reading Poetry*. New York: Farrar and Rinehart, Inc., 1941, pp. 195-226.

Lee, Charlotte I., *Oral Interpretation*. Boston: Houghton Mifflin Co., 1952, pp. 230-242.

Tresidder, Argus, *Reading to Others*. Chicago: Scott, Foresman & Company, 1940, pp. 72-84.

# The Expansive Paraphrase as an Aid to Assimilation

THE RECALL OF A SPECIFIC IMAGE IS IMPORTANT IN ASSIMILATION, BUT just as important is the re-creation of the entire background of personal feelings that must have motivated any piece of writing, whether it is a recorded, simple, spontaneous statement of your own or the words of a writer you have never known, in a period with which you are unfamiliar, and in a setting you have never experienced. A valuable technique is the recall of the image and the re-creation of the background in the expansive paraphrase. This technique is valuable also as a test of the thoroughness with which assimilation has taken place, for unless the passage is understood fully you cannot execute an expansive paraphrase.

To paraphrase is to put into your own words the writings and utterances of another person or of an earlier statement of your own. The expansive paraphrase not only translates the language into your own, but it fills in the background of thought and feeling from which the utterance sprang, as well as the omitted but implied thoughts and feelings from between the lines and the words.

Rarely does the speaker express all he has in mind. Still less often does the writer express everything he has thought. Art is selective. Many details are suggested; others are not even suggested but left for the reader to supply. An author gives details and uses language that will stimulate a reader to fill in the picture from his own experiences from the larger context of the selection and from what he can learn of the writer and his way of thinking. Expansive paraphrase is this filling in of the picture. You describe, in greater detail than the text, the experience that the author has set down. You do it from the point of view of the author, but in your own words. It is as if you, as the author, were asked just what you mean by a particular passage, and you, as the author, explain in greater detail just what you do mean. The author's words are not yours, and they often need to be explored for the experience they represent before they mean as much to you as the author intended.

For instance, Tennyson says in "Crossing the Bar":

> *Twilight and evening bell,*
> *And after that the dark!*

Put yourself in Tennyson's place, and describe in detail how you think and feel. You may want to say something like this, "It's almost dark, and very quiet. The birds have settled down for the night and I can hear the church bell from the village clearly and sweetly. There is still a trace of sunset along the horizon. The air is cool and fresh. It will soon be night, and I am ready for peaceful, tranquil sleep." Tennyson says all this in nine words because he has made careful selection of the details that enable us to fill in the entire picture. But the picture should be complete for every interpreter, and sometimes it is not. You should be prepared to paraphrase any time you are asked to do so, and should be alert in your preparation for interpretation to those times when your re-experiencing of the text does not go beyond the words set down.

Sometimes the language of literature is not only condensed and highly connotative, but it comes from an era different from our own. Capulet, in *Romeo and Juliet*, says, "God's bread! It makes me mad." You might say, "Ye gods! It makes me furious!" This is not much change in language, and it does not involve expansion, but because it is your own it brings the experience to you. Macbeth says:

> *If it were done when 'tis done, then 'twere well*
> *It were done quickly.*

Someone else might say, "If I could only be sure that when I kill the old man that would be the end, and there would be no repercussions, then the quicker it's done, the better. If I could just be sure nobody would investigate to see what has happened to him, or, more than that, if I could be sure that killing him wouldn't haunt me and that I'd not have nightmares about this, I'd go ahead."

When you are asked to paraphrase, observe the following rules:

1. Put yourself in the place of the person speaking and speak in the first person.
2. Use your own words.
3. Go into much greater detail than does the text.

# EXERCISES

*1.* To be sure you understand and can employ this aid to assimilation, paraphrase the following:

> There is a pleasure in the pathless woods,
> There is a rapture on the lonely shore,
> There is a society where none intrudes
> By the deep sea, and music in its roar.
> > Childe Harold's Pilgrimage, LORD BYRON

> Something there is that doesn't love a wall,
> That sends the frozen-ground-swell under it.
> > "Mending Wall," ROBERT FROST

> Miniver Cheevy, child of scorn,
> Grew lean while he assailed the seasons.
> > "Miniver Cheevy," E. A. ROBINSON

> Four score and seven years ago our fathers
> brought forth on this continent a new nation,
> conceived in liberty, and dedicated to the
> proposition that all men are created equal.
> > "Gettysburg Address," ABRAHAM LINCOLN

> From you have I been absent in the spring,
> When proud-pied April, dress'd in all his trim,
> Hath put a spirit of youth in everything,
> That heavy Saturn laugh'd and leap'd with him.
> > Sonnet XCVIII, WILLIAM SHAKESPEARE

You will note that you must know what the words mean, you must understand the grammar, and you must often read the entire selection in order to understand any of the above fragments well enough to paraphrase them. That is why the author and selection title are given.

2. Paraphrase the following statements. Try to preserve the full meaning, direct and implied, that each statement carries.

> You've made your bed; now lie in it.
> Politics makes strange bedfellows.
> A stitch in time saves nine.
> All the world's a stage.
> If wishes were horses, then beggars could ride.
> Give him enough rope and he'll hang himself.
> Set a thief to catch a thief.

## Additional Readings

Clark, S. H., and Maud May Babcock, *Interpretation of the Printed Page.* New York: Prentice-Hall, Inc., 1940, pp. 21-29.

Henneke, Ben Graf, *Reading Aloud Effectively.* New York: Rinehart & Company, Inc., 1954, pp. 43-45.

Winans, James A., *Speech-Making.* New York: D. Appleton-Century, 1938, pp. 421-425.

# Phrasing: Getting Off the Page

WHEN WE SPEAK SPONTANEOUSLY WE HAVE AN IDEA, A SOMETHING TO say, and the words to express that idea usually come so immediately and miraculously that we are only aware of words as such when they do not come without conscious effort. In reading from a text, we have words before us that we pronounce aloud, but how many readers are not fully aware of the idea until all the words are pronounced! To learn to group words of a text together into ideas, and to learn to grasp each idea *before* any words that express it are uttered, is the aim of this project. If the idea is grasped fully, in all its detail, the words that express that idea will come as spontaneously and inevitably as they do in conversation.

We all know that the words in any piece of writing or utterance fall into related groups and that the ideas contained in the discourse become clear to us largely as we discern the relationships between the words. Chapters are divided into paragraphs, paragraphs into sentences, sentences into clauses, clauses into functioning parts of subject, verb, object, modifiers, and these parts into words. The eye or the ear picks up the material word by word, then almost as quickly begins to sort out the words which belong together and to group them into relationships which reveal the structure of the thought. Just as the syllables of a word have little meaning alone, so words in isolation fail to mean very much to us. Nor do we give them meaning merely by adding what little meaning there is in each word to what has gone before. Instead we build up meaning out of patterns of relationship. We perceive that the whole essay is, let us say, about the deliciousness of roast pig, as it is in Charles Lamb's "A Dissertation upon Roast Pig." We note that all parts of the essay lead to or from that central idea. Our minds dwell longest on that idea. Sections within the essay develop other ideas. There is a story of how roast pig was discovered. There is a section on not giving the dish away even to one's best friend. There is a paragraph on the idea that everybody likes roast pig, another on the idea that it is good throughout, etc. Each section has a central idea around which the section is organized, sometimes stated in words, sometimes not. Each sentence in the paragraph or section is in turn organized around a central or dominant idea. For example, central in the following sentence is the idea that Mr. Lamb *shares* his "good things" with friends: "I am one of those, who freely and ungrudgingly impart a share of the good thing's of this life which fall to their lot (few as mine are in this kind) to a friend." Again, parts of the sentence are organized around or focused upon smaller ideas: the good things of this life; few as mine are in this kind; to a friend. Each contains a concept, an idea, a feeling, a reaction. To break it down further is to destroy almost all its meaning. To relate it to the central idea of the whole sentence is to give it greater meaning. These smallest word groups we call phrases.

Determining the word content of each phrase is a process of discerning the concept or idea or other mental and emotional unit being expressed, then noting which words are directly related to it. In the process we note at once that some words are quite unimportant: in "to a friend," *to* and *a* are relatively unimportant, but to *friend* we give attention because it is the focal point. In "the good things of this life" we find ourselves giving attention to the "good things" concept while the other words do their work unobtrusively and quietly. These other words contribute but they do not dominate.

So it is that language is constructed. Subordinate units contribute to dominant units or controlling ideas. These in turn contribute to the larger ideas of the selection. The process of identifying the word that controls the idea is usually called centering. The process of selecting the words to be grouped with the central-idea word is called phrasing. Before he can group words into phrases the interpreter must analyze the thought of every sentence, searching for the key words and ideas, deciding which other words are related to the idea words, and noting the relationships between groups.

*This is a class in oral interpretation* is a very simply structured sentence with one image, one idea, one thought expressed. Some ideas may be expressed even more simply. One may say "Help!" or

"Ouch!" or "Stop!" and express a complete idea. Other sentences may reflect complex thought with many ideas, images, fractions of the whole thought—but each a unit by itself—to be analyzed and handled. And it makes a difference how words are grouped and how many key words are chosen. There is a subtle difference between *That's my last* DUCHESS/ *painted on the wall/ looking as if she were* ALIVE, and *That's my last* DUCHESS *painted on the wall/ looking as if she were* ALIVE. Often the difference is not so subtle:

Give up, John.
Give up John.
Honest Mr. Markham?
Honest, Mr. Markham?
Honest? Mr. Markham?

The process of grouping words into thought units is called phrasing, a process essential not only to analysis for the interpreter, but also to his delivery. It is with these phrases that he builds the series of mental, emotional, physical, and vocal reactions which convey the meaning to an audience. He does not read words, but rather groups of words as units, by which he directs the attention of his listeners and helps them to give structure to their thoughts. It is as if the reader were inviting his listeners to concentrate now on a small group of trees in the forest, now on a larger group, and then again on a single tree.

The number of groups and the number of words in a group are controlled by the key ideas, expressed most commonly by key words, and they normally reflect the structure of the thought processes as first the author and now the interpreter build up phrase by phrase the central or dominating idea of the whole selection. Analysis of any sentence of more than a word in length reveals that the number of phrases in a sentence is not fixed, that one may phrase in different ways, and that the number of minor ideas that may be grouped together is influenced by several factors.

In consideration for the listener, word groups are normally made smaller as the ideas and the vocabulary are less familiar, as the content is more complicated and difficult, as the word order in the sentence departs from the normal order, and as grammatical structure becomes more complex. In a mechanical sense, grouping is also influenced by the number of words a reader can deliver comfortably on one breath. With these limitations in mind the reader groups the words of his sentences in such a way as to cause them to carry the meaning as he has found it in the passage. Putting too few words in a group results in a choppy effect and tends to direct the listener's attention to words rather than ideas. In dwelling on minutiae he may miss the point. Putting too many words in a group results in the listener's failure to comprehend the thought. If the reader phrases at every bar in the following sentence the result is unpleasant: *As the embarrassed young man came/ wheeling around the corner/ from his girl's house/ on his battered old red bicycle/ his cap caught the wind/ blowing in his face/ and sailed back/ onto Clara's lawn.* The sentence is divided too many times. As one after another of the breaks is eliminated, however, it becomes apparent that all but the break after *bicycle* can in ordinary circumstances be taken out. This sentence reads well in two relatively long phrases. Observe, however, that in the sentence, "But, Sir Anthony, I would send her, at nine years old, to a boarding school, in order to learn a little ingenuity and artifice," needs several breaks. Here a long sweeping phrase tends to camouflage the relationships of ideas and the niceties of emphasis in Mrs. Malaprop's speech.

It is important not to distort the thought of a writer by phrasing in places unrelated to the structure of the idea relationships. For instance, we all have a tendency to group at the end of a line of print, probably because, if the eyes are not on the paper continually, there is a slight searching for the next line. For that reason, run-on lines of poetry are often read badly. Inadequate understanding of meaning often results in phrasing that distorts, if it does not totally destroy, the meaning. Careful study of a passage will result in an analysis and a grouping of words that illuminate meaning as a carefully lighted stage illuminates the scene. The whole picture is clear; points of emphasis stand out clearly from other elements in the scene; the relationships between the parts in the scene, the meanings, are sharply revealed.

Once you have completed your analysis of the selection and divided it into phrases, you should begin mastering the technique and forming a habit of grasping the ideas before they are spoken aloud.

Therefore, in preparation, scan the words of the first thought, then look away from the page and try to image the idea. If your mind is blank, or you simply recall one or two words and no ideas, repeat the process until you overcome your habit of reading words and not ideas. When the idea is grasped, speak it aloud to an imaginary listener. Both imagery and paraphrase will help in this process. Go on to the other ideas. If any group gives particular difficulty, put a check mark beside it and give it particular attention.

The following is a grouping of Browning's *Rabbi Ben Ezra* prepared for oral reading with one thought to a line:

> *Grow old along with me!*
> *The best is yet to be,*
> *The last of life,*
> *For which the first was made:*
> *Our times are in his hand who saith,*
> >*"A whole I planned,*
> *Youth shows but half;*
> *Trust God:*
> *See All,*
> *Nor be afraid!"*

A little practice with this selection will show you that the technique is not difficult. The key step, and the one where you are most likely to forget yourself, is the one of looking away from the page while you are imagining the idea and before you speak. But this is a crucial step and one you must master. Resist any tendency to glance at the script for the next idea while you are still speaking the last.

Practice will also reveal some other facts to you. For instance, you can often grasp more than one idea with one glance at the script. Your developing powers of concentration and your greater familiarity with the selection will have increased the power of your eye and mind to take in and to retain. Another discovery will be that the reading process works more easily if you hold the script high enough so that you do not need to move your head to glance at the next thought unit. Only the eyes need to move. If you tend to lose your place, keep your thumb under the line you wish to read next.

## EXERCISES

*1.* Prepare a script of the following poem, giving a separate line to each phrase, as in the example from *Rabbi Ben Ezra* above. Practice reading it aloud, remembering not to speak while you refer each time to the script for the next phrase, nor yet while you are forming the idea in your mind. (The pause is probably not nearly so long as you think it is.)

> One word is too often profaned
>   For me to profane it,
> One feeling too falsely disdain'd
>   For thee to disdain it.
> One hope is too like despair
>   For prudence to smother,
> And pity from thee more dear
>   Than that from another.
> I can give not what men call love;
>   But wilt thou accept not
> The worship the heart lifts above
>   And the Heavens reject not;
> The desire of the moth for the star,
>   Of the night for the morrow,
> The devotion of something afar
>   From the sphere of our sorrow?
>             "To ———," SHELLEY

*2.* Prepare your script of one of the following selections by separating one thought unit from another by means of a bar (/). Again practice to read the selection for the class with your eyes off the page at all times you are speaking.

### A.

The airs were very light; their speed was small; the heat intense. The decks were scorching underfoot; the sun flamed overhead, brazen out of a brazen sky; the pitch bubbled in the seams, and the brains in the brainpan. And all the while the excitement of the three adventurers glowed about their bones like a fever. They whispered and nodded and pointed and put mouth to ear with a singular instinct of secrecy, approaching that island underhand, like eavesdroppers and

thieves, and even Davis, from the cross-trees, gave his orders mostly
by gestures. The hands shared in this mute strain, like dogs, without
comprehending it; and through the roar of so many miles of breakers,
it was a silent ship that approached an empty island.

"The Ebb Tide," STEVENSON

### B.

The gray sea and the long black land;
And the yellow half-moon large and low;
And the startled little waves that leap
In fiery ringlets from their sleep,
As I gain the cove with pushing prow,
And quench its speed in the slushy sand.
Then a mile of warm sea-scented beach;
Three fields to cross till a farm appears;
A tap at the pane, the quick sharp scratch
And blue spurt of a lighted match,
And a voice less loud, through its joys
    and fears,
Than the two hearts beating each to each!

"Meeting at Night," BROWNING

### C.

The English language befriends the grand American expression—
it is brawny enough, and limber and full enough. On the tough stock
of a race, who through all change of circumstance was never without
the idea of political liberty, which is the animus of all liberty, it has
attracted the terms of daintier and gayer and subtler and more elegant tongues. It is the powerful language of resistance—it is the dialect of common sense. It is the speech of the proud and melancholy
races, and of all who aspire. It is the chosen tongue to express growth,
faith, self-esteem, freedom, justice, equality, friendliness, amplitude,
prudence, decision and courage. It is the medium that shall well nigh
express the inexpressible.

"The English Language," WALT WHITMAN

### D.

I remember, I remember
The house where I was born,

The little window where the sun
Came peeping in at morn;
He never came a wink too soon,
Nor brought too long a day;
But now, I often wish the night
Had borne my breath away.
I remember, I remember
The roses red and white,
The violets, and the lily-cups,
Those flowers made of light;
The lilacs where the robin built,
And where my brother set
The laburnum on his birthday,—
The tree is living yet!
"I Remember," THOMAS HOOD

## Additional Readings

Clark, S. H., and Maud May Babcock, *Interpretation of the Printed Page.* New York: Prentice-Hall, Inc., 1940, pp. 3-21; 29-33; 46-65; 73-92.

Crocker, Lionel, and Louis M. Eich, *Oral Reading* (ed. 2). New York: Prentice-Hall, Inc., 1955, pp. 113-117.

Henneke, Ben Graf, *Reading Aloud Effectively.* New York: Rinehart & Company, Inc., 1954, pp. 88-91.

Lowrey, Sara, and Gertrude E. Johnson, *Interpretative Reading: Techniques and Selections* (rev. ed.). New York: Appleton-Century-Crofts, Inc., 1953, pp. 157-167.

McLean, Margaret Prendergast, *Oral Interpretation of Forms of Literature.* New York: E. P. Dutton & Co., Inc., 1942, pp. 53-59; 67-74.

Parrish, Wayland Maxfield, *Reading Aloud* (ed. 3). New York: The Ronald Press Company, 1953, pp. 24-30.

Tresidder, Argus, *Reading to Others.* Chicago: Scott, Foresman & Company, 1940, pp. 30-40.

# Relating Phrases

WHEN YOU HAVE LEARNED TO GRASP IDEAS, NOT WORDS, AND THE IDEA is so clear that you do not need to refer to the text but can speak it directly to the audience, the next step is not difficult if you have assimilated the material well and if you have a good ear for the variations in human speech. You have already noted that it is often possible to grasp more than one thought at a glance. This technique helps to relate the units mentally. You have also noted that some units have so natural and logical a relationship that you relate them without being conscious that you have done so.

Many kinds of relationships are possible between phrases. Extremely subtle and complex ideas can be expressed through the arrangements of phrases, and in involved material one may need to search closely for the nature of the relationship that exists between units. Often one phrase is subordinate to another:

The man he wants, *who has never been a criminal,* is in the next room.

The old tin can *in the corner of the back lot* was what he had been looking for all afternoon.

Other phrases show contrast:

Not the old, *but the new*

She sat in a chair; *he stood on one.*

Some phrases show a comparison:

*Like a rowboat in choppy water, the old* Ford bounced to the top of the knoll.

Some phrases indicate thoughts in a series:

*... of the people, by the people, for the people ...*

Some phrases indicate transitions:

*In the second place ...*

*After the shoe has been cleaned,* it is time to start the polishing
process.
There are phrases of condition:
*If you can pay the rent,* you may stay in the house.
Some phrases are repetitions for emphasis:
*You, and I do mean you,* keep out of here.
These are repetitions of importance. They restate something that has
gone before, calling attention to it, pressing it upon our consciousness. Other repetitions are often not so important. For purposes of
clarity or rhythm the author may repeat an idea or a phrase in what
is often called an echo. The repetition for emphasis demands stress;
the repetition for clarity or rhythm is normally touched lightly or
thrown away. While the former repetition is usually spoken with a
drop in pitch and a prolongation of sound, the latter is often delivered
more quickly than the surrounding material and not uncommonly
with a repetition of the vocal patterns used in the first statement of
the idea. There are many more relationships which phrases may
indicate—relations of climax, anticlimax, amplification, modification,
interpolation, etc.—and each must be discovered before the meaning
is clear.

But it is the expression of these relationships that is important
to us here. If you have read aloud the examples presented above, and
especially if you have read them with any force of feeling, you have
noted that each calls for a different manner of reading—of length of
pause before or after or both, of shift in pitch upward or downward
at the beginning, of rising or falling inflections from beginning to end
of the phrase, of changes or repetitions of quality, pitch, or tempo
used in preceding or following phrases, or any number of other variations from the rest of the material to the phrase under consideration.
If you will go further and listen with great care to the way people
relate phrases by voice and to the language of melodic line and tempo
in our speech, you cannot but be astonished at the myriad ways we
convey meaning by relating phrases. There seem to be several basic
patterns and thousands upon thousands of variations upon these patterns. To try to record them all would be futile. To try to record
"the most common ones" would take many, many pages. Yet every
interpreter must become skillful in the ability to reproduce even the

most subtle variation at will and to make totally clear to an audience the relationship of phrases he intends. In spontaneous speech, unless English is not his mother tongue, he has no problem. The variations have been learned along with the language. In the "willed" speech of the interpretative situation, he may need to give his techniques some thought and practice.

The interpreter has two sources upon which to draw in developing accurate expression for the relating of phrases. One of these is observation and the other is feeling. As he listens to his own speech and to the speech of his friends, with an ear specifically tuned to catch the patterns of voice and use of time in handling meaning, he becomes increasingly aware of phenomena that had worked their magic on him without his having been conscious of it before. If he is thorough in the study of his art, he will try out these patterns on his own voice.

The second source is his own feelings. Once he has assimilated his material into his own thought and emotions, once he has re-created the imagery within himself, he can depend in large part upon the habits of a lifetime to guide him to an accurate basic pattern. He may have to increase its intensity or degree of variation, he may have to develop the subtlety of its expression, but the rich store of experience he has had with the language all his life, in talking and in hearing others talk, in emotionally quiet and in emotionally stormy times— this experience is the storehouse from which he will draw expression when he permits feelings to guide him.

Three very basic and much needed skills in relating phrases must be mastered, however, without fault. These occur so often and are the framework upon which so many variations are woven that no interpreter can succeed without them. These are expressions of relationships which give an impression of continuity or that there is more to come, of finality or that this is the end of this idea, and of momentary completeness or that the listener is invited to dwell on this thought for a moment but that there is more to come. Though it would be dangerous to assume that any one voice movement or vocal inflection will express each of these relationships, it will probably be useful to point out a few tendencies people exhibit in common.

Compare your expression of these two sentences:

*I must go now.*

*I must go now but I want you to wait for me.*

Pay particular attention to your expression of the word *now* in both sentences. On *now* in the first sentence, the pitch drops perceptibly lower than in the second. The *now* in the second sentence is not only higher in pitch, but the dying out of intensity is not so obvious. Read the same sentence again, this time putting primary emphasis on *now* instead of on *go*. Though, in addition to added intensity, the length of the inflection is greater and more time is given to *now*, the inflection of the first *now* seems to drop lower in pitch, while it drops and then rises slightly on the second *now*, and there is greater relaxation of energy at the end of the first *now*. The patterns of the first sentence are the basic patterns of finality. The patterns through *now* in the second sentence are the basic patterns of continuity.

By using the continuity inflection it is quite possible to keep an audience waiting for you to complete your thought. Practice the following sentences to see how long the class will wait for you to go on when you use vocal continuity as compared with their satisfaction with the completeness of the idea when you use vocal completeness. Alternate the sentences you read so that the class will not know which to expect.

1. *It's a beautiful day.*
   *It's a beautiful day (but rain is predicted).*
2. *I have to study now.*
   *I have to study now (but I can go with you later).*
3. *That was a fine performance.*
   *That was a fine performance (and I wish we could have more like it).*
4. *What are you going to do tonight?*
   *What are you going to do tonight (after you finish your paper)?*
5. *What a concert!*
   *What a concert (that was)!*

Between these two vocal effects is momentary completeness. Mentally, we dwell on each image or idea and invite the listener to savor it with us. For instance, a child has spent a dime, and reports each item bought as a wonderful thing in itself, "I got a jawbreaker!—and a stick of candy!—and an ice cream cone!"

If the child had bought only a jawbreaker, his inflection at the end of the phrase would have had the sharp drop in pitch characteristic of finality. But he had also purchased other items. When he has savored the pleasure of the jawbreaker, his mind races on to the stick of candy. And, again after a pause, the ice cream cone flashes into his attention. For the moment each idea is complete and the voice drops at its end. But back further is a consciousness of the other items which prevents the degree of pitch drop indicative of complete finality. There is something complete about each idea, but at the same time there is more to come. If, however, the child had thought of all three items as a collective whole and combined the phrases in a parallel series, he would vocally have used the rising inflections between the phrases characteristic of continuity. Momentary completeness is indicated by a middle ground of inflectional drop—not so far as to indicate a full period, but not so high to preclude the listener pausing for a while and contemplating what has just been said as an idea in itself before he connects it with a subsequent idea.

In the following passage, determine where you want finality, continuity, and momentary completeness. Practice until you can let an audience know with your voice whether the idea is finished, whether it continues, or whether you want them to stop and dwell on the thought just completed, yet there is more to come that is related.

*Let me picture to you the footsore Confederate soldier, as buttoning up in his faded gray jacket the parole which was to bear testimony to his children of his fidelity and faith, he turned his face southward from Appomattox in April, 1865. Think of him as—ragged, half-starved, heavy-hearted, enfeebled by want and wounds, having fought to exhaustion—he surrenders his gun, wrings the hands of his comrades in silence, and lifting his tear-stained and pallid face for the last time to the graves that dot the old Virginia hills, pulls his gray cap over his brow and begins the slow and painful journey. What does he find—let me ask you who went to your homes eager to find, in the welcome you had justly earned, full payment for four years' sacrifice—what does he find, when, having followed the battle-stained cross against overwhelming odds, dreading death not half so much as* surrender, he reaches the home he left so prosperous and beautiful? He finds his house in ruins, his farm devastated, his slaves free, his stock killed, his barns empty, his trade destroyed, his money worthless; his social system, feudal in its magnificence, swept away; his people without law or legal status; his comrades slain, and the burdens of others heavy on his shoulders. Crushed by defeat, his very traditions gone; without money, credit, employment, material, or training; and besides all this, confronted with the gravest problem that ever met human intelligence—liberated slaves.

"The New South," HENRY W. GRADY

## Additional Readings

Dolman, John, *The Art of Acting*. New York: Harper & Brothers, 1949, pp. 101-117.

Henneke, Ben Graf, *Reading Aloud Effectively*. New York: Rinehart & Company, Inc., 1954, pp. 91-95.

Parrish, Wayland Maxfield, *Reading Aloud* (ed. 3). New York: The Ronald Press Company, 1953, pp. 30-34.

Tresidder, Argus, *Reading to Others*. Chicago: Scott, Foresman & Company, 1940, pp. 30-40.

Winans, James A., *Speech-Making*. New York: D. Appleton-Century, 1938, pp. 404-415.

Woolbert, Charles H., and Severina E. Nelson, *The Art of Interpretative Speech* (ed. 4). New York: Appleton-Century-Crofts, Inc., 1956, pp. 158-161.

## [PROJECT 2.6]

# Synthesis and Evaluation of Progress

NONE OF THE SKILLS DISCUSSED SO FAR WILL BE VERY USEFUL UNTIL it is fully habituated. The good reader is unsatisfied until his material is thoroughly assimilated, and consciously or unconsciously he strives to image and "talk" his material until it seems to be the expression of his own thought. He adjusts his thought groups until he feels audience attention is directed just as it should be. He distinguishes, almost automatically, between reading aloud to himself and reading to and for an audience. If he cannot see their eyes and faces, actually or in imagination, he is uncomfortable. Lastly, he is fully aware when his voice finishes a thought; if he finds he has made a mistake and that the thought is too closely connected with the next, he re-expresses the whole idea.

Divide the following selection into thought units and mark them with bars, or type one group to a line. Image and paraphrase each thought. Determine the center for each thought, where ideas end, where ideas continue, and if there is any momentary completeness. Mark your script, if necessary, with code letters, such as *F* (finality), *C* (continuity), or *MC* (momentary completeness). Practice reading aloud to a real or imagined audience until a glance at the script will produce the idea or image and it can be spoken without further reference to the script.

### To A Fish

You strange, astonished-looking, angle-faced,
Dreary-mouthed, gaping wretches of the sea,
Gulping salt-water everlastingly,
Cold-blooded, though with red your blood be graced,
And mute, though dwellers in the roaring waste;

And you, all shapes beside, that fishy be—
Some round, some flat, some long, all devilry,
Legless, unloving, infamously chaste:—

O scaly, slippery, wet, swift, staring wights,
What is't ye do? what life lead? eh, dull goggles?
How do ye vary your vile days and nights?
How pass your Sundays? Are ye still but joggles
In ceaseless wash? Still nought but gapes, and bites,
And drinks, and stares, diversified with boggles?

### A Fish Answers

Amazing monster! that, for aught I know,
With the first sight of thee didst make our race
For ever stare! O flat and shocking face,
Grimly divided from the breast below!
Thou that on dry land horribly dost go
With a split body and most ridiculous pace,
Prong after prong, disgracer of all grace,
Long-useless-finned, haired, upright, unwet, slow!

O breather of unbreathable, sword-sharp air,
How canst exist? How bear thyself, thou dry
And dreary sloth? What particle canst share
Of the only blessed life, the watery?
I sometimes see of ye an actual pair
Go by! linked fin by fin! most odiously.

"The Fish, the Man, and the Spirit," JAMES HENRY LEIGH HUNT

Many people find memorization automatic when they prepare the reading in the way that has been outlined. The assimilation and effective communication of *ideas* are the aim of oral interpretation, and whether one is more comfortable with or without a script is a matter of personal preference. It needs to be emphasized, however, that using a script does not, in any way, lessen the time, thought, and imagination necessary for good interpretation.

As a test unit, select a humorous essay from one of the following authors and prepare it for reading aloud to the class.

| | |
|---|---|
| Clarence Day | Cornelia Otis Skinner |
| Stephen Leacock | James Thurber |
| Betty MacDonald | Mark Twain |
| Dorothy Parker | |

# 3

## PROJECTS IN

# Analysis

# [PROJECT 3.1]

# Nature and Mood of the Speaker

SO FAR PROJECTS TO MASTER THE MOST FUNDAMENTAL ASPECTS OF ORAL interpretation have been studied. The idea most basic to them all is that the reader *must* have something to say for successful communication. The next six projects are directed toward enrichment of meaning and appreciation of meaning.

It is quite possible to assimilate the meaning of "My Last Duchess" through imagery and paraphrase, to phrase it properly and to relate phrases, yet to express the whole poem, not from the point of view of a cruel, cold, proud aristocrat of the Renaissance but from the point of view of attractive, modest Susie Jones. It is equally possible, and it has been done, to read the lines of Queen Elizabeth at the height of her power as she is presented in Maxwell Anderson's *Elizabeth the Queen* as if she were a lovesick teen-age girl. For some reason it is more obviously ludicrous for an actor to do this than for an oral reader, probably because the nature and point of view of the speaker in the selection is suggested rather than presented literally in interpretation. It is no less necessary to take on the nature and point of view of the writer (speaker) than it is to assimilate the ideas.

An author may be writing his own ideas, impressions, emotions, or experiences from his point of view, or he may create a character and write the ideas, impressions, emotions, and experiences of that character. The identity of the speaker must be determined first. Along with his identity must come a determination of his nature, of his attitudes, his feelings, his beliefs.

Determining the identity of the speaker normally presents little difficulty unless you are working with excerpted or anonymous materials. In that event a little detective work may be required. In any case, the speaker must be either the writer speaking directly to the reader or a character he has created. If the latter is the case, the character will usually be identified. If he is not, sufficient details will usually be presented for you to be able to construct his identity.

Determining the nature of the speaker, however, can be more elusive and at times it may tax your ingenuity and skill as a researcher and reader. Your goal is to discover the unique qualities of the speaker, those elements in him, related to the subject matter of the selection, that mark him as an individual and reveal to you how he approaches what he is saying, how he feels about it, what attitudes of his may illuminate the passage.

Though human nature and emotions have probably not changed a great deal since the age of Pericles, manners, education, and customs have changed, and people have always differed one from another. T. S. Eliot and Lew Sarett were born the same year. They are both writers and both American born. Both have taught in great American universities. Yet Sarett, the woodsman and appreciator of nature, was very, very different in his nature, his point of view, his every aspect from Eliot, the scholar and sometimes cynical seeker after the meaning of life and living. In order to read either truthfully, it is necessary to understand each as fully as is possible. Longfellow, the children's poet, was very different from the sensitive, almost psychopathic Poe; David, the shepherd boy, was very different from St. Paul, the evangelist.

In the short time allowed for the preparation of classroom selections, it is a problem to get background information to guide an oral interpretation. However, there are a number of helps. For material about the author, *Who's Who* will give the most condensed and basic information on when an author lived, where, his occupation and chief interests. An encyclopedia will give more detailed information of the same sort, with some critical evaluation. Prefaces and introductions to collected works of the author will often provide facts and opinions that are helpful. Usually, however, only the most detailed, intimate biographical materials present the completed emotional-intellectual portrait that is desired by the interpreter. Without them, he must use his skill in reading between the lines, in making syntheses of his own from the facts available, in supplying background out of the reservoirs of information he has at his command as a result of his own educational experiences.

If only the place and time in which an author lived are known, the interpreter will lean heavily on broad generalizations he has learned. For instance, it is probable that contemporary living is far more casual and informal than it was before the first world war. Education today is, by and large, more practical and less classical than before the twentieth century. European culture is older than American, and the frontier spirit is less in evidence. Even through generalizations such as these the interpreter can usually avoid gross errors and arrive at something approaching the spirit of a writer, especially when this knowledge is associated with the specific content of the selection. But the more one knows about the author, the more accurate the conception of the personality is likely to be. A knowledge of the writer's personality will provide insights into how he felt about his subject matter and assist you to a proper emotional and intellectual interpretation.

It is doubtful if much about the writer's personality can be discerned from his picture except in rare instances (artists' interpretations may reveal more than photographs), but many people feel they know an author better and are more comfortable reading his work after they have seen his picture. Pictures of the greatest authors are readily available in libraries or even on the cards of the well-known children's game, "Authors."

If a selection is part of a larger work, the rest of the work should be scanned, at least, to get a proper perspective for the fragment. Good students will read the entire work carefully and with pleasure. If the selection is complete in itself, it is always well to read a few more selections from the same author to understand how the particular unit reflects his thinking.

The interpreter will gather all the information he can about the personality of the author and about the ideas and attitudes common in the place and time in which he lived, in the author's other work, and in the whole selection. He will then form from this information a synthesis, an interpretation of the nature and mood of the speaker in the selection under consideration. In turn he will attempt to assimiliate that nature and that mood, to make them his own.

When an author creates a character, and expresses his ideas, then it is far more necessary to understand the character than the author, though some knowledge of the author—whether he treats things lightly or seriously, whether he is formal or informal in his habitual approach—will be useful. But unless you can gain intimate insights into the creative processes of the author your knowledge of him and his period will serve only to help you to set very general patterns of attitude and feeling. The far more important source of information is the selection itself.

To understand the character speaking, what he says, his ideas and language must be studied very closely. In Amy Lowell's "Patterns," for instance, we know it is wartime. We know that a woman is speaking, and that her lover has been killed in action. The poem tells us how this tragedy has changed her from a warm, impulsive person to a person shocked into walking through life as if she were only part of a pattern. We know the time is not modern or contemporary. The lover wore a sword and buckles on his shoes. Since we know that the lover was Lord Hartwell and that word of his death came from a Duke, the formal garden is probably not American but possibly is English. Part of what we show the audience in the very first lines of the poem is the effect the word of her lover's death has had on the speaker. She is not weeping and she is not responding to her beautiful garden. She is responding only to memories of her experiences with her lover.

Close study of the selection and an alert eye for the details that reveal time, place, mood, and attitude tell much more about the speaker in the poem than do the details of Miss Lowell's life. The play must be studied more than Shakespeare if we are to know Hamlet. This is not to say, however, that the thorough and intelligent interpreter will not study both. To study *Hamlet* out of the context of Shakespeare and his times could result, indeed has resulted, in some Danes so melancholy as to strain the credulity of those who also know that "the glass of fashion and the mold of form" had a far more vigorous and bold aspect to his character. To read Mrs. Sullen or Dorinda in *The Beaux' Stratagem* without knowledge of Farquhar or his times has resulted in characters much too troubled, much too quarrelsome, much too impelled by Freudian impulses to be acceptable to anyone who is informed about London in the early eighteenth century.

# EXERCISES

1. In the following selections, who is speaking? When and where did he live? What do you think he looks like? What clothes do you think he wore? How would he approach people? What kinds of things in the world around him would interest him most? What did he value most in his experiences?

"Mending Wall," Robert Frost

"The Hollow Men," T. S. Eliot

"The Raven," E. A. Poe

*Romeo and Juliet* (Capulet) Shakespeare

"Chicago," Carl Sandburg

*Ile* (the captain) Eugene O'Neill

"Richard Cory," E. A. Robinson

"Dilemma," John V. A .Weaver

2. Choose one of the above selections to read aloud to the class. Through your reading, make the speaker's nature, point of view, and mood very clear to your listeners.

3. Make a selection of material of your own choice to read aloud to the class. Determine who is speaking. Answer the questions posed above in regard to the speaker. From the speaker's point of view, image, paraphrase, and phrase the selection. Practice it aloud.

## Additional Readings

Henneke, Ben Graf, *Reading Aloud Effectively*. New York: Rinehart & Company, Inc., 1954, pp. 126-130.

Lowrey, Sara, and Gertrude E. Johnson, *Interpretative Reading: Techniques and Selections* (rev. ed.). New York: Appleton-Century-Crofts, Inc., 1953, pp. 218-227.

Tresidder, Argus, *Reading to Others*. Chicago: Scott, Foresman & Company, 1940, pp. 61-65.

Woolbert, Charles H., and Severina E. Nelson, *The Art of Interpretative Speech* (ed. 4). New York: Appleton-Century-Crofts, Inc., 1956, pp. 48-87.

# To Whom He Speaks: The Role of the Audience as Listener

ONCE THE IDENTITY OF THE SPEAKER HAS BEEN DETERMINED, HIS NATURE and his mood have been sought out, it is time to consider the role of the audience as listener and the ways in which that role is determined by the author of the material to be presented and by the sometimes delicate adjustments of relationship between the audience, the occasion, the speaker, and the material. Several factors involved in any decision as to the role of the audience are a matter of taste and judgment. A few items are matters of fact discovered after an examination of the materials.

Matters of fact are involved with the determination of the one to whom the author is addressing his materials. The source of this information is usually in the selection itself. In a play one character normally addresses another character who is on stage. Identification of the listener is, in this case, easy, as it is in certain passages of novels and stories where characters are presented addressing other characters. Not quite so easily identified, but nearly so, are the ones addressed in certain lyrical and narrative poetry. One does not need to do much research into literary history and the personal lives of the poets to discover the identity of "thee" in Elizabeth Barrett Browning's poem, "How Do I Love Thee," or of the girl in Paul Laurence Dunbar's "Discovered" with its refrain of "Nevah min', Miss Lucy." Perhaps more often direct address is aimed at a lover, an athlete, a fellow poet, a personification a little less specific. This is the case in such poems as A. E. Housman's "To an Athlete Dying Young," Elinor Hoyt Wylie's sonnet sequence *One Person*, and Edna St. Vincent Millay's "I Know I Am but Summer to Your Heart." Determining the identity and the nature of the one addressed in this kind of material is often a little more difficult. Usually answers to these problems can be determined only by piecing together clues given in the material.

Perhaps the most common practice of the writer is to address no one in particular but anyone who establishes rapport with him. Narrative and expository passages in the novel and short story usually fall into this category. So do most lyrical, philosophical, and narrative poems, whether they be of the length and power of Milton's *Paradise Lost* or the brevity and flippancy of a quatrain or a couplet by Dorothy Parker, Arthur Guiterman, or Ogden Nash. The identity of the listener does not supposedly enter into the meaning of the communication here. What is important is that *some* listener respond.

In some materials more than one person is addressed. Several people may speak. There may be complex interchanges. Sometimes it is easy, sometimes difficult, to identify the persons to whom these statements are made, but usually a little study reveals who they are.

The interpreter will make use of his information about the identity and nature of the one addressed in his selection when he determines the role expected of the audience as he presents the materials to them. He may choose to be the writer speaking directly to the audience; he may elect to be a character speaking to the audience as another character; he may elect to be a character addressing another character imagined to be present while the audience only listens in upon the conversation. He may elect to be a character speaking to another character imagining themselves in complete privacy. In any case, the members of the audience, separately and collectively, take on an identity of their own, an identity which the successful interpreter controls within certain ill-defined limits. This identity often changes from one person to another, preferably at the will of the interpreter and usually with little conscious effort on the part of either. But the assumption of some identity by the audience is in part what makes an audience of them, each thinking and reacting in some kind of harmony with all the others rather than each in his own individual way.

The audience has come prepared to play a game of make believe with you. It sees the interpreter as the guest who has come to entertain it. At his will and direction it also sees him in its imagination as the speaker in the selection. Then the audience wants to know, "Who shall I be? What character am I? Shall I be myself, reacting as myself to what you say? Or shall I imagine I am Juliet and you are Romeo saying goodnight to me? Or do you want me to imagine I am myself, listening to Romeo saying goodnight to Juliet, whom we both imagine to be present?"

Normally the audience will fall into whatever role you, the interpreter, suggest for it. But there are certain demands you must be careful not to make. If the audience feels silly or out of character in its role, if the situation becomes too embarrassingly intimate, if for any reason at all the audience becomes self-conscious in its role, the game of make believe is called off and you encounter resistance. This resistance is not so often overt as it is a withdrawal into an inflexibility of response, outwardly polite, perhaps, but inwardly uncooperative. In "To Helen," Poe could only be speaking to his remembered image of Helen. It would probably embarrass an audience to address its members directly as if they were Helen. This is private and personal speech. The audience recognizes it as such and much prefers that the privacy be symbolically respected and that a little distance be maintained between them and it. Here the audience prefers to maintain its own identity and hear, in imagination, Poe as he addresses his remembered image.

Whether or not speech is too private for direct communication depends often on the mood of the reader and on his success in establishing rapport with his audience. On some occasions, with the mood carefully established, and with the confidence of the audience won, the audience is willing to play Juliet to the reader's Romeo and hear the familiar lines:

> *Sleep dwell upon thine eyes, peace in thy breast!—*
> *Would I were sleep and peace, so sweet to rest!*

The same kind of problem must be faced if you are reading Elizabeth Barrett Browning's love poem to Robert. Will the audience be willing to imagine that it is Robert as you read the following?

> *I love thee with the passion put to use*
> *In my old griefs, and with my childhood's faith.*
> *I love thee with a love I seemed to lose*

*With my lost saints,—I love thee with the breath,*
*Smiles, tears, of all my life!*

In each of the examples quoted above the identity of the listener is clear. Whether or not you will address the audience as if it were that listener is a matter of taste, determination of which will be made in accordance with the nature of the occasion, the characteristic attitudes and feelings to be encountered in the audience, the skill of the reader in establishing mood, and the amount of esthetic distance desirable.

Esthetic distance refers to the amount of direct involvement of the audience in the material to be presented. If the reader addresses the audience as individuals in their own usual identities, if he invites their responses to himself by look, by pause, by directness, the amount of esthetic distance is small. The material is a personal matter to each member of the audience, in this case, immediate and pressing. If, however, the reader assumes a character, he has to that degree withdrawn from the audience, reduced in a real sense its directness of involvement, increased the esthetic distance. If he moves further away by assuming a role, as the interpreter might do if he were reading Browning's "My Last Duchess" and the character he has become is addressing an imaginary being, the esthetic distance has become still greater. In an increasing degree the audience has become observer, witnessing the events and the conversation, less and less involved in a way that demands its direct action and reaction.

The actor is even further removed in esthetic distance when he enters a world of make believe where he is costumed, placed in a setting to represent the surroundings suggested by the author, given another character, or characters, to talk to, and where they in turn respond to him. The audience merely sits outside the pool of light and watches the events transpire.

The amount of esthetic distance desirable is determined by weighing several factors. The first to be considered is, of course, the identity of the one addressed in the material itself. But alongside that consideration should go the one of examining the size of the audience. Generally speaking, the larger the audience, the greater the esthetic distance desired and the less intimate the attempted contact—unless the audience becomes so small that each member is aware of every other member as an individual. Then intimacy or directness of involvement may be a cause of self-consciousness and is to be avoided.

The occasion makes a difference, too. Whether you are reading to a class or a group assembled for a gala dinner, an afternoon study club or a group who has paid to hear you perform makes a difference in the directness of your approach, the kinds of roles the audience can play with ease, and the degree of intimacy or personal involvement you can safely expect.

The interpreter must examine carefully all the elements involved in the selection, his own reputation and skill as a performer, the intangibles in the occasion which affect the mood and temper of the audience, the habitual attitudes and the artistic sophistication of the audience, the size of the audience, and any other elements that would affect the interrelationship of interpreter, material, occasion, and audience in such a way as to color, heighten, or weaken the interaction between them at the moments of performance. When all things have been carefully considered, the interpreter must make a judgment and a decision as to the role the audience is to play, the degree of its emotional and intellectual involvement in the performance, the relation of speaker to listener.

Whatever the decision, it is imperative that there be no doubts in the minds—the feelings—of the audience as to precisely what its role is. By look, by voice, if necessary by word, the audience is informed of its role. And there must be no wavering, no uncertainty, no faltering on the part of the interpreter in keeping the role of the audience clear and consistent. These faults confuse. They result in an insecurity which in turn usually results in a withdrawal from participation. If the interpreter distrusts his own judgment, he may seek advice from teachers, students, other readers, even members of his future audience, but advice should not be treated as law. The final decision rests with the interpreter and is based on his knowledge, his intuitions, his feelings, his sensitivity to other people's feelings. His purpose is to make perfectly clear to the audience what its role is and to establish the esthetic distance in such a way as to provide the audience with the greatest possible amount of satisfaction. Increasing the esthetic distance does not necessarily in itself decrease or increase the emotional and intellectual reaction of the audience. But achieving an adjustment which the audience feels is just right for a particular selection is the interpreter's aim, for in that feeling the audience finds satisfaction.

# EXERCISES

1. In the following selections, to whom is the material addressed? Assuming that the audience is a class of twenty people, meeting regularly three times a week in the middle of the morning, what role would you expect the audience to play in each selection? Is there more than one choice possible?

"Mending Wall," Robert Frost

"The Hollow Men," T. S. Eliot

Juliet, beginning "Farewell! God knows when we shall meet again," Shakespeare

"Weeng" (an Indian slumber-song) from *Slow Smoke*, Lew Sarett

"University Days," from *My Life and Hard Times*, James Thurber

"Oh, My Beloved, Have You Thought of This?" Edna St. Vincent Millay

"Meditation on Saviors," Robinson Jeffers

2. Prepare to read Hamlet's "To be or not to be" soliloquy, first as if Hamlet were speaking to himself and the audience is not even assumed to be present. Now prepare it to be read in the same way except that the reader recognizes that the audience is present and overhearing but maintaining its role as "the audience." Last, prepare it to be read as if the audience were a very intimate friend of Hamlet with whom he talks over the most private of his thoughts. Note the differences in your own manner, in the direction of your glance, in the "eye contact" with your audience, in your vocal quality.

3. Prepare a reading of a selection in which the role of the audience and the direction of the speaker's speech are a complex problem. Try something like one of the following selections:

"Soliloquy of the Spanish Cloister," Robert Browning
"Pictor Ignatus," Robert Browning
"The Bishop Orders His Tomb at Saint Praxad's Church," Robert Browning
"Terence, This Is Stupid Stuff," from *A Shropshire Lad*, A. E. Housman
"Rubáiyát of Omar Khayyám of Naishápúr," Edward Fitzgerald
"Sister Helen," Dante Gabriel Rosetti
"Night," Robinson Jeffers
"West Running Brook," Robert Frost
"How Beautiful With Shoes," Wilbur Daniel Steele

If the real audience is being addressed, make it feel it is being talked to. If an imagined character is addressed, make the audience see that character, too. If a remembered character is being addressed or a remembered scene or experience has your attention, make your audience see and experience with you.

## Additional Readings

Dolman, John, *The Art of Acting*. New York: Harper & Brothers, 1949, pp. 13-21.

Dolman, John, *The Art of Play Production* (rev. ed.), New York: Harper & Brothers, 1946, pp. 27-47.

Langfeld, Herbert Sidney, *The Aesthetic Attitude*. New York: Harcourt Brace and Howe, 1920.

Lowrey, Sara, and Gertrude E. Johnson, *Interpretative Reading: Techniques and Selections* (rev. ed.). New York: Appleton-Century-Crofts, Inc., pp. 176-178.

# Language of the Speaker

SURELY NO ONE WOULD SERIOUSLY DISPUTE THE STATEMENT THAT AN audience must know what the words are and what they mean before it can even follow the performance of an interpreter, much less react to it in any desirable or satisfying way. Yet many kinds of phenomena often interfere with the audience's reception and comprehension of the words and their meanings. One of these phenomena is failure on the part of the speaker to pronounce the words in such a way that the audience can easily identify them as the ones the author wrote. Another is failure on the part of the speaker to discern, and thus to convey, the full freight of meaning carried by the words.

To avoid both of these dangers the interpreter must pay careful attention to the language of the selection, being sure that he can pronounce every word correctly, that he knows what every word denotes and what it connotes, that he has explored and recognized the significance of the order and relationships of the words, and that he is aware of the special weight of meaning in the figures of speech and other devices the author has used.

Probably little needs to be said about the importance of correct pronunciation. Anyone who has found himself in a foreign city away from the obliging native people who speak his language and who has tried to make himself understood through inaccurately pronounced words can testify to the importance of saying the word as the natives say it. The man who is struggling with a language other than his native tongue can, however, usually be forgiven for making his listener struggle to identify his words. But the person who mispronounces words in his own tongue risks not only failure to communicate but loss of face or respect as well. The listener can only conclude that the speaker is insufficiently prepared, that he doesn't know accurately what he is talking about, and that, perhaps, his background of education and experience are not up to the challenge of the material he is attempting to present. The unkind listener will mark him down as ignorant. An ear trained to listen with discrimination to the speech of educated people around him and a mind trained to send him searching in a pronouncing dictionary whenever he encounters a word in his selection with which he is in the least unfamiliar will soon prepare the interpreter to pronounce his words correctly and permit his audience to identify those words accurately.

In these days of rapid reading of quantities of material, it is not unusual to guess at the meaning of unfamiliar words from the context in which they are found, and to be able to make a reasonably accurate guess at definition even though the pronunciation of the word is unknown and the reader would hesitate, therefore, to add the word to his speaking vocabulary. His guess, the guesses of roommates and friends may not be relied upon. Only the dictionary can always offer an authoritative pronunciation. Anything less is very obvious to listeners. A radio station program director once commented that the station could go on for weeks with a certain volume of mail, but let one person on one program, staff member or not, mispronounce one word, and the volume of mail doubled from the cards and letters mailed to call attention to the mispronunciation.

Understanding the meaning, however, is a more complex matter since words take on meaning and color in several different ways, some assigned to the words by a sort of common practice of people, some by personal association and experience with the words, some by the way words are associated with one another in the sentence, some by the psychological effect of the sounds of the words upon listeners, some by the larger context of the whole work and even the occasion on which it is being presented, some by the experiences of our lives, direct or through conversation and reading, which the words cause us to recall. All our lives we have been building up a larger and larger storehouse of words and their meanings. But since each time a word is employed in a new context it takes on a slightly different meaning, we must remain constantly alert.

That aspect of a word's meaning called its denotation is probably the easiest aspect to identify, and is probably the least changeable.

This is what is often referred to as the "dictionary meaning," but it is more accurate to say that it refers to those experiences, those things, those processes (which the dictionary meanings try to describe with other words) to which the words have been assigned by human experience, to which the words refer. S. I. Hayakawa in his *Language in Action* suggests that if we will cover our mouths with our hands and point we will be closer to the denotation of the word than if we try to use other words. Of course not all denotations can be pointed to. Some are in the realm of feeling, of idea, and of imagination. But there is always some thing, feeling, relationship, experience, or phenomenon to which a word has been assigned in the common experience of people. In all our experiences with animals we have as a community of English-speaking peoples assigned the word *dog* to a particular class. We have all, through experience, learned the limits of the word. Some animals may be nearly like dogs but enough different that we call them foxes or wolves or cats. If the word is a familiar one everyone understands the limits and the extent of the word's meaning. What the word refers to changes little from one context to another, from one year to another. If it is an unfamiliar word we may seek to find the word being applied to what it refers to (as when the animal's name appears on its cage at the zoo), consult the experience of others, piece out its meaning from many uses in the writings of people familiar with it, or figure out what it refers to by consulting the dictionary. The first of these approaches takes a long time, although it is, of course, the best way to learn the denotation of a word. The last is probably the quickest and most common method for the interpreter to use as he prepares to read his selection. It is perhaps least safe to depend on the one context within the selection as sufficient to piece out the meaning of the word.

The connotation of a word is more difficult to discover, for it is made up of the associations people have with the word, their feelings when they see or hear the word, their visions, their recollections. Some words are happy words, some are sad, some are naughty. Some words have connotations so unpleasant they cannot be uttered in the presence of other people. Some words cause a kind of warmth to pervade the person who hears or sees them.

This freight of feeling which words carry and which results from the experiences and verbal contexts people associate with them, is best learned through long use of and association with the word. Next to that it is best to observe the emotional quality of the contexts in which it is used. But for a quick grasp of the word, consult the dictionary. Read not only the definition but, if there is one, also the section which discriminates between the uses of the synonyms and antonyms. The connotation of the words begins to become clearer when one reads that

*Enough* is relative, denoting a supply equal to a given demand. A temperature of 70° Fahrenheit is *enough* for a living-room; 212° *enough* to boil water; neither is *enough* to melt iron. *Sufficient*, from the Latin, is an equivalent of the Saxon *enough*, with no perceptible difference of meaning, but only of usage, *enough* being the more blunt, homely, and forcible word, while *sufficient* is in many cases the more elegant or polite (*College Standard Dictionary*, Funk and Wagnalls, 1940).

Not all words are accompanied by such full descriptions, but the sensitive reader can discern a great deal about the connotation of any word in the dictionary.

There is never in the dictionary, however, sufficient space available to convey the full connotation of any word. Volumes would be required to describe all the feelings and associations the simple and familiar word *home* calls up for all of us. It means a house or several houses; it means parents, brothers, sisters, friends; it means Christmases and Thanksgivings and Fourths of July; it means chores and disciplines, love and rebellions; and it means all the other associations we have with it. Some aspects of the word's connotation most of us share in common. Other aspects are different for each of us because no person's experience ever duplicates another's. Therein lies the interesting, usually challenging, and often baffling aspect of connotation for the interpreter. He must solve the riddle of the word's connotation for other people as well as himself; he must avoid the trap of assuming the connotation is identical for all people. And since he cannot know entirely what is in the minds of his audience, he must be so sensitive to his own connotation for the word that he colors and enriches the word for his audience.

Everyone is aware that the order of the words also determines meaning in the English sentence. It makes a difference whether we say, "The man killed the bear," or "The bear killed the man." The words are the same; only the order has been changed. The form of the word also alters the meaning: *bear, bears, bear's; is, are, was, been; kill, kills, killed.* A third element which alters meaning is the class functions of the word: *part* as a noun and *part* as a verb have different meanings; so also do many other words which can serve as more than one part of speech.

The complex relationships between the forms of words, the order of the words, and the class functions of the words make up what is called the grammatical structure of the sentence. From this structure and the denotations and connotations of the words we discern the meaning. If, however, we have overlooked any part of the significance of those relationships, if we have not found for every element of the sentence a relation to some other element in the sentence, our understanding is incomplete or inaccurate. There is usually very little difficulty in finding the relationships in the short sentence, but it takes careful analysis to be sure when the structure is long or complicated:

> *Over the dark mountain, over the dark pinewood,*
> *Down the long dark valley along the shrunken river,*
> *Returns the splendor without rays, the shining of shadow,*
> *Peace-bringer, the matrix of all shining and quieter of shining.*
>
> > "Night," ROBINSON JEFFERS

*Would that the structure brave, the manifold music I build,*
> *Bidding my organ obey, calling its keys to their work,*
*Claiming each slave of the sound, at a touch, as when Solomon willed*
> *Armies of angels that soar, legions of demons that lurk,*
*Man, brute, reptile, fly,—alien of end and of aim,*
> *Adverse, each from the other heaven-high, hell-deep removed,—*
*Should rush into sight at once as he named the ineffable Name,*
> *And pile him a palace straight, to pleasure the princess he loved!*
>
> > "Abt Vogler," ROBERT BROWNING

Analysis of the first quotation in the context of the poem reveals that *splendor, shining, Peace-bringer,* and *matrix* are all substitute words for *night,* the subject of the poem. *Returns* is the verb. The phrases beginning with *over* and *down* are adverbial phrases modifying *returns.* The phrase beginning *along* modifies *Down the long dark valley* and is also adverbial in function. We recognize this sentence as being constructed not in normal order, although not in an uncommon reversal of normal order either. As soon as the functions of the parts and the relations between the parts become clear, the meaning begins to emerge.

The passage from Browning is more difficult, for the verb is left unfinished.

"*Would that the structure brave, the . . . music . . . I build . . .*"

would do what? Browning doesn't complete that thought until he begins the next stanza. There he begins

"*Would it might tarry like his, the beautiful building of mine . . .*"

Now the relationships of the parts begin to become clear when the basic subject-verb structure has been discovered. Most of what he wills his music to do is compared to an experience of Solomon who once willed a palace of pleasure. Other phrases, parentheses, clauses take on meaning as a result of their relationship to other words, phrases, and clauses.

While all language carries with it a weight of meaning in the connotations of the words and of the imagery, some devices of language, the various figures of speech, carry an especially heavy burden and deserve particular attention. Literature is concerned, in large part, with man's feelings and aspirations. It strives to express in words and in concentrated form the most fundamental truths. These truths are deeply important to people, yet are extremely difficult to express in words for they are so often a matter of our most fundamental thoughts and most basic feelings. The literary artist is not content simply to tell us about these thoughts and feelings. He attempts the much more subtle and satisfying task of creating in a poem or story or play or dance or musical composition or painting an art object which will show us through our own experience with the piece the thought and feeling he had in mind. We will have experienced what something in man's life *feels like*.

To accomplish this calling up and intensification of feeling the literary artist uses figurative language. There are a great many different figures of speech—Porter G. Perrin says in his *Writer's Guide and Index to English* (Scott, Foresman and Co., 1942, p. 234) that over two hundred have names—but the most common types are allusion, metaphors, similes, analogies, metonymy, irony, exaggeration, and understatement. Each of these devices serves the function of making clearer or intensifying a meaning or a feeling by transferring the image and usually the feeling associated with the image to the new subject.

The allusion refers to a remembered experience of the family, the group, the culture, of a person, place or event. Nearly every American knows what we refer to when we say of a youngster who has kicked his football through the neighbor's window, then confessed that he was responsible: "he has chopped down his cherry tree and he has not told his lie." Most of us recognize the references in these allusions: *He met his Waterloo; he is a Jeremiah and she is a Cassandra; my father had the patience of Job.* Here in a word or phrase the allusion calls up a wealth of associations in each example which gives the statement meaning.

The simile is a simple comparison: *My father was like a caged lion after the fourth day of the flood; the bride's first biscuits used to be like rocks, now she opens a package of mix; out like a light; up above the world so high, like a diamond in the sky.*

The metaphor is also a comparison, but the *like* or *as* of the simile is omitted. *Peace-bringer* and *matrix* are metaphors in the selection from Jeffers' "Night" quoted above. Sandburg calls Chicago, in a series of metaphors,

> *Hog Butcher for the World*
> *Tool Maker, Stacker of Wheat,*
> *Player with Railroads and the Nation's Freight Handler ...*

We speak of the *rubberneck, baloney, dead fires, hot music,* and *wet blankets.*

Analogies are comparisons, too, but they are extended comparisons of one idea or situation to another. The comparison of Abt Vogler's *structure* of music with Solomon's *palace* of pleasure is an analogy. So is the description, "Our house is built in the form of an H. The living room forms the cross bar, the bedrooms form the right upright line and the kitchen and dining room form the left one." The following passage from Morgan Farrell's "Fog's Thickening, Sir," first published in *Scribner's Magazine*, December, 1934, illustrates how the analogy not only clarifies but also gives a feeling for the subject.

*The same principle [the electrically rotated gyroscopic compass] operates the automatic steering machine, whose stout pedestal, two compasses and pair of spoked wheels occupy the place of honor in the exact center of the bridge. It is known to its human companions as "Iron Mike."*

*Like the flesh and blood quartermaster in the wheelhouse back of him, when Mike is once set to steer a certain course, he will steer it through hell, hurricane, and high-water. Unlike the quartermaster, however, the voice of authority means nothing to Mike. So if the keen eye of the commodore should detect a ghostly white mountain dead ahead and the commanding voice of the commodore roar in Mike's metal ear: "Hard right—hard," that placid robot would continue to steer straight for the iceberg, which is one reason why the gyroscopic steering machine is uncoupled and out of use on a thick night like this.*

Metonymy, the use of one word for another, is quite like metaphor. We ask after the condition of the *rubber* (the tires) when we buy a used car; we speak of *Shakespeare* for Shakespeare's plays, of *dish* for something to eat, of *mouths* to feed, of *Iowa* for the University of Iowa football team, and of *have a heart* for be lenient.

Irony implies something different, often opposite from what is said: *That's a fine kettle of fish; the Podunk Shakespeare.* E. E. Cummings uses irony for the basis of a poem called "Nobody Loses All the Time," in which his uncle Sol, who wanted to be a farmer, failed at vegetable farming and then chicken farming. But at his funeral (after death by drowning himself in the watertank)

> somebody pressed a button
> (and down went
> my Uncle
> Sol
>
> and started a worm farm)

Light irony is usually comic; severe irony often becomes heavily sarcastic or satiric.

Exaggeration, often called hyperbole, is a most common figure of speech in our conversations: *I'm dead!; Her face would stop a clock; He's rolling in money; a lump on his head as big as a goose egg.* Exaggeration, and its counterpart, understatement, are often used by the writer for humorous effects. Robert Frost uses the understatement of the New England farmer for comic effect in "Brown's Descent." After Brown has slid, reeled, lurched, bobbed, and fallen two miles down the slippery mountainside from his home one evening, he looks back up the slope and all he says is "Well—I—be—."

Each of these figures of speech reveals feelings it would otherwise take many more words to reveal. They are a kind of shorthand language, enriching our enjoyment and appreciation of conversation and literature. To be sure, their success usually depends on a common background of reading and experience, but the literary artist sprinkles them liberally through his material. If the interpreter would understand the full import of his materials, he will study carefully the figures of speech he encounters there, searching diligently for the full impact each one carries. He will recognize that the major function of a figure of speech is usually connotative, and until he has found its full emotional content he has failed to appreciate the full meaning of the text.

Lastly, the interpreter needs to appreciate and respect the language the author used to express the exact shading of his thought and feeling. A writer is not only skilled in his choice of words but he has a special ability and concern for the exact word to express the precise shading of his thought. Hamlet says,

> How weary, stale, flat and unprofitable
> Seem to me all the uses of this world!

Can you say it as well in your most discouraged moments? Try! Consider all the implications or connotations of weariness, staleness, flatness, and unprofitableness. What does *uses* mean in this context? Why did Hamlet say *weary* instead of *tired, stale* instead of *useless?* Sometimes there is a slight difference in the denotations of the words used, sometimes the difference is largely in the connotations. Sometimes the word is more suggestive of the emotion because of its sound (onomatopoeia). Sometimes the word fits into the rhyme or rhythm pattern better. Sometimes the word is used simply because it seems right and inevitable for the speaker to use it in the context. Whatever the reason for the choice, the words of the artist need to be respected and savored for they are the basic units for appreciation and understanding of the essential truths of literature.

# EXERCISES

1. In the following selections, be sure of your pronunciation of the capitalized words, of their exact meanings and their connotations in the context:

> My heart is like a singing bird
>   Whose nest is in a WATER'D SHOOT;
> My heart is like an apple-tree
>   Whose boughs are bent with thick-set fruit;
> My heart is like a RAINBOW SHELL
>   That paddles in a HALCYON sea;
> My heart is gladder than all these
>   Because my love is come to me.
>     "A Birthday," CHRISTINA ROSSETTI

> Daughters of Time, the HYPOCRITIC Days,
> Muffled and dumb like barefoot DERVISHES,
> And marching single in an endless file,
> Bring DIADEMS and FAGOTS in their hands.
> To each they offer gifts after his will,
> Bread, kingdoms, stars, and sky that holds them all.
> I, in my PLEACHED garden, watched the pomp,
> Forgot my morning wishes, hastily
> Took a few herbs and apples, and the Day

Turned and departed silent. I, too late,
Under her SOLEMN FILLET saw the scorn.

"Days," EMERSON

And now, as the night was SENESCENT
And STAR-DIALS pointed to morn—
As the star-dials hinted of morn—
At the end of our path a LIQUESCENT
And NEBULOUS LUSTRE was born,
Out of which a MIRACULOUS CRESCENT
Arose with a DUPLICATE HORN—
ASTARTES'S BEDIAMONDED crescent
Distinct with its duplicate horn.

"Ulalume," POE

2. Explain the figures of speech in the following, and what they add to the passage so far as you are concerned:

You are beautiful and faded,
Like an old opera tune
Played upon a harpsichord;
Or like the sun-flooded silks
Of an eighteenth-century boudoir.

"A Lady," AMY LOWELL

Look at the stars! look, look up at the skies!
O look at all the fire-folk sitting in the air!
The bright boroughs, the circle-citadels there!
Down in dim woods the diamond delves! the elves'-eyes!
The grey lawns cold where gold, where quickgold lies!
Wind-beat whitebeam! airy abeles set on a flare!
Flake-doves sent floating forth at a farmyard scare!—
Ah, well! it is all a purchase, all is a prize.
Buy then! bid then! —What? —Prayer, patience, alms, vows.
Look, look: a May-mess, like on orchard boughs!
Look! March-bloom, like on mealed-with-yellow sallows!
These are indeed the barn; withindoors house
The shocks. This piece-bright paling shuts the spouse
Christ home, Christ and his mother and all his hallows.

"The Starlight Night," HOPKINS

See, what a grace was seated on this brow;
Hyperion's curls, the front of Jove himself,
An eye like Mars, to threaten and command,
A station like the herald Mercury
New-lighted on a heaven-kissing hill.

Hamlet, SHAKESPEARE

Well, son, I'll tell you:
Life for me ain't been no crystal stair.
It's had tacks in it,
And splinters,
And boards torn up,
And places with no carpet on the floor—
Bare.
But all the time
I'se been a-climbin' on,
And reachin' landin's,
And turnin' corners,
And sometimes goin' in the dark
Where there ain't been no light.
So, boy, don't you turn back.
Don't you sit down on the steps
'Cause you finds it kinder hard.
Don't you fall now—
For I'se still goin', honey,
I'se still climbin',
And life for me ain't been no crystal stair.

"Mother to Son," LANGSTON HUGHES

3. Choose one of the above selections, or some other if you prefer, to read aloud to the class. Let your reading tell the class what you see and feel from the way you read the words and figures of speech.

## Additional Readings

Aggertt, Otis, and Elbert R. Bowen, *Communicative Reading*. New York: The Macmillan Co., 1956, pp. 55-87.

Clark, S. H., and Maud May Babcock, *Interpretation of the Printed Page.* New York: Prentice-Hall, Inc., 1940, pp. 199-242.

Crocker, Lionel, and Louis M. Eich, *Oral Reading* (ed. 2). New York: Prentice-Hall, Inc., 1955, pp. 94-117.

Hayakawa, S. I., *Language in Action.* New York: Harcourt, Brace & Co., 1941, pp. 55-101; 186-213.

Kenyon, J. S., and Thomas Albert Knott, *A Pronouncing Dictionary of American English.* Springfield, Mass.: G. & C. Merriam Co., 1944.

Langer, Susanne K., *Problems of Art.* New York: Charles Scribner's Sons, 1957, pp. 13-26.

McLean, Margaret Prendergast, *Oral Interpretation of Forms of Literature.* New York: E. P. Dutton & Co., Inc., 1942, pp. 23-27.

Parrish, Wayland Maxfield, *Reading Aloud* (ed. 3). New York: The Ronald Press Company, 1953, pp. 21-24.

Perrin, Porter G., *Writer's Guide and Index to English* (rev. ed.). Chicago: Scott, Foresman & Company, 1950, pp. 318-326; 332-356.

Woolbert, Charles H., and Severina E. Nelson, *The Art of Interpretative Speech* (ed. 4). New York: Appleton-Century-Crofts, Inc., 1956, pp. 136-158; 180-191.

# Purpose and Theme of the Speaker

POEMS AND STORIES AND PLAYS HAVE PURPOSES OR REASONS FOR HAVING been composed and audiences are always eager to identify that purpose. Until the listener discovers what the whole selection is about he is restless; if he never does find out the purpose of the selection, he is frustrated and disappointed.

The purpose is the objective the author wanted to accomplish with his reader or listener, the idea he wanted to put across, the topic he wanted to introduce and the impression or attitude he wanted to leave concerning it, the intellectual or emotional or esthetic experience he wanted to create within his reader or listener, or the meaning he wished to convey. Analyzing a selection to find the purpose leads the interpreter in several directions. In order to be sure he has not overlooked any important aspect of the material, he must search for the subject or theme. He must find the attitude toward the subject, the conclusions concerning the subject or thesis and the intended emotional, intellectual, or esthetic experiences which underlie the selection.

Identifying the subject is the simplest part of the process of finding what it is all about. The title often states the subject. See, for instance, Amy Lowell's "Patterns," Sandburg's "The People, Yes," Milton's "Lycidas," William Blake's "The Tiger," or Robert Frost's "Mending Wall." Some selections state the subject within the text. Robert Frost begins his poem entitled, "To Earthward" by telling us of his reactions to sensations—"love at the lips," odors of musk and honeysuckle, the touch of rose petals—when he was young. Then he speaks of the fact that

> Now no joy but lacks salt
> That is not dashed with pain
> And weariness and fault; . . .

He needs stronger sensations as he grows older to satisfy his desires for sense experiences. The topic is clear within the text: sense experiences. Sometimes an author states his topic, sometimes he permits the reader to discover it in the context of what he writes. Such, for instance, is the case in A. E. Housman's "When I was One and Twenty." The subject of this poem is the feeling of youth that it knows a great deal. Housman never says that is his subject, but the reader discovers it when he says

> But I was one-and-twenty,
> No use to talk to me.

And again when he says

> And I am two-and-twenty,
> And oh, 'tis true, 'tis true.

Several readings may be required of some poems before the subject or topic about which they were written emerges. The following poem by Edith Sitwell is an example. The title, "Trio for Two Cats and a Trombone," you will discover has little if anything to do with the subject.

> Long steel grass—
> The white soldiers pass—
> The light is braying like an ass.
> See
> The tall Spanish jade
> With hair black as nightshade
> Worn as a cockade!
> Flee
> Her eyes' gasconade
> And her gown's parade
> (As stiff as a brigade).
> Tee-hee!
> The hard and braying light
> Is zebra'd black and white;
> It will take away the slight
> And free
> Tinge of the mouth-organ sound
> (Oyster-stall notes) oozing round

Her flounces as they sweep the ground.
The
Trumpet and the drum
And the martial cornet come
To make the people dumb—
But we
Won't wait for sly-foot night
(Moonlight, watered milk-white, bright)
To make clear the declaration
Of our Paphian vocation,
Beside the castanetted sea,
Where stalks Il Capitaneo
Swaggart braggadocio
Sword and mustacio—
He
Is green as a cassada,
And his hair is an armada.
To the jade 'Come kiss me harder'
He called across the battlements as she
Heard our voices thin and shrill
As the steely grasses' thrill,
Or the sound of the onycha
When the phoca has the pica
In the palace of the Queen Chinee!

The title, the verse form with its heavily marked rhythms, the repetitions and variations of sounds (phoca, pica, onycha, Chinee) in nonsense words add up to nothing in identifying the subject. But an analysis of the people of the poem, the tall Spanish jade, she, and Il Capitaneo, and their actions reveals a triangle love affair as the subject of the poem.

It is when we pursue the problem of meaning past the stage of identifying the subject or topic that all the other trappings of the poem begin to make their contributions to our understanding. Here analysis reveals a mocking, harsh attitude toward the lovers. The one is a jade with hair worn like a knot of ribbon on his head. She, with boastful eyes and overdress, is a picture of pride. The second lover and rival is presented as swaggart, green, with hair like a fleet of war vessels. The combination of the mockery with the romantic love elements, phrased in the cheap jazz sounds and rhythms of the poem, presents not only the subject of love but reveals a bitter, mocking attitude toward this world of romantic faith.

The poem of Robert Frost, "To Earthward," referred to above, not only discusses the subject of sensations but also reveals an attitude toward them: they have been, and still are, a source of much pleasure to Mr. Frost. The poem of Mr. Housman reflects an amused attitude toward his youthful superiority and certainty. These attitudes color the treatment of the subject and prepare the reader or the listener for the thematic conclusions.

In some poems, such as the Frost selection, the thematic conclusion is clearly stated

> When stiff and sore and scarred
> I take away my hand
> From leaning on it hard
> In grass and sand,
> The hurt is not enough:
> I long for weight and strength
> To feel the earth as rough
> To all my length.

These last three lines carry the summing up of his reactions to his subject; they are his conclusion. Housman's "When I Was One and Twenty" does not state its conclusion. Instead what seems to be a conclusion (And oh, 'tis true) turns out to be irony and drives home further by its indirection Housman's point that the young are amusingly sure of themselves. Miss Sitwell's "Trio" does not state its conclusions, either. Nor can we discover any line or lines that epitomize the point of the whole poem. The whole poem forms a complex mixture of incompatible materials through which we read her attitude toward her subject and from which, in turn, we assume a conclusion: romantic love and all its trappings are false, feelingless, meaningless, and even comic.

There may be, and in much good literature there is, a further, a deeper meaning in the selection which can rarely be described adequately in words but which often represents the specific purpose of the artist in creating his story, poem, or play. This meaning is the esthetic experience to be found in the piece: the creation of a feeling, the revelation of a truth with emotional as well as intellectual dimensions, the flash of an insight into something unique and fresh, an experience of what life or something in life feels like. For the accomplishment of this deeper meaning the writer has marshalled all his forces. His story, if he has a story, his characters, if he uses characters, the thematic conclusions, the attitudes, the subject—all these are the structure and the flesh of his piece. The words, the sentences with their specially selected forms, the figures of speech, the rhythms and the rhymes, the sounds—all these are the affective coloring materials which he combines with the structure and the flesh of his selection to create for his audience an experience often too subtly based in the deeper and wordless life of the emotions to be expressed in any other way than through the complex combination of materials which go into a work of art.

If Frost has been successful in "To Earthward" he has given us the feel of once intense reactions to sensations, now meager reactions to stimuli of equal strength, and the hunger of his whole body for strong, even rough and hurtful, sensations. The very attempt to phrase the esthetic experience Frost sought does violence to the feeling in the poem. This is something we "know" as much with our inner sensations as with the language and reasoning level of our minds. If Housman has been successful, we feel our amusement at our own youth even, somehow, if we ourselves are only one-and-twenty! The many harsh images in Miss Sitwell's poem (light . . . braying like an ass; mouth-organ sound . . . oozing round her flounces; where stalks Il Capitaneo; to the jade "Come kiss me harder"), the strong rhythms, the obvious romantic story, the vigorous repetitions of sound (See, Flee, Tee-hee!, But we, He, etc.) all combine to give us a new feeling, a new sensation, a new attitude toward her subject.

The pursuit and discovery of these elements in the selection—subject, attitude toward the subject, conclusions of the writer about his subject, and the esthetic purpose of the writer—constitute the very heart of the analysis task of the interpreter. The discovery of these elements makes clarity of presentation possible. They guide him in selecting and building the emotional tone of his presentation. They assist him to clarify his own specific purpose which will be, of course, to bring to the audience the experience the author intended.

There will be an over-all or general purpose to be considered. The dominant general purpose may be to entertain, to instruct, to persuade, to inspire. Paul's letter to the Corinthians on charity (I Corinthians xiii) teaches through inspiration. James Thurber's "University Days" from *My Life and Hard Times* amuses by means of satiric overstatement of some alleged university practices. Robinson Jeffers' main purpose in "The Trap" is to persuade us that

> Blind war, compared to this kind of life, [Toys,
> motors, fine clothes, leisure, diversion]
> Has nobility, famine has dignity.

This general purpose provides a sort of key, a framework within which is to be found the specific purpose. It is, perhaps, more important to the artist who created the selection than to the interpreter, but it does provide some broad guidelines.

If there is an esthetic experience in the selection, it should be the specific purpose of the interpreter to cause this experience to be re-created in his listeners. He will bend every effort, he will select and discipline his every technique, so that the experience is created in each member of his audience with all the clarity and intensity he can discover in the selection. This is not a vague sort of experience with dimly defined limits. It may not be possible to describe it accurately in words, but if the writer is a writer of quality, the experience he intends is clearly discernible and not to be trifled with. Discovering it demands close study and consideration of every element followed by a careful tuning in of yourself to these elements in order that you may create for yourself an accurate synthesis. Outlining the thought, analyzing the structure, noting patterns of sound, paraphrasing—all the aids to assimilation may have to be called into service. One of the most helpful is often the condensative paraphrase wherein you condense the words of the author into a very few words. But the real synthesis will probably be only partly a matter of words and largely a matter of feeling.

If the selection's major emphasis is on a thesis or conclusion, the task is a more intellectual one and involves the use of words primarily. The condensative paraphrase is doubtless the most useful tool in determining the specific purpose in this kind of material. Statement of specific purpose here often follows some such form as "What I want the audience to have clear in its mind is that war is curious, since you shoot a person down you'd treat if you met him in ordinary circumstances" (Thomas Hardy's "The Man He Killed"). The statement of specific purpose is simple, clear, and to the point. It states precisely what it is the interpreter wants to have happen to the audience.

Whatever the specific purpose, whether it be to make the audience visualize children swinging from birch trees (Robert Frost, "Birches"), sense the frustration of any man with a sense of beauty in his effort to achieve "a lasting haven of happiness, an elysium in life" (as we are made to feel it through the love story of Ashurst and Megan in Galsworthy's hauntingly beautiful novelette, *The Apple Tree*), or catch the feeling of human dignity and personal pride in a woman with a desire to give in to the demands of an autocratic and overly proud person of whom she is extremely fond (in *The King and I*)—whatever the specific purpose it must coincide precisely with that intended by the author, it must be simply and clearly identified, and it must be the lodestar which determines every turning in the preparation and presentation of the selection. There may be many minor themes, there may be several aspects of the emotional content, there may be turns of thought, but there is one central or focal purpose—one specific purpose—by which the interpreter will set his sights.

## EXERCISES

1. Condense the emotional and logical sense of each of the following selections and then formulate and write down a statement of general and specific purpose for each:

"The Jumping Frog," Mark Twain
"Journey," Edna St. Vincent Millay

Meeting at Night, Robert Browning
Gloucester's opening speech ("Now is the winter of our dis-
content") Richard III, Shakespeare
"The World Is Too Much With Us," Wordsworth

2. Select one of the above selections to prepare and read aloud
to the class. Watch the class for evidences that your purpose is being
accomplished. Remember that there are other evidences of amusement than roars of laughter.

3. Make your own choice of material to read to the class pur-
posefully.

## Additional Readings

Cunningham, Cornelius C., Literature As a Fine Art. New York: Thomas
    Nelson & Sons, 1941, pp. 233-258.
Daniels, Earl, The Art of Reading Poetry. New York: Farrar and Rine-
    hart, Inc., 1941, pp. 252-343.
Edman, Irwin, Arts and the Man. New York: The New American Li-
    brary of World Literature, Inc., 1949, passim.
Langer, Susanne K., Problems of Art. New York: Charles Scribner's Sons,
    1957, pp. 13-58.
Lowrey, Sara, and Gertrude E. Johnson, Interpretative Reading: Tech-
    niques and Selections (rev. ed.). New York: Appleton-Century-
    Crofts, Inc., 1953, pp. 197-228.
Woolbert, Charles H., and Severina E. Nelson, The Art of Interpretative
    Speech (ed. 4). New York: Appleton-Century-Crofts, Inc., 1956,
    pp. 47-76.

# Organization of the Selection

AFTER THE SUBJECT OF THE SELECTION HAS BEEN IDENTIFIED, THE
author's attitude toward the subject determined, the author's conclusions about his theme noted, and the nature of the esthetic experience
contained in the selection defined, the interpreter seeks the means to
make these things clear and effective for the audience. One of the
elements to be found in the selection which is of particular significance in this respect is its organization.

The organization of anything is the way its parts are arranged in
relation to one another. The arrangement may be very simple or very
complex, but if there is organization there is always a meaningful
relationship involved in the arrangement of the parts. One brick
standing alone is not an organization. But two bricks, side by side,
end to end, end to side, one on top of the other, or in any other
meaningful relationship are an organization of bricks. Hundreds of
thousands of bricks arranged in complex patterns make a Windsor
Castle for Queen Elizabeth II and her family. One word may have
meaning, but alone it has no organization. Two words juxtaposed may
or may not have a meaningful relationship. There is little meaning
in *six the*. But the unknown poet who wrote

*I!*

*Why?*

arranged his words meaningfully. Any change in their arrangement
changes their meaning. "Why I?" does not produce the same effect.
Nor does

*Why?*

*I!*

Nor even "I! Why?" Each may be a meaningful arrangement, an
organization, but each differs from the others.

The painter arranges his space in the painting. He arranges the relationships of color. The architect arranges his building blocks. The musician arranges his sounds. The poet arranges his words in order, even to their placement on the page. He chooses to present his ideas in a particular order, he arranges his rhythms and sounds, his imagery, his stanzas, his verses in a selected relationship one to another. The dramatist arranges his acts and scenes and episodes, his crises and climaxes, his exposition and his action, his revelations of character in a systematic, meaningful order.

While it is true that most of man's activity is organized—he arranges the parts of his automobile, he arranges the order of his worship services, he arranges his day's work—his artistic production depends highly on its ordering and arrangement for its effectiveness.

One of the most important functions of organization is to give and clarify meaning. The interpreter's audience will have little success in finding meaning in the selection until it has perceived and noted the significance of the arrangement in the selection. The very essence of meaning lies in the perception of relationships with dimensions of length, breadth, height, and time, of cause and effect, stimulus and response, hotter and colder, of home and country, the world, the universe, the Mind of God. Any phenomenon takes on meaning as we see its relationship to us or to something else. This statement is equally true of the elements in a speech, poem, story, or play.

A second important function of organization is the building up of emotional effect. By withholding some images or ideas until others have had their effect, the emotional impact is often heightened. Such is the case in Housman's poem "When I Was One and Twenty." He develops his thoughts around the errors of thought at one-and-twenty through fourteen lines. Then he adds the two lines beginning "And I am two-and-twenty" with their ironical turn of thought, providing the poem with its amusing quality. Had he begun with the last thought, the fun would have been destroyed and the result a dull moralizing. A short story such as Charlotte Perkins Gilman's "The Yellow Wallpaper" builds its effect of horror at the insanity of the person presumably telling the story by starting out in a quiet, reasonable manner, then adding detail after detail each of which reveals more and more that the person speaking is entirely the victim of dreadful hallucinations, until finally we realize that she believes she is caged behind the pattern in the wallpaper and that the mark on the wall is the result of her crawling round and round the room, trying to get out. By organizing the details of her story in a climactic order, the whole experience of the reader is intensified.

There are many kinds of organization, of organization within organization, and of interrelated organizations. It is impossible to describe all the kinds, for the material and the mind of the artist impose on every new poem, story, or play, every new speech or essay, a new solution of the problem, new possibilities of organization. It may be useful, however, to note a few of the types of organization most commonly encountered in order that we may see more clearly how to find the organization in the selections we expect to present.

Everyone, in writing compositions, making and hearing public speeches, and in reading, has had experience with the "introduction—body—conclusion" type of organization. In this order of materials the subject is introduced first, with whatever history, definition, and analysis it needs, grouped with attention-getting remarks; in the body the subject is developed; in the conclusion, by summary, questions, anecdotes, quotations, or striking statements, the subject is finished and the whole given a closer sense of unity. This form lends itself to the prose expository and persuasive discourse rather easily; it is often applied to other forms as well, but not so often to poetry. It is an over-all form within which other methods of organization are usually developed.

A very common organization of a story, whether it be in the form of a novel, a play, a short story, or a fable, is for the author to provide exposition of place, time, characters, and background information. Into this combination of elements is next introduced the situation, a sort of definition of the relationships of these elements to one another, particularly the characters. Next the author introduces a disturbance in the life of one or more of his characters. The disturbed ones decide to do something about this new and painful state of affairs and set out to accomplish a goal (get engaged to the girl, prevent the villain from foreclosing on the mortgage, get elected, find the lost child). Next, obstacles and complications rise to block the disturbed ones. And finally the goal is achieved or the disturbed ones clearly defeated.

This pattern may be varied from story to story. Or the author may choose to present events in a simple time sequence without other relationships. First event A happens, then event B, then event C. "At eight o'clock he took the bus; at 8:15 the bus broke down; at 8:30 he walked toward the office, at 9:00 he met his brother; at 9:30 he arrived at the office." There is little relationship between these events except a time relationship (plus the further but not unimportant fact that *he* is involved in each happening).

A more common organization is the cause-to-effect relationship. "He left the lights turned on which caused the battery to run down which prevented the starter from turning over the motor which...."

Another organization frequently encountered is the contrast or comparison. Sometimes it is as brief as a metaphor or a simile, sometimes it is an extended analogy.

> *The fog comes*
> *on little cat feet.*
> *It sits looking*
> *over harbor and city*
> *on silent haunches*
> *and then moves on.*
> "Fog," CARL SANDBURG

or

> "*A snake is as round as a hole in the ground;*
> *Weasels are wavy and sleek;*
> *And no alligator could ever be straighter*
> *Than lizards that live in a creek.*
>
> *But a Camel's all lumpy*
> *And bumpy and humpy—*
> *ANY SHAPE does for me!*"
> "The Plaint of the Camel," CHARLES EDWARD CARRYL

From these simple comparisons and contrasts the materials of literature range through longer analogies to very complex compositions. The comparison by Jesus of Himself to the true vine and His Father to the husbandman (John 15: 1-17) is a simple one. Plato's "Allegory of the Cave" (*The Republic*, Book VII) is considerably more complex. But Plato's analogy seems child's play alongside Edmund Spenser's *Faerie Queene*.

Another organization quite commonly found is the question and answer:

> *Tell me where is fancy bred,*
> *Or in the heart or in the head?*
>> *How begat, how nourished?*
>> *Reply, reply.*

> *It is engender'd in the eyes,*
> *With gazing fed; and fancy dies*
> *In the cradle where it lies.*
>> *Let us all ring fancy's knell;*
>> *I'll begin it,— Ding, dong, bell.*
>>> *Ding, dong, bell.*
>>> The Merchant of Venice, SHAKESPEARE

> *'Is my team ploughing,*
>> *That I used to drive*
> *And hear the harness jingle*
>> *When I was man alive?'*

> *Ay, the horses trample,*
>> *The harness jingles now;*
> *No change though you lie under*
>> *The land you used to plough.*
>> "Is My Team Ploughing," A. E. HOUSMAN

Some selections have long answers and short questions, some the reverse. But the basic structure is the same.

Another common organization is the statement of subject or situation followed by comment on it or what it seems to be, followed in turn by some development of thought or event or revelation which puts new light on the subject and adds to our insights:

> *I hate and love—the why I cannot tell,*
> *But by my tortures know the fact too well.*
>> "Love's Unreason," CATULLUS

Having this day my horse, my hand, my lance
Guided so well that I obtained the prize,
Both by the judgment of the English eyes
And of some sent by that sweet enemy, France;
Horsemen my skill in horsemanship advance,
Town folks my strength; a daintier judge applies
His praise to sleight from which good use doth rise;
Some lucky wits impute it but to chance;
Others, because of both sides I do take
My blood from them who did excel in this,
Think Nature me a man-at-arms did make.
How far they shot away! the true cause is,
Stella looked on, and from her heavenly face
Sent forth the beams which made so fair my race.

Sonnet XLI, *Astrophel and Stella*, SIR PHILIP SIDNEY

There are many other kinds or methods of organization: association of ideas, space relationships, "not this . . . , but this . . . ," the
series (1st, 2nd, 3rd), etc. Some kind of structure is in every successful
piece of writing and this ordering of the materials lends clarity, meaning, and emotional impact to the selection. When the reader and his
audience both see clearly what the structure is, they follow more easily
the author's meaning.

Many signs and marks of structure help the reader to identify the
organizational pattern. Most important of these is the order in which
the words and sentences are set down on the page. Other signs include
the mechanical devices of stanza divisions, paragraph divisions, and
indentations; the time signs of *then, and, later, now, soon, when, after,
before,* etc.; the comparison signs of *like, as;* the contrast signs of *yet,
but, not only . . . but also, not . . . but,* etc.; the direction signs in space
arrangement of *right, left, over, beyond, north, south, east, west, up,
down,* etc. The playwright uses entrances, exits, dimouts, and curtains
to help indicate the major structure units. The novelist divides his
work into chapters.

A transitional or marking device does not always guide the listener through the movement from section to section of the selection's
structure. If this is the case, the interpreter must project a sense of

organization to his audience by means other than words. One of these means is called "building" (sometimes, more narrowly, "topping," especially in dialogue), which is accomplished by progressively increasing the intensity of tone, raising the pitch, increasing the intensity of emotion, or any combination of these. This progressive change of pitch and loudness from point to point or section to section or idea to idea can give a sense of change or movement in structure. It can be accomplished by reversing these processes, too, until the main point is reached.

A transition that is not part of a progression of transitions can be indicated by almost any means, vocal or physical, which indicate a change: shift of pitch, shift of loudness, pause, change of emotional quality in the voice, change in direction of attention, change in position of the body. All of these may be used to signal a change, a move to another aspect of the structure or organization of the selection.

All of these signs and devices help the reader and his audience to orient themselves, to answer the questions, Where are we? When do these events take place? What does this have to do with that? What does it mean? The reader will take care not only to find these devices for himself, but to see to it that his audience does not overlook them. ∎

# EXERCISES

1. Organize the following speeches so there will be a background or introduction, a series of points, and a conclusion:

Henry V's speech before Harfleur, Act III, Scene 1, *Henry V*, Shakespeare

John Brown's speech to the jury from *John Brown's Body*, Benét

Mark Anthony's funeral speech, *Julius Caesar*, Shakespeare

2. Prepare one of the above to read aloud to the class, making your organization definite enough so they can list your major points.

3. Make your own selection of material and deliver it so the class can list your major points.

## Additional Readings

Boardman, Gail, *Oral Communication of Literature*. New York: Prentice-Hall, Inc., 1952, pp. 97-190.

Cunningham, Cornelius C., *Literature As a Fine Art*. New York: Thomas Nelson & Sons, 1941, pp. 91-132.

Daniels, Earl, *The Art of Reading Poetry*. New York: Farrar and Rinehart, Inc., 1941, pp. 344-421.

McLean, Margaret Prendergast, *Oral Interpretation of Forms of Literature*. New York: E. P. Dutton & Co., Inc., 1942, pp. 121-127.

# Making Points

THE ORGANIZATION OF THE SELECTION IS OF GREAT IMPORTANCE IN guiding the listener to an understanding; it is, of course, only the guide, the series of arrows pointing the way. What is being organized is the basic units of thought, the sentences. Individually and in groups sentences carry the ideas and the feelings which have the final impact of accomplishing the esthetic, intellectual, and emotional purpose of the author.

Many elements influence the meaning of a sentence: the context of the whole selection, the place of the sentence in relation to the structure of the piece, its juxtaposition to other sentences, the words and their order within the sentence, and not least, certainly, the emphasis or focus on words within the sentence. Our language is a marvelously flexible instrument so cleverly devised that the same words in the same order can be made to mean many different things by shifting the emphasis from one word to another, a practice called "making points."

The simple sentence, "I will walk home now," may be read with five different purposes, each of which will result in emphasis of a different word, as follows:

1. Purpose: to make clear my intention as contrasted with that of others.
   I will walk home now.
2. Purpose: to make clear my determination.
   I WILL walk home now.
3. Purpose: to make it clear I want to walk and not to ride.
   I will WALK home now.
4. Purpose: to make my destination clear.
   I will walk HOME now.
5. Purpose: to make it clear I will depart immediately.
   I will walk home NOW.

Though we often think of nouns and verbs as carrying the most meaning, emphasis may fall on any part of speech—noun, pronoun, adjective, verb, adverb, conjunction, or preposition. Lincoln spoke of government "of the people, by the people and for the people." One might speak of "liberty and union." A boy might say, "She is the girl for me."

You may demonstrate this change of meaning if you will make up three sentences to read to someone else. In several readings shift your purpose (and emphasis) from point to point and see whether your different purposes can be understood. Then try to read each word of each of the sentences with equal emphasis, first with little emphasis on each word, and then with a great deal of emphasis. You will note interesting changes in opinion as to what your purpose is.

When all words are given equal emphasis, it is useful to note that the audience tends to interpret your mood rather than your meaning. When little, but equal, emphasis is given, the reader sounds dull, and when much but equal emphasis is given each word, the speaker sounds angry. There are, indeed, times when the speaker's purpose may be an emotional and not a logical one, but when an entire reading is read with so little emphasis that points are not clear to an audience, the reading is simply dead and dull. If, on the other hand, a selection is read with too many words receiving equal emphasis, the listener will feel that too much is being thrown at him and will stop trying to sort out for himself what is important and what is not. Generally speaking, making too many points is a harder habit to break than making too few. A good general rule to remember (though there are exceptions) is to make only one major point in each phrase.

Note how emphasizing the lightly capitalized words in the following short passage almost magically clarifies the meaning and helps the listener through the shifting thought.

PETRUCHIO.

> Good morrow, KATE;
> for that's your NAME, I hear.

KATHERINE.

> Well have you HEARD,
> but something HARD of HEARING:
> They call me KATHERINE that do talk of me.

PETRUCHIO.

> You LIE, *in faith;*
> *For you are call'd* PLAIN *Kate,*
> *And* BONNY *Kate,*
> *And sometimes Kate the* CURST:
> *but* KATE,
> *the* PRETTIEST *Kate in Christendom.*

If one goes further and heavily capitalizes some words, such as NAME, KATHERINE, KATE (next to last line), to indicate heavier pointing, the meaning becomes even clearer.

The old verse

> *I used to think I knew I knew*
> *But now I must confess,*
> *The more I know I know I know*
> *I know I know the less.*

makes little if any sense at all until certain *know's* are singled out for emphasis. The second *I know* in the third line needs to be focused upon with energy. Then all else begins to fall in place.

It becomes apparent that there is a significance not only in what is emphasized, but also in what is not. On the opposite side of this fabric of emphasis is de-emphasis. Compared to some other languages, English is very heavily de-emphasized. One of the most important things foreigners must master when they learn English pronunciation is how *not* to emphasize. A common instruction in the theater is to "throw away" certain words and phrases, because they are not important. Similarly, though they must be heard by the audience, the reader needs barely to touch or "throw away" the words in a phrase that are not "pointed up." Read the selection above with this in mind.

To find the word to be emphasized in a phrase normally requires only a little thought and study of the selection, for our experience with language, since before we learned to talk, guides us. There are some kinds of difficulties, however, some especially important practices, and some results of bad judgment and habit which merit special consideration.

When there are several possible choices of words to be emphasized in a phrase, the reader sometimes needs to take counsel with himself, and ask, "Just what do I mean? What is important to me?" In the first line of Masefield's "Sea Fever," he writes:

> I must go down to the seas again, to the lonely sea
> and the sky.

What is important in reading this? Is it the compulsion, the place one must go, or the loneliness? It should be noted here that *I* seldom receives emphasis unless very definite contrast is implied. That is a word to "throw away" because it is so obvious. The most common way that teachers elicit emphasis, aside from reading lines for the student, is to ask questions the answers to which must be the points desired. Sometimes the interpreter can use that technique on himself. "*Where* must you go? To the *seas*. Where? To the SEAS again. What kind of sea? The *lonely* sea. What kind? LONELY. Now try the line.

> I must go down to the SEAS again, to the LONELY
> sea and the sky.

In this example *seas* turned out to be more important; for another reader *lonely* might have taken the stronger emphasis.

Some points of emphasis are difficult to locate because the meaning of the sentence is obscure. In that case there is no alternative to ferreting out the meaning, from word to word, from phrase to phrase, from subject to verb to object to modifier. Sometimes the quest leads beyond the selection to the life and times of the author, but until the points of emphasis are clear the meaning remains clouded.

Once a point has been made, it should not be made again in the same way. If an author repeats a phrase or sentence precisely, it should be read differently the second time, as a sort of thoughtful echo or to reinforce the emotional effect, or it should be read with a different point of emphasis. Poetry, with its refrains and repetitions, is often particularly troublesome to the reader. Thomas Hardy's "Waiting Both" is an example:

> A star looks down at me,
> And says: "Here I and you
> Stand, each in our degree:

*What do you mean to do,—*
*Mean to do?"*

*I say: "For all I know,*
*Wait, and let Time go by,*
*Till my change come,"—"Just so,"*
*The star says: "So mean I:—*
*So mean I."*

Repetition of the same degree of emphasis on all words in the refrains would spoil it. Reducing the emphasis on the echo line is probably the best solution since changing points results in a mechanical, artificial sound. A poem like E. A. Poe's "The Bells" has taxed the skill of readers for generations.

Contrasts and comparisons are made clear by emphasizing the contrasted words. This seems to be self-evident, yet how many people fail to emphasize the second member of a comparison as much as the first! Only equal emphasis on the contrasting words in these lines from Edwin Arlington Robinson's "Luke Havergal" can make clear that the solution to the mystery of the meaning of Luke's quest— Is it life? Is it the love of a dead sweetheart?—must be found in death, not in life:

*No, there is not a dawn in* EASTERN *skies*
*To rift the fiery night that's in your eyes;*
*But* THERE, *where* WESTERN *glooms are gathering,*
*The dark will end the dark, if anything.*

Eastern is contrasted with there and western, two words for the same idea, and if the reader fails to lift these words into focus the passage is lost.

Contrast is the major method in this poem by Vachel Lindsay. If the contrasted elements set in capitalized type are not equally emphasized the poem loses its point:

THE LEADEN-EYED

*Let not young souls be smothered out before*
*They do quaint deeds and fully flaunt their pride.*
*It is the world's one crime its babes grow dull,*
*Its poor are ox-like, limp and leaden eyed.*

Not that they STARVE, but starve SO DREAMLESSLY,
Not that they sow, but that they seldom REAP,
Not that they SERVE, but have no GODS to serve,
Not that they DIE, but that they die like SHEEP.

Emphasis is achieved by changing loudness, duration, pitch, or quality (or any combination) to make the word stand out from surrounding words. The more obvious the change, the more obvious the emphasis. The popular assumption is that loudness is by far the most important and frequently used to achieve emphasis, and that a pause before the word to be emphasized is next in importance. Actually, good readers prolong emphasized words and syllables most often. Linked with this prolongation (and possibly because of it) pitch change is the second most frequently used means of emphasis. Prolong the italicized words in the following sentences and shorten the others. What is the result? Now prolong and inflect the italicized words. Now speak the italicized words loudly, but give them the same amount of time and inflection given the other words.

1. I don't *want* it.
2. What are *you* going to do?
3. *When* did you say you would go?

The most obvious result of bad judgment or carelessness in emphasis is vocal patterns, which may become so habitual that they are extremely hard to break up. Because poetic stresses usually fall on the emphasized syllables of words, it is not uncommon to hear poetry read so that all poetic stresses receive precisely the same kind and amount of emphasis. Generally, people call this a "sing-song" reading. We are aware of the same pitch, loudness, and timing on each poetic stress regardless of sense stress.

A second pattern that may become habitual is to so overuse loudness as a means of emphasis that everything sounds angry and "pounded out." This is usually linked with a tendency to make too many points as follows: I cannot *think* that *you* would do *this* to *me*. To correct this pattern, the first step is to determine just what the big point is you wish to make, and then to use prolongation and pitch change to make the point.

The most common pattern habit and the most difficult to correct is to attack each sentence, phrase, or line of poetry strongly and then gradually let it die out so that it is almost a murmur at the end. Such a reader needs to become aware of his habit, first of all, and then to consider what the points are. How many times are the first word or two "thrown away" if one considers the sentence logically! Again and again the points to be emphasized occur later in the sentence, even at the end of the sentence. This periodic or climactic development of the sentence is characteristic of much dramatic dialogue. It is not uncommon to any type of discourse. The reader must recognize that all important elements do not appear in first position and he must learn to conserve energy for the points which come late in the line or sentence.

## EXERCISES

*1.* Select two or three nursery rhymes or other very familiar verse and underline the points of emphasis. Note your tendency, in this kind of familiar material, to overpoint. Try, by changing emphases, to vary the meaning. When you believe it is exactly right, present your reading to the class for their reactions to your choices.

*2.* Read the following passages and their repeats, either as echo or with different stress. Can you explain your choice?

> *God of our fathers, known of old,*
> > *Lord of our far-flung battle-line,*
> *Beneath whose awful Hand we hold*
> > *Dominion over palm and pine—*
> *Lord God of Hosts, be with us yet,*
> *Lest we forget — lest we forget!*

> *The tumult and the shouting dies;*
> > *The captains and the kings depart:*
> *Still stands Thine ancient sacrifice,*
> > *An humble and a contrite heart.*
> *Lord God of Hosts, be with us yet,*
> *Lest we forget — lest we forget!*

Far-called, our navies melt away;
   On dune and headland sinks the fire:
Lo, all our pomp of yesterday
   Is one with Nineveh and Tyre!
Judge of the Nations, spare us yet,
Lest we forget — lest we forget!

If, drunk with sight of power, we loose
   Wild tongues that have not Thee in awe,
Such boasting as the Gentiles use,
   Or lesser breeds without the Law—
Lord God of Hosts, be with us yet,
Lest we forget — lest we forget!

For heathen heart that puts her trust
   In reeking tube and iron shard,
All valiant dust that builds on dust,
   And guarding, calls not Thee to guard,
For frantic boast and foolish word—
Thy Mercy on Thy People, Lord!
              "Recessional," KIPLING

           Sweet Portia,
If you did know to whom I gave the ring,
If you did know for whom I gave the ring,
And would conceive for what I gave the ring,
And how unwillingly I left the ring,
When nought would be accepted but the ring,
You would abate the strength of your displeasure.
           Merchant of Venice, SHAKESPEARE

Give me the splendid silent sun with all his beams full-
   dazzling,
Give me juicy autumnal fruit ripe and red from the
   orchard,
Give me a field where the unmow'd grass grows,
Give me an arbor, give me the trellis'd grape,
Give me fresh corn and wheat, give me serene-moving
   animals, teaching content,

Give me nights perfectly quiet as on high plateaus west
 of the Mississippi, and I looking at the stars,
Give me odorous at sunrise a garden of beautiful flowers
 where I can walk undisturb'd,
Give me for marriage a sweet-breath'd woman of whom
 I should never tire,
Give me a perfect child, give me, away aside from the
 noise of the world a rural domestic life,
Give me to warble spontaneous songs recluse by myself,
 for my own ears only,
Give me solitude, give me Nature, give me again
 O Nature your primal sanities!

      "Give Me the Splendid Silent Sun," Whitman

    Give thy thoughts no tongue,
Nor any unproportion'd thought his act.
Be thou familiar, but by no means vulgar.
Those friends thou hast, and their adoption tried,
Grapple them to thy soul with hoops of steel;
But do not dull thy palm with entertainment
Of each new-hatch'd, unfledg'd comrade. Beware
Of entrance to a quarrel, but being in,
Bear't that th' opposed may beware of thee.
Give every man thy ear, but few thy voice;
Take each man's censure, but reserve thy judgment.
Costly thy habit as thy purse can buy,
But not express'd in fancy; rich, not gaudy;
For the apparel oft proclaims the man,
And they in France of the best rank and station
Are of a most select and generous chief in that.
Neither a borrower nor a lender be;
For loan oft loses both itself and friend,
And borrowing dulleth edge of husbandry.
This above all: to thine own self be true,
And it must follow, as the night the day,
Thou canst not then be false to any man.
Farewell: my blessing season this in thee!

        Hamlet, Shakespeare

To be, or not to be: that is the question:
Whether 'tis nobler in the mind to suffer
The slings and arrows of outrageous fortune,
Or to take arms against a sea of troubles,
And by opposing end them. To die: to sleep;
No more; and by a sleep to say we end
The heart-ache and the thousand natural shocks
That flesh is heir to, 'tis a consummation
Devoutly to be wish'd. To die, to sleep;
To sleep: perchance to dream: ay, there's the rub;
For in that sleep of death what dreams may come
When we have shuffled off this mortal coil,
Must give us pause: there's the respect
That makes calamity of so long life.

Hamlet, SHAKESPEARE

When all the world is young, lad,
  And all the trees are green;
And every goose a swan, lad,
  And every lass a queen;
Then hey for boot and horse, lad,
  And round the world away:
Young blood must have its course, lad,
  And every dog his day.

When all the world is old, lad,
  And all the trees are brown;
And all the sport is stale, lad
  And all the wheels run down;
Creep home, and take your place there,
  The spent and maimed among:
God grant you find one face there,
  You loved when all was young.

"Young and Old," CHARLES KINGSLEY

3. Read the following phrased passage with the pattern described above. Read it again, and make your points where your purpose places them:

I went to the doctor yesterday,
to see about my hay fever,
mechanically
and without much hope of relief,
an attitude which the worthy practitioner did little to change.
His office,
up two flights of stairs
in a decayed region near Golden Square,
is full of large, broody furnishings
which make the room navigable only by persons of a very
    light draft.
The doctor himself is gaunt as a totem pole.
He wore an antiquated black suit,
The lapels of which had been dragged together in a reluctant
    rendezvous just over his collarbone.
When I rehearsed my ailment,
he listened with an attention which seemed too mournful
    and elaborate for a trifling tale of catarrh.
I felt ashamed not to have a life-size, three-dimensional ill-
    ness to offer him,
something with a fair prospect of taking me off.
After I had finished my apologetic plaint,
he looked sadly up my nose
and said in a stifled voice
that there was nothing to be done for hay fever,
if it were hay fever,
but that I might try smelling salts.

              With Malice Toward Some, MARGARET HALSEY

## Additional Readings

Clark, S. H., and Maud May Babcock, *Interpretation of the Printed Page.*
    New York: Prentice-Hall, Inc., 1940, pp. 46-68.
Dolman, John, Jr., *The Art of Acting.* New York: Harper & Brothers,
    1949, pp. 107-112.

Fairbanks, Grant, *Voice and Articulation Drillbook.* New York: Harper & Brothers, 1940, pp. 218-227.

Ortleb, R., "An Objective Study of Emphasis in Oral Reading of Emotional and Unemotional Material," *Speech Monographs,* 4:56-68, 1937.

Tiffen, J., and M. D. Steer, "An Experimental Analysis of Emphasis," *Speech Monographs,* 4:69-74, 1937.

# Synthesis and Evaluation of Progress

SELECT FOR PRESENTATION TO THE CLASS A SOMEWHAT MORE AMBITIOUS project in literature than you have chosen so far which will give you an opportunity to exhibit your skills of analysis and your ability to carry on a sustained effort. Your selection should be a piece of literature which does not yield its meaning at a first or second reading, but one which demands research into backgrounds, close study of the text for organization and purpose, careful analysis of language and a nice attention to making points. Look to the dramatic monologues of Browning, the works of John Milton, Shakespeare, Marlowe, Shelley, Keats, Wordsworth, Jeffers, Matthew Arnold, James Joyce, or others whose intellectual demands on the reader are strong and whose accomplishments in artistic achievement have been recognized as of very high quality.

Prepare your reading with thoroughness, leaving no aspect of the analysis unfinished. Study to make your reading reveal not only the author's ideas, but his attitudes, his particular individuality, his style, and his specific purpose. Decide on the desirable esthetic distance, who is being addressed, the role of the audience. Pay attention to emphasis and the making of points.

Your practice should be thorough enough so that you feel kinship with the author. Assimilate his words, his ideas, his imagery into your own person. Re-create the selection. Experience it yourself. Then try to project the whole complex experience and personality of the author, as they are revealed in the selection, to your audience.

You may want to use a brief introduction. Sometimes an announcement of the author's name and the title of the selection is sufficient. For other materials a few very brief remarks may be required to orient the audience.

Your performance will be judged on the following points:

1. Selection of material
2. Analysis of material: language, structure, nature and mood of speaker
3. Definition of specific purpose: clarity, effectiveness
4. Assimilation of material: imagery and sincerity
5. Directness: proper direction of the selection; rapport with audience
6. Delivery: phrasing, emphasis, pronunciation, clearness of relationships
7. General effectiveness: ability to hold involuntary attention.

# 4

## PROJECTS IN
# Physical
# Expressiveness

[PROJECT 4.1]
### The Role of Physical Behavior in Communication

[PROJECT 4.2]
### Relaxation and Poise

[PROJECT 4.3]
### Concentration and Abandon

[PROJECT 4.4]
### Descriptive and Emphatic Movement

[PROJECT 4.5]
### Judgment and Physical Response

[PROJECT 4.6]
### Synthesis and Evaluation of Progress

# The Role of Physical Behavior in Communication

THERE HAS PROBABLY BEEN MORE CONTROVERSY REGARDING THE physical behavior of the oral interpreter than regarding any other phase of his art. Glaring bad taste and poor judgment on the part of some interpreters have led their observers to make dogmatic statements and rules such as that there are distinct divisions between "acting," "impersonation," and "oral reading," or that all action should be reduced to a minimum in oral reading. Officials of reading contests have even ruled that there should be no action and that readers who move should be penalized by the judges. Fortunately, appropriate physical response seems so right and natural that it usually goes unnoticed.

Without reference to any particular piece of literature, let us recognize a number of facts that relate to the problem of physical behavior. First, all of us, interpreters included, are here in the flesh and people recognize and respond to our physical presence. Without quite realizing how, we notice that our friends seem sad, gay, tired, or bored because we look at them and note their physical responses. Whatever a person's mood or emotion, whatever his attitude, he carries it with him and it is reflected in his physical appearance, generally so clearly that we "sense" it immediately. Second, people generally are sensitive to appearances and feel considerable confidence in their ability to interpret them; they commonly make judgments about the general character of others from their appearance. Some of us judge whether or not we like a person simply on the basis of his looks. Americans, especially, are very conscious of cleanliness and good grooming. Employers are not usually content with letters of application, pictures, and recommendations. They want a personal interview —a chance to see the candidate and his reactions. Whatever physical appearance the interpreter takes before his audience makes an impression as to the kind of person he is. Third, since we both hear and see the interpreter, what we see contributes importantly to our experience. Every project we have discussed so far has been considered on the basis of seeing and hearing. We know if a reader is imaging by watching his face and eyes and sometimes we are aware that his hands are helping his imagery. We know how he is directing attention by watching him. We judge from what point of view he is speaking by watching him. We sense much of the esthetic distance he is attempting to establish from his appearance and his actions. We recognize that some action communicates ideas or helps to clarify and reinforce ideas, that some action communicates emotion. At the play, in the lecture hall, at the interpreter's lecture recital we strain to see, if an object or another person intervenes. People flocked to radio broadcasts to see the artists. Television was hailed as a great step forward because we could both hear and see.

Physical appearance as an indication of an interpreter's background and habits of person needs little comment. By long experience we have learned that cleanliness, good grooming, taste in the selection of clothing appropriate to the person, the occasion, and the place, posture, control of movement to the point of gracefulness and efficiency are generally companions to traits of personality which we approve and usually admire. We have learned to read from its appearance the disciplines the body has been given.

Nor is there anything unfamiliar or difficult to understand about the function of the body in helping to communicate ideas. Although the body does not have as many idea resources as the tongue nor so wide a vocabulary, there is a language of physical action as specific as the language of words. Nodding and shaking the head, turning toward or away, pointing directions, measuring of size with the hands, shaking the fist, shaking a finger—all these communicate ideas. Some actions are complete by themselves in conveying meaning; others are employed to reinforce or clarify the word language they accompany.

The functions of the body in the communicative process that have to do with emotions and emotional responses are perhaps a little less understood and bear examination, since it is upon this part of the process and the principles involved therein that so much of the actor's, the dancer's, the speaker's and the interpreter's art rests. Our concern here is with the part the body plays in eliciting an emotional response from members of the audience.

Three important characteristics of human behavior are related to the problem. One of these is the fact that the physical behavior that accompanies any emotion tends to be much the same from one experience of the emotion to the next and from one person to another. A second of these characteristics of human behavior is that a person tends to imitate the physical action he observes in another. And a third is that not only does the emotion tend to cause the physical behavior characteristic of that emotion, but the physical behavior characteristic of a given emotion tends to result in the production of that emotion.

That there is similarity of physical behavior from incidence to incidence of our anger (or any other emotion), or from one man's anger to another's, is a fact we are all aware of very early in life. This fact is perhaps more apparent in the actions of others than it is in ourselves. Before we could talk we had begun to learn the emotional meaning of other people's actions: the rough, hard actions and muscular tensions of anger, the soft, gentle, yielding actions and muscular tensions of love, the quick movements and rising tensions of terror. Continued experience has assured us that we are rarely in error as to what the emotion is. Occasionally we are astonished to have "read" or discerned the true emotion in spite of a "cover-up" of actions designed to look like something else. Our carefully trained eyes have observed while our attention has been directed elsewhere. In part what we have seen is the evidence of muscular tensions, of big muscles and little, in combination and alone, that produce the motion or outward movement of the person. We have also noted the motions of countertensions and the tiny movements in the smaller muscles. We have not only seen these evidences of tension, but we have also recognized them as the tensions that go with some specific emotion. We may or may not have observed other kinds of evidence—changed color, words —but these signs have told their tale because they are always nearly the same: anger has its characteristic muscular tensions; sorrow, joy, love, distrust—each creates almost the same pattern every time it occurs.

It should also be noted at this point that the voice is a physical instrument and that what we hear by way of quality, pitch, loudness, and rate is the result of a great complex of muscular tensions. The muscles of voice production respond with great sensitivity to our emotions and we are so attuned and so sensitive to the voices of others, we have trained our own vocal mechanisms so thoroughly and so wonderfully to imitate what we hear even to the minutest changes in quality and pitch, that we have only to hear to be able in an instant to adjust the complex musculature of abdomen, chest, larynx, pharynx, tongue, and jaws to similar tensions, with the resultant feeling. We can reproduce the feelings and tensions of others or "read" their feelings from their voices.

The second characteristic, our tendency to imitate the actions of others, we can observe in ourselves and our friends, sometimes to the embarrassment of all concerned. If we are not alert to the danger we may find ourselves walking like the man with the limp just ahead of us, scratching our ears like the man at the next table, cocking our heads like the hard-of-hearing gentleman at the dinner party, or peering over our glasses like the lady behind the desk at the library. This tendency to imitate is called empathic response and is a physical, nonthoughtful reaction to the behavior of others. While it is true that our tendency to imitate extends to animals, machines, and even objects, that some authorities claim we imitate inanimate, nonmoving objects, our concern here is only with the tendency to imitate other people and our discussion is limited to that. Were it not for the inhibitions placed upon us by our training, the tendency toward imitation would no doubt lead us into many more comic and tragic situations than it does. It is also to be noted that many factors call on our attention at once and the imitation tendency is usually considerably dissipated before we have completely given in to it.

The third characteristic, the fact that there is a direct relationship between feeling or emotion and muscular tension or physical behavior, a fact known as the James-Lange theory of emotion, we can observe in our actions from time to time. Arise in the morning feeling in low spirits, force a smile, a light step, and lifted shoulders; shortly the low spirits have evaporated and a happier feeling has taken over. Beware the friendly sparring match, for it often turns into a fight in good earnest. Force yourself into friendly actions and gestures, and you often see your enemy as someone you like. This approach to the production of feeling is less common than the more familiar "experience the feeling, then note the physical behavior changes" process, but it is nonetheless real.

With these principles clearly in mind it is not difficult to trace the body's function in the communicative process. Assume that the interpreter stands before an audience to read. The materials before him, his preparation for reading them, the images he is calling up, all result in an emotional response or feeling within him. As a result of this feeling his muscles take on the tension pattern characteristic of that feeling. The audience observes him and unconsciously tends to assume the same set of muscular tensions it has consciously or unconsciously observed. Since this is the set of muscular tensions characteristic of the emotion felt by the interpreter, the audience soon experiences that same emotion. If this feeling is a proper companion for the emotional quality of the imagery and ideas of the selection being read, then it reinforces what the interpreter is trying to get done—it assists the interpreter in accomplishing his specific purpose.

Whatever emotions the audience holds, with their accompanying muscular tensions, will have an effect upon the interpreter in return, for he is subject to the same empathic responses to the audience that they are subject to from him. If he receives a strong impression of muscular tensions like the ones he already is experiencing, his own are reinforced.

Only in rare, somewhat magic, moments in the theatre, in the lecture-recital hall, or any other place where an interpretative event occurs does the process just described take place with the directness, the force, and the clarity described above. The careful reader will have noted the qualification *tends to* in several places. Many elements in the situation prevent the total empathic response to the interpreter which he would like to elicit from his audience. Many circumstances prevent the complete correlation between muscular tension patterns and our feelings or emotions.

There are probably many reasons why we do not imitate the

actions we see. It takes effort to imitate. We may be imitating or carrying out actions of our own, actions and muscular tensions that are characteristic of our own thinking, our own will, and our own emotions. Besides, we have been taught that direct imitation is in most circumstances discourteous.

But in the interpretative situation where the audience willfully gives its attention to the interpreter, where it is invited, in miniature, to imitate the muscular tensions of the artist, and where it wants to "feel" with him, we might expect a greater degree of response than usual. The reasons for failure of response furnish interesting clues to the nature of the physical behavior training we will want to engage in.

One important deterrent to a desirable empathic response is stage fright. The interpreter who feels insecure, nervous, frightened, or inadequate will, in spite of all he can do, have these muscular patterns mixed in with those of the emotion of the selection, if indeed he is able to respond to his selection at all. His feelings and fears he telegraphs to his audience, which in turn telegraphs them back again. This is a vicious circle.

In some of us emotional patterns are so habitual that there is a sort of residue, a carry-over, at all times. If this is true of the interpreter, he will be mixing the wrong with the right, and the audience response will be confused.

Some people seem to live thin, even arid, emotional lives. Habit, inhibitions, incapacity perhaps, inexperience—many factors may be responsible, but the interpreter who does not respond emotionally to his material is unable to set the chain of reaction in motion. There is no source, no first cause.

The interpreter may also err in presenting muscular tensions and vocal qualities that are an inaccurate representation of the more usual manner of expressing a particular emotion. This error is possible because the interpreter's emotion is at least in part a selected, formulated, or manufactured one. If the judgment of the interpreter is faulty in defining the emotion, if his memory of sensory images is not exact, if his ability to eliminate other feelings is incomplete, he will most probably telegraph the wrong impressions to his audience.

Within audiences other deterrents exist. The feelings they bring with them into the room, the distractions and discomforts audiences may encounter, their empathic responses to one another—these are important, but somewhat outside the control of the interpreter. Wherever he can he will work in a situation where these elements are minimized, but he must depend on the force and vitality of his performance, coupled with the usual willingness of the audience to cooperate, to win the day.

At first thought one might assume then that all that is necessary to achieve a desirable response is for the interpreter to "feel" his material and everything else that is controllable will take care of itself, that if the reader learns to assimilate his material thoroughly, if he analyzes well and directs his attention properly, then his voice and body will take care of themselves. Such is not the case, however. Very few young men and women have mastered the habit of good posture, for example. Few but the seasoned professionals can relax at will or put their musculatures in a condition for instant and complete response to their minds and feelings. The degree of response in muscular tensions and the fine quality of control are both, at least in part, functions of practice and training. The interpreter, as much as the singer or other musician or the athlete, needs a disciplined body. In an interpretation course there is, naturally, no point in training the voice and body unless it be to express something. Vocal and physical techniques are meaningless here unless they are considered as a method to convey meanings found in literature. But this does not at all obviate the need for the student to practice, even drill, those physical and vocal skills which improve his range, accuracy, and effectiveness.

Our training of physical responsiveness is based on three factors. First of all, a listener is merely embarrassed or uneasy if a reader's body suggests nervousness, uncertainty, affectation, contempt for him, the listener, or anything else not directly concerned with what the reader has to say. Therefore, our first project will be directed toward relaxation and poise, or "presence," a term actors like to use. Though he is relaxed and well-balanced, we feel the latent energy. Second, a reader's face and body should be responsive enough to his thought that an audience can interpret his behavior. Conditions that most often interfere with his reactions are his inhibitions, his fear of making a fool of himself and overdoing, or "hamminess." Therefore, the second unit of training will be to teach the reader to abandon himself, give himself up utterly to what he is doing. Third, a reader's physical responsiveness may help emphasize his points, or it may help to clarify his points, or it may do both at the same time. Therefore, descriptive and emphatic action will be considered. It must be remembered that a reader's particular responsiveness arises from and is dependent on the literature he is reading and the occasion on which he is reading. Therefore, he should learn good judgment and good taste as to what is appropriate, and not rely solely on rules.

## EXERCISES

1. Observe your own feelings—note very carefully the feeling of your *muscles*—as you watch a heavy man working about his house or yard or car. Watch him for some length of time, giving him your full attention. Now observe a highly trained swimmer or golfer or dancer or skater. Note the difference in your own *muscular* responses.

2. Take note of your physical and emotional changes as you move into the presence of people in heightened emotional states: at a victory celebration, at a disaster scene, at a funeral, at a fight.

3. Try acting proud, sad, happy, bright and alert, dull and drowsy, angry.

4. Prepare the following selection, first as if it were to be acted and then as a platform reading. Note the extreme differences in gross movement about the stage. At the same time, however, note the similar, if not identical, qualities of the inner feelings and the muscular tensions which accompany them. The selection will need thorough preparation, including a reading of the entire play. It will demand much of you by way of analysis in re-creating the imagery, assimilating the material, phrasing it, and in developing the techniques for presentation. Note there is a wide range of emotion, most of it rather intense. See if you can create some of this emotion in your audience.

[... The clock strikes eleven.

FAUSTUS.    Ah, *Faustus*,
*Now hast thou but one bare hour to live,*

And then thou must be damned perpetually!
Stand still, you ever-moving spheres of heaven,
That time may cease, and midnight never come;
Fair Nature's eye, rise, rise again, and make
Perpetual day; or let this hour be but
A year, a month, a week, a natural day,
That Faustus may repent and save his soul!
O lente, lente currite, noctis equi!
The stars move still, time runs, the clock will strike,
The devil will come, and Faustus must be damned.
O, I'll leap up to my God!—Who pulls me down?—
See, see, where Christ's blood streams in the firmament!
One drop would save my soul, half a drop: ah, my Christ!—
Ah, rend not my heart for naming of my Christ!
Yet will I call on him: O, spare me, Lucifer!—
Where is it now? 'tis gone: and see, where God
Stretcheth out his arm, and bends his ireful brows!
Mountains and hills, come, come, and fall on me,
And hide me from the heavy wrath of God!
No, no!
Then will I headlong run into the earth:
Earth, gape! O, no, it will not harbor me!
You stars that reigned at my nativity,
Whose influence hath allotted death and hell,
Now draw up Faustus, like a foggy mist,
Into the entrails of yon lab'ring clouds,
That, when you vomit forth into the air,
My limbs may issue from your smoky mouths,
So that my soul may but ascend to heaven!
       [The clock strikes the half-hour.
Ah, half the hour is past! 'twill all be past anon.
O God,
If thou wilt not have mercy on my soul,
Yet for Christ's sake, whose blood hath ransomed me,
Impose some end to my incessant pain;
Let Faustus live in hell a thousand years,
A hundred thousand, and at last be saved!

*O, no end is limited to damnéd souls!*
*Why wert thou not a creature wanting soul?*
*Or why is this immortal that thou hast?*
*Ah, Pythagoras' metempsychosis, were that true,*
*This soul should fly from me, and I be changed*
*Unto some brutish beast! all beasts are happy,*
*For, when they die,*
*Their souls are soon dissolved in elements;*
*But mine must live still to be plagued in hell.*
*Cursed be the parents that engendered me!*
*No, Faustus, curse thyself, curse Lucifer*
*That hath deprived thee of the joys of heaven.*
　　　[The clock strikes twelve.
*O, it strikes, it strikes! Now, body, turn to air,*
*Or Lucifer will bear thee quick to hell!*
　　　[Thunder and lightning.
*O soul, be changed into little water-drops,*
*And fall into the ocean, ne'er be found!*
　　　[Enter DEVILS.
*My God, my God, look not so fierce on me!*
*Adders and serpents, let me breathe a while!*
*Ugly hell, gape not! come not, Lucifer!*
*I'll burn my books!—Ah, Mephistophilis!*
　　　[Exeunt DEVILS with FAUSTUS.

　　　　　　　*The Tragical History of Doctor Faustus*, Scene XIV,
　　　　　　　　　　　　　　　CHRISTOPHER MARLOWE

## Additional Readings

Chekhov, Michael, *To the Actor*. New York: Harper & Brothers, 1953, pp. 1-20.

Cunningham, Cornelius C., *Literature As a Fine Art*. New York: Thomas Nelson & Sons, 1941, pp. 271-278.

Dolman, John, *The Art of Acting*. New York: Harper & Brothers, 1949, pp. 45-49; 238-257.

James, William, *Psychology: Briefer Course*. New York: Henry Holt & Co., Inc., 1920, pp. 373-390.

Lee, Charlotte I., Oral Interpretation. Boston: Houghton Mifflin Co., 1952, pp. 75-88.

Lowrey, Sara, and Gertrude E. Johnson, Interpretative Reading: Techniques and Selections (rev. ed.). New York: Appleton-Century-Crofts, Inc., 1953, pp. 46-52; 61-68.

Oliver, Robert T., Training for Effective Speech. New York: The Cordon Co., 1939, pp. 452-486.

Sarett, Lew, and W. T. Foster, Basic Principles of Speech. Boston: Houghton Mifflin Co., 1936, pp. 114-137; 155-191.

Tresidder, Argus, Reading to Others. Chicago: Scott, Foresman & Company, 1940, pp. 215-219.

Woolbert, Charles H., and Severina E. Nelson, The Art of Interpretative Speech (ed. 4). New York: Appleton-Century-Crofts, Inc., 1956, pp. 213-226.

# Relaxation and Poise

Too much tension appears to be the great American affliction today. It shows in our faces, our headaches, and even in the diseases that put us in hospitals and mental institutions. It inhibits us from free motion, it saps our energy, it colors our emotions. But the interpreter has more to overcome than the tensions generated by his regular daily living. He has also the tensions to guard against or to release that are caused by his appearance in front of an audience, for an audience that has gathered to be entertained wants the reader to exhibit the same kind of poise and balance and ease of motion that it expects in its dancers or its athletes.

Good posture, a necessary element in physical poise, becomes important to the reader for several reasons. One reason we want good posture is that we believe it looks good. Another is that it reflects a disciplined, even proud personality. A third is that it leaves the muscles of breathing unhampered for action, a most important reason for the speaker, interpreter, or singer. A fourth reason is that all muscles not needed to maintain posture or carry on life-supporting activities of the body are free to respond easily to the play of emotional change. Good posture is efficient and economical in that the body is so held and carried that the centers of weight are balanced one over the other in a column and little effort is then expended in maintaining one's erect carriage. As soon as we slump, the head leans forward, the chest droops forward, or the hips tip backward, muscles are called to work to prevent our falling over. Working muscles are tensed muscles. Tensed muscles are not completely free to respond. It is possible, however, for people to control their gross muscles when they know how, and it is to that end that the exercises in this project have been devised. They are directed toward acquiring a well-balanced physical posture that is alert but does not appear to involve tension.

Muscular tensions in addition to those required for good posture are to be watched and disciplined. Those which represent undesirable emotions should be eliminated as far as they can be: tensions of fear, frustration, boredom, irritation, hurry. These nearly always get in the way of free response in the interpreter. But it is also true that although an audience wants to see an entertainer relaxed, it does not want to see him collapsed! There is a balance, a poise, required which keeps him alert and ready. The physical disciplines and exercises suggested below should help to correct extremes in either direction. They are the kind of exercises that should not only be learned and practiced today, but should precede, whenever possible, any public performance, and should be daily routine until satisfactory posture and "presence" are acquired.

# EXERCISES

*1.* Stand against a wall with enough room so that you can swing your arms and body without hitting any individual or object. Place your feet apart and about a foot away from the wall. Now lean back against the wall and try to make each part of the spine touch the wall, beginning at the bottom. Roll the spine up against the wall. Pay particular attention to straightening the lower spine. Now push yourself away from the wall with your hands so the body, still with straightened spine, is balanced over the balls of the feet. Rise up and down on the balls of your feet to test your balance. The body should not rock back and forth, but move straight up and down.

2. Rag doll exercise. Put feet apart and drop chin toward the chest. Let its weight pull the head over, and then let the weight of the shoulders and hanging arms pull them over until the entire body is hanging from the waist. Gradually straighten the spine from the bottom until the body is upright. Feel that the lower spine is straight, shoulders are balanced on top of the spine, and the head is balanced, not held, on top of the shoulders. Rather than hold the shoulders back, broaden them. Hold the chin up easily. From this

position, let the upper body collapse and dive forward, so the torso is hanging from the hips and bounces three times, with the head flopping loosely like a marble on the end of a string. Have a friend test the looseness of neck muscles by touching the head gently to see if it is loose or being held rigidly. Raise the body as before.

3. Sitting on a chair, drop the chin on the chest and pull forward until stretching along the back muscles is felt. Then drop the right ear toward the right shoulder and pull until stretch on the left shoulder is felt. Point your chin to the ceiling until stretch is felt along the sternum. Drop your head to the left shoulder until stretch is felt on the right shoulder. Drop your head forward, and then balance it upright. Gently nod the head up and down as if to "oil the joint." Now rotate the head forward, right, back, left and forward by moving the spine and shoulders and letting the head roll of its own weight. Do this twice to the right and twice to the left.

4. Still in a sitting position, lean your elbows on your knees and let your head hang loosely toward your knees. Now shake your head so vigorously that your jaw and the skin of your face move independently of the skull.

5. Stand up in place, straighten the lower spine until a slight pull is felt in the thighs and there is a slight tension around the hips. Balance the shoulders on the spine and broaden them. Balance the head on the shoulders with the chin well up. Feel as if you were a person of consequence. Test posture by moving straight up and down on the balls of the feet so that the body does not rock. Sit down with a minimum of jack-knifing by moving one foot back to the chair, shifting some of the weight to it, and lowering the body. Maintain the same straight spine and balance of the torso while sitting, but relax the hands and arms by shaking them if necessary. Shift one foot back and let it support the weight of the body as you rise straight up, trying to keep the spine straight and balanced.

6. Maintaining this same balance, go up and down stairs. Keep the torso upright and motionless, and let the legs do the work.

7. Finally, rise from your chair as you would for a performance, go to the front of the room or to the lectern. Be sure you have plenty of room around you. Look at your audience in the friendliest possible way and smile. Consider yourself a success if they smile—not laugh—back.

## Additional Readings

Fink, David Harold, *Release From Nervous Tension*. New York: Simon and Schuster, Inc., 1943, pp. 67-113.

Franklin, Miriam, *Rehearsal* (ed. 3). New York: Prentice-Hall, Inc., 1950, pp. 109-122.

Jacobson, Edmund, *You Must Relax*. New York: McGraw-Hill Book Co., 1957, pp. 84-139.

Woolbert, Charles H., and Severina E. Nelson, *The Art of Interpretative Speech* (ed. 4). New York: Appleton-Century-Crofts, Inc., 1956, pp. 222-223.

# Concentration and Abandon

A READER NEEDS TO CONCENTRATE HIS ATTENTION AS COMPLETELY AS he is able on what he is saying. Since there are such close links between the content, both intellectual and emotional, the reader's feelings, his physical responses, and the total reaction of the audience, and since attention to ideas and the experiencing of feelings foreign to the content of the selection are reflected in the performance, the reader must find means to establish habits that eliminate undesirable concerns from his thoughts, and furnish his mind with relevant materials to react to. He must develop techniques that not only free but reinforce his own responses. The skilled reader has learned to concentrate on his materials and to abandon himself to the demands they make upon him.

The beginner commonly shows evidences of uncertainty or dissatisfaction with his performance, but once he has started he must suppress not only the evidence that he feels he is not doing well enough, but even the temptation to let the critic in him have any say until the performance is over. A reader cannot look to his instructor or any other member of an audience with a questioning, "Is that all right?" or "How am I doing?" in his eyes and attitude and still present Robert Frost's ideas and attitudes. He cannot grimace, shake his head, or snap his fingers in dissatisfaction without destroying the illusions he is creating. He must give over every part of himself to what he is doing while he is before an audience. The mind that wanders to concerns over dress, the impression the reader is making, the distractions from outside the room, even to what is coming next leaves a telltale trace in the physical behavior of the performer, be he speaker, reader, or actor.

Some inappropriate physical response results not so much from self-consciousness or the wandering mind as from consciousness of lack of sufficient knowledge of the character or situation or idea. The reader, instead of responding, feels a vast, uneasy blankness akin to the feeling of being confronted by an important question in an examination he cannot answer. The interpreter who has written his own material rarely is faced with this difficulty, for people find it comparatively easy to recall their own reactions and impulses, and the feelings of their own bodies responding. But it is not so easy to respond as somebody other than himself. This takes practice in finding what should be reacted to in the feelings of the author or his character and in forming those feelings within himself.

Probably the greatest help in this last situation is an understanding and awareness of one's own empathic responsiveness. Since it is a natural imitative impulse one must be careful not to embarrass oneself or others by indulging in the impulse, but one does want to feel the peculiarity in one's own muscles of the rolling gait, the head lifted to look under a pair of glasses, the contorted face, or the hunched body of the shiverer on the street corner, and one wants to feel how these peculiarities of muscular action make one feel emotionally. Increasing the intensity of response by giving fuller attention to one's observations, and by being aware of the nature of the responses, can be highly instructive and of great assistance to the interpreter anxious to improve his empathic and emotional responsiveness. Once we take the trouble to observe, we discover behavior and feelings we are astonished to find are there. People have a wide range of reactions to various experiences—reactions they had not quite realized existed— and the subtlety of the changes in reaction and the combination of feelings to be found are a constant source of wonder and instruction to the careful observer. There is also the further bonus of personal enrichment and the intensification of the observer's own reactions. When he has learned to give undivided attention to his observations and to encourage his own responses, the interpreter is well on the way to strengthening the emotional aspects of his physical behavior and of creating habits that will permit him to project with clarity and power the emotional content of his material. Recalling your own responses and impulses, and feeling into a character or feeling the character in your own muscles, are the aims of the pantomimes and monologues that follow. To accomplish this goal, abandoning yourself to the exercises will be essential. Memory of your own responses, direct and empathic, will be important aids, assuming that the situations and characters are understood.

## EXERCISES

1. Walk, until you are told to change moods by a teacher or assistant, in the following ways:
   a. Terribly tired and completely depressed.
   b. Full of vigor and vitality. You never felt better in your life.
   c. Wrestling with a knotty problem.
   d. Angry at yourself.
   e. Angry at someone else.
   f. Responding to nature—trees, clouds, flowers, sunset. Choose some one object.
   g. Afraid of something behind you.

2. You are on your way to the registrar's office for your grades. You know you have not put enough time and thought on any of your courses and could even be in danger of flunking out. You wait in line, get your grades, open them, and find you got low C's in three courses and a low B in the fourth. You never felt so wonderful in all your life. Reverse the situation.

3. Put yourself in one of the following situations and talk extemporaneously as the situation develops.
   a. You are trying to study for an important examination. People come in to gossip, to borrow things, or to ask questions about their assignments. You finally do something about the situation.
   b. You are waiting for a date, and getting more and more impatient as various people chat with you and make comments.
   c. You have horrible stage fright. You practice your selection with a friend. You go to class, wait to be called, have some terrible moments before the class, and gradually become engrossed in your selection.

4. Walk around the room, the men as women and the women as men. The men should imagine they are wearing girdles and medium or high heels. They should be as anxious not to appear flat-chested as most women are. They should be aware that their imaginary dresses are pretty and clean and will not hang well unless they hold themselves well. The consciousness of the imaginary girdle should shorten the stride. The women should imagine themselves in slacks, flat shoes, and loud sports shirts worn out. Entire freedom from any confining about the hips should lengthen the stride and loosen the hips. Be at least six feet tall in imagination and remember that girls, children, animals, and objects are correspondingly lower.

5. With imaginary aids like those above, walk as a little boy or girl of pre-school age. (You may have to observe and respond empathically.)

6. Walk as a person of 70 or so who, though not altogether decrepit, shows that he is not so young as he once was.

7. Pantomime three different characters sitting at a desk trying to compose a letter. They cannot find the words to say what they mean. They rise and walk about the room or look out a window.

8. Present three different characters or one character in three different moods and situations through their speeches. Give the audience the setting and background for each character and speech. Some suggestions of possible characters and speeches are as follows:

  a. Gloucester's soliloquies, *Richard III*, Shakespeare
  b. Hamlet's soliloquies, *Hamlet*, Shakespeare
  c. Jacque's philosophical speeches, *As You Like It*, Shakespeare
  d. Christina's speeches to her husband and mother-in-law, *The Silver Cord*, Sidney Howard
  e. Mrs. Phelps' justification, *The Silver Cord*, Howard
  f. Katherine's last long speech on obedience, *Taming of the Shrew*, Shakespeare
  g. Maurya's last speech, *Riders to the Sea*, Synge
  h. Mrs. Tancred, *Juno and the Paycock*, O'Casey

(Many others can be found easily by thumbing through an anthology.)

## Additional Readings

Chekhov, Michael, *To the Actor*. New York: Harper & Brothers, 1953, pp. 47-62.

Woolbert, Charles H., and Severina E. Nelson, *The Art of Interpretative Speech* (ed. 4). New York: Appleton-Century-Crofts, Inc., 1956, pp. 218-222.

# Descriptive and Emphatic Movement

ATTENTION HAS BEEN GIVEN TO ACQUIRING VITALITY WITH STRENGTH IN the posture muscles along the lower spine and around the hips, together with ease in the face, neck, and shoulders. This sort of posture should discourage shifting of the feet and tense, random movements of the hands and arms which, when present, can only suggest that the reader is uneasy and self-conscious. In other words, one purpose is to eliminate distractions. Another purpose is to free the body from the tensions of poor posture and other bad physical habits and thus prepare it for free and easy physical responses to the materials the reader wants to present. Since the mere physical presence of the interpreter conveys meanings to an audience, he should be sure that his physical responses make his meanings as clear as possible, and that whenever he can he will use physical responses not only to help illuminate the idea expressed but to reinforce or emphasize it as well.

In a very general way it may be said that a reader's movements are either emphatic or descriptive. People regularly accompany their speech with movement and gesture. Sometimes this movement is primarily an emotional reinforcement: pounding a fist on a table, shaking a fist in someone's face, vigorous bobs of the head on words to be emphasized, shakes and nods of the head, hand slaps, skips, jumps, stamps, slouches, stiffenings, and all sorts of movements which add emotional emphasis. At other times the movement is primarily descriptive: a hand raised to indicate height, two hands held apart to indicate size, a finger pointed in the indicated direction, gestures of up, down, around, square, long, round, demonstrations that the thing to be done is to be done thus and so, imitations of another's actions. People want to communicate ideas and to express their feelings

124

through their physical behavior. It is only rarely that they use descriptive movement that is not also emphatic. As often as not emphatic movement is also descriptive. There is no clear line of demarcation between the two, for human expression of ideas is always accompanied by emotion of some kind and in some degree of intensity.

Some material lends itself to strongly emphatic movement. In Capulet's "God's bread!" speech in *Romeo and Juliet* we know he is exasperated and angry. In fact, he is about to "blow his top." We know from the very first scene of the play that he is inclined to be choleric. His wife is used to it. When he calls for his sword, his wife says, "A crutch, a crutch! Why call you for a sword." In the fifth scene of Act I Capulet gets so angry when Tybalt wants to drive out the Montagues, who have crashed Capulet's party, that he is actually reduced to sputtering. In the fifth scene of Act III Capulet's anger and frustration grow until his wife warns him, "You are too hot [angry]." So he definitely is emphatic when he says, "God's bread! it makes me mad." Just as you do when you are angry, Capulet wants to do something violent—kick something, or beat his head with his fists. He shakes his finger at Juliet, pounds the table. Certainly the violence of his feelings would be expressed physically.

Other material lends itself to strongly descriptive movement. Cyrano de Bergerac, in the first act of Rostand's play by that name, has a speech about his nose that offers wonderful opportunities for descriptive responses. In fact, it is hard to understand how it could be delivered any other way. The scene is the great hall of the Hotel de Bourgogne, where plays are performed. The lords and ladies have assembled in their finery, and fruit sellers and pickpockets have made their appearance. Cyrano has just made good his promise to drive a certain fat actor off the stage if he tried to appear in another romantic role, and so has stopped the play. Valvert, feeling that Cyrano has become too cocky, and in an attempt to humiliate Cyrano in the eyes of the assembled crowd, says, lamely, "Your nose—is very large!" Cyrano answers gravely, "Very." Valvert laughs feebly. Then Cyrano shows him all the various manners in which he might have delivered clever insults: aggressive, amicable, descriptive, dramatic, etc. He announces with voice, body, and word what the manner could be.

The effective interpreter takes care, through constant observation and practice, to develop his own physical responsiveness. It is his objective to respond vigorously and positively, to eliminate anything from his responses that destroys or muddles the clarity of what he intends his responses to communicate, and to reinforce the content of his selections through the empathic impact of what he does. The exercises listed below are designed to increase the interpreter's range and force of physical responsiveness.

## EXERCISES

1. Prepare Capulet's "God's bread!" speech for delivery to an audience. Note how much of the speech is delivered to his wife and how much to his daughter. Could any of it be delivered to the audience, the observers? Where do the climaxes of his feelings come? Read the play up to this point to see what kind of a man Capulet is. Show then his exasperation, frustration, and rage. You will find it necessary to memorize this speech and give it without a manuscript.

2. Prepare Cyrano's speech on his nose. Look for every opportunity not only to describe the various moods which you pantomime, but to make clear such images as the nose as a roost for birds or as a chimney. In fact, it should be possible to pantomime the entire speech. This speech is best memorized, although it is a difficult one to memorize. (The mood for each insult could be listed on a card, but use the card as little and as unobtrusively as possible.)

3. Feel your way through one of the following speeches without speaking any words aloud. Speak the words only when you have worked out physical responses that express the meaning all the way through the selection. This is a good test for physical responses.

A.

... *but when the wary chief*
*Had poised and shrewdly scanned the mighty bow,*
*Then, as a singer, skilled to play the harp,*
*Stretches with ease on its new fastenings*
*A string, the twisted entrails of a sheep,*

Made fast at either end, so easily
Ulysses bent that mighty bow. He took
And drew the cord with his right hand; it twanged
With a clear sound as when a swallow screams.
The suitors were dismayed, and all grew pale.
Jove in loud thunder gave a sign from heaven.
The much-enduring chief, Ulysses, heard
With joy the friendly omen, which the son
Of crafty Saturn sent him. He took up
A winged arrow, that before him lay
Upon a table, drawn; the others still
Were in the quiver's womb; the Greeks were yet
To feel them. This he set with care against
The middle of the bow, and toward him drew
The cord and arrow-notch, just where he sat,
And, aiming opposite, let fly the shaft.
He missed no ring of all; from first to last
The brass-tipped arrow threaded every one.

*Odyssey*, HOMER

### B.

ORLANDO: Good-day and happiness, Dear Rosalind!....

ROSALIND: Why, how now, Orlando! where have you been all this while? You a lover! An you serve me such another trick, never come in my sight more.

ORL.: My fair Rosalind, I come within an hour of my promise.

ROS: Break an hour's promise in love! He that will divide a minute into a thousand parts and break but a part of the thousandth part of a minute in the affairs of love, it may be said of him that Cupid hath clapp'd him o' the shoulder, but I'll warrant him heart-whole.

ORL.: Pardon me, dear Rosalind.

ROS: Nay, an you be so tardy, come no more in my sight: I had as lief be wooed of a snail.

ORL.: Of a snail!

ROS: Ay, of a snail; for though he comes slowly, he carries his house on his head; a better jointure, I think, than you make a woman.

... Come, woo me, woo me; for now I am in a holiday humour and like enough to consent. What would you say to me now, an I were your very very Rosalind?

ORL: I would kiss before I spoke.

ROS: Nay, you were better speak first, and when you were gravelled for lack of matter, you might take occasion to kiss. . . .

ORL: How if the kiss be denied?

ROS: Then she puts you to entreaty, and there begins new matter.

ORL: Who could be out, being before his beloved mistress?

ROS: Marry, that should you, if I were your mistress, or I should think my honesty ranker than my wit.

ORL: What, of my suit?

ROS: Not out of your apparel, and yet out of your suit. Am I not your Rosalind?

ORL: I take some joy to say you are, because I would be talking of her.

ROS: Well, in her person I say I will not have you.

ORL: Then in mine own person I die.

ROS: No, faith, die by attorney. The poor world is almost six thousand years old, and in all this time there was not any man died in his own person, videlicet, in a love-cause. . . . men have died from time to time, and worms have eaten them, but not for love.

ORL: I would not have my right Rosalind of this mind, for, I protest, her frown might kill me.

ROS: By this hand, it will not kill a fly. But come, now I will be your Rosalind in a more coming-on disposition, and ask me what you will, I will grant it.

ORL: Then love me, Rosalind.

ROS: Yes, faith will I, Friday and Saturdays and all.

ORL: And wilt thou have me?

ROS: Ay, and twenty such.

As You Like It, SHAKESPEARE

## C.

IAGO: My noble lord,—

OTHELLO: What doest thou say, Iago?

IAGO: Did Michael Cassio, when you woo'd my lady, Know of your love?

OTH: *He did, from first to last: why does thou ask?*

IAGO: *But for a satisfaction of my thought;*
No further harm.

OTH:       *Why of thy thought, Iago?*

IAGO: *I did not think he had been acquainted with her.*

OTH: *O! yes; and went between us very oft.*

IAGO: *Indeed!*

OTH: *Indeed! ay, indeed: Discern'st thou aught in that? Is he*
not honest?

IAGO: *Honest, my lord!*

OTH: *Honest! ay, honest.*

IAGO: *My lord, for aught I know.*

OTH: *What dost thou think?*

IAGO:       *Think, my lord!*

OTH: *Think, my lord!*
By heaven, he echoes me,
As if there were some monster in his thought
Too hideous to be shown. Thou dost mean something.

Othello, SHAKESPEARE

## D.

ELLINGHAM: Kerchival!

KERCHIVAL: (Under the handkerchief.) *Eh? H'm!*

ELLING: *Can you sleep at a time like this? My own nerves are*
on fire.

KER: *Fire? Oh—yes—I remember. Any more fire-works, Bob?*

ELLING: *A signal rocket from one of the batteries, now and then.*
(He goes up beyond the window. Kerchival arouses himself, taking
the handkerchief from his eyes.)

KER: *What a preposterous hour to be up. The ball was over an*
*hour ago, all the guests are gone, and it's nearly four o'clock.* (Looking at his watch.) *Exactly ten minutes of four.* (He takes out a cigar.)
*Our Southern friends assure us that General Beauregard is to open*
*fire on Fort Sumter this morning. I don't believe it.* (Lighting the
cigar and rising, he looks out through the window.) *There lies the*
*old fort—solemn and grim as ever, and the flag-staff stands above it,*
*like a warning finger. If they do fire upon it* (shutting his teeth for
a moment and looking down at the cigar in his hand) *the echo of*

that first shot will be heard above their graves, and Heaven knows how many of our own, also; but the flag will still float!—over the graves of both sides.

(Ellingham enters from the central door and approaches him.) Are you Southerners all mad, Robert?

ELLING: Are you Northerners all blind? (Kerchival sits down.) We Virginians would prevent a war if we could. But your people in the North do not believe that one is coming. You do not understand the determined frenzy of my fellow Southerners. Look! (Pointing toward the rear of the stage.) Do you see the lights of the city, over the water? The inhabitants of Charleston are gathering, even now, in the gray, morning twilight, to witness the long-promised bombardment of Fort Sumter. It is to be a gala day for them. They have talked and dreamed of nothing else for weeks. The preparations have become a part of their social life—of their amusement—their gayeties. This very night at the ball—here—in the house of my own relatives— what was their talk? What were the jests they laughed at? Sumter! War! Ladies were betting bonbons that the United States would not dare to fire a shot in return, and pinning ribbons on the breasts of their "heroes." There was a signal rocket from one of the forts, and the young men who were dancing here left their partners standing on the floor to return to the batteries—as if it were the night before another Waterloo. The ladies themselves hurried away to watch the "spectacle" from their own verandas. You won't see the truth! I tell you, Kerchival, a war between the North and South is inevitable!

KER: And if it does come, you Virginians will join the rest.

ELLING: Our state will be the battle ground, I fear. But every loyal son of Virginia will follow her flag. It is our religion!

KER: My State is New York. If New York should go against the old flag, New York might go to the devil. That is my religion.

ELLING: So differently have we been taught what the word "patriotism" means!

Shenandoah, HOWARD

4. Prepare a selection of your own choosing to deliver to the class. Look for opportunities to describe physically what you are saying and how you feel.

## Additional Readings

Albright, H. D., *Working Up a Part*. Boston: Houghton Mifflin Co., 1947, pp. 24-35.

Selden, Samuel, *The Stage in Action*. New York: F. S. Crofts & Co., 1946, pp. 41-98.

Tresidder, Argus, *Reading to Others*. Chicago: Scott, Foresman & Company, 1940, pp. 219-227.

# Judgment and Physical Response

PHYSICAL RESPONSES TO ANY SELECTION MAY VARY THROUGH A WIDE range from large to small, from energetic to weak, from colorful to reserved. Sometimes they attract attention, sometimes the audience is scarcely aware of them. The use of physical responsiveness is somewhat like the use of medicine, however. It is not necessarily true that where a little is good, a lot is better. It is interesting to observe that different kinds and different degrees of action in response to identical material very often elicit equally satisfactory responses from an audience. This is a particularly common phenomenon when different interpreters present the same selections. Beginners in the art of interpretation, particularly actors who perform the same role through a run of several performances, are frequently puzzled to discover that the same pattern of behavior is not always equally effective on different occasions. It soon becomes clear to the student that more than one element is involved which determines the effectiveness of physical behavior, that he has no simple yardstick by which to measure what is appropriate, and that he must make a judgment based on a consideration of the relative importance of the several factors involved.

Good physical behavior should be clear as to its meaning, sufficiently vigorous to cause a physical response (empathic) in the audience, and leave an impression of rightness and propriety. Clarity of meaning and vigor of action are achieved by techniques discussed in the foregoing projects. An impression of rightness and propriety is our major concern in this project.

It is true that choice of physical behavior is a matter of taste but, as in so many other choices where taste is involved, one is not reduced to consulting a crystal ball. The interpreter can make a thoughtful evaluation of the variable factors—speaker, situation, audience, and material—that affect his decision. Each has its special influences and each demands its own special adjustments.

Physical behavior that is natural to one performer is often wrong for another. One person may use sweeping gestures and many of them. Another may, with very slight movements of his hands, tell the same story and be equally effective. Sizes and shapes of people affect their movements; relationships of size of body parts vary from one person to another; habitual ways of self-expression, relation of physical behavior to personality pattern, strength, grace—dozens of elements in people's physical and mental make-up affect what is natural in their physical behavior. Any movement that looks unnatural or awkward or forced calls attention to itself, distracts an audience from attending to what is being interpreted, and decreases the effectiveness of the performance. Movement that employs the natural rhythms of the interpreter's body and reflects his personality improves his effectiveness. It should be pointed out, however, that *natural* does not necessarily mean *habitual*. People develop many bad habits of movement, sometimes from inhibition, sometimes from laziness, that are not natural to or right for them. The serious student is always working to discipline his body in the direction of its own most effective performance.

Another important factor that affects our judgment is the situation—the formality or informality of the occasion, the place, the time, etc. Reading in a church sanctuary might not permit of movement that would be fitting on a theatre stage. Reading at a gathering of friends calls for a different kind of movement, perhaps, than reading for a group of school officials. Reading to children invites the reader to sit with the children or to take them on his lap, if there are only one or two. Reading in the living room of someone's home demands far less movement than reading to a large audience in a large auditorium. Reading in poor light demands more movement than reading in a brightly lighted area. These and other aspects of the situation in which the interpreter appears all affect judgment of movement.

A third factor that affects the interpreter's choice of action is the audience itself. It may come with preconceived notions about what is right for the performer. The degree of total attention it offers the interpreter, its mood, its physical condition and comfort, its experience with interpreters, even its prejudices are involved in its judgment of physical behavior. There are conventions of behavior that change from place to place in the world. Some are generally recognized— hand-shaking, nose-rubbing, body-scratching, kissing, etc. Others are not so easily discovered, for they may not be clearly understood even among those who use the conventions. But failure to observe taboos and conventions is dangerous in that it may embarrass or even insult the observer. Usually, however, these are no problem, for the interpreter is normally as much a part of the cultural pattern in which these attitudes and conventions exist as his audience. If he appears away from home, however, he will be wise to be alert.

The material the interpreter presents is the most influential factor in determining physical behavior, of course. The formality or lightness of the material, the character or characters being presented, the situation within the material—all these are major determinants of not only the kind of action but of the degree as well. In Hamlet's first soliloquy, "Now I Am Alone," he was too wrought up by seeing his resented stepfather performing the duties of his recently dead father to want to lean on anything or to relax in any posture. But in "To Be or Not to Be" his posture could be comtemplative and relaxed. For "Mending Wall" one could very well be leaning on a reading stand, but "How Do I Love Thee," a different kind of contemplation, is too intense to suggest leaning.

The literature itself will for the most part suggest the manner the reader needs to use, and the reader's sense of appropriateness can be guided by what he does in similar situations, or what people generally do. If one were reporting a wedding and said that the bride and groom knelt, he would hardly kneel to illustrate the action. Yet ludicrous actions similar to this have been reported in reading situations. Even if one were showing the audience (impersonation) how scared the groom was, it is quite certain he would eliminate kneeling from the act.

A fifth factor that affects movement is the general mode or manner or style of the presentation. There is often much discussion about this problem, for it is difficult to explain the very real differences between the points of view of the actor, the impersonator, and the one who suggests with little, if any, overt movement, without erasing the equally real similarities. However, acting among children and impersonation among adults are so common that it is not hard to point out how people actually behave. A few very simple exercises may make this clear.

## EXERCISES

1. Go to a wall and push as hard as you are able. Say, "I am *pushing* as hard as I can" and push especially hard on that word. Now, come back before the class and with little if any overt movement, but all the effort of actual pushing, say the same thing. This is the difference between "suggesting" and "acting out." The acting-out is a definite aid to the suggesting, but they both feel about the same inside. The act of pushing gets the emphasis in the one situation, and the feeling of effort is important in the other.

2. Tell the class briefly about a very interesting or odd person that you know. Now *show* the class how he behaves and talks. In the second instance you are impersonating. Combine the two manners. Talk, suggesting what the person is like and how he behaves, then say, "Watch, and I'll show you."

3. Work out a short pantomime (it may have some exclamations or other words) in which you have this same person walk into a room, sit down at a desk or table, and compose a letter with considerable difficulty. He might even ball up the paper and throw it vehemently into the waste basket before he leaves the room, or he may finish the letter successfully. Use all properties necessary. This is acting. Knowledge about the person, suggestion, and impersonation are all used, but now you want actual doors, chairs, tables, pen, ink, paper. You want the proper clothes and make-up, while in impersonation you are concerned, almost entirely, with how your individual reacts and not so much with the things he reacts to. However, acting out a scene almost always seems to help impersonation. Its literal nature makes necessary the externalization of nebulous ideas.

Although this unit is devoted to the thesis that it is more important to develop judgment of what is suitable and in good taste considering the material, the occasion, and the reader, and that audience response is the ultimate test of appropriateness, nevertheless a few specific suggestions for behavior may be made.

First of all, the reading is for the benefit of the audience. It is being told or shown something. Therefore, everything that is done should be directed to and clearly visible to the audience. The reader will be seen best if he is standing, and it is seldom if ever necessary to show only the profile. An audience will allow the reader to imagine characters in front of him, even though, were they real, they might have to be to the side if the reader is to be seen by the audience. The reader should learn to keep his head up unless the material clearly demands that he hide his face. There could be times, of course, when turning the face and head away from a gruesome sight might be more telling than letting the face express horror. But generally speaking the audience should see the face and eyes of the reader.

Usually, impersonative and dramatic materials tend to demand more physical freedom than any other sorts of materials. Therefore, a reading stand is not desirable here. Many students prefer to memorize dramatic materials because they find the manuscript distracting and in the way.

Lastly, avoid any action that is awkward in the reading situation. Narrate or cut it. Imaginary properties are often especially difficult to project, and are seldom, if ever, essential to the reader.

# EXERCISES

1. With the material and the situation (both real and that presented in the material) in mind, what manner and action would you consider appropriate for any three of the following selections? Be ready to defend your opinions and be ready to demonstrate your ideas in your reading, for audience reaction is important in determining what is proper and appropriate for you.

"The Waltz," Dorothy Parker

"Jenny Kissed Me," Leigh Hunt

"The Last Leaf," Oliver W. Holmes

"In a Laboratory," Robert Browning
Twenty-Third Psalm, The Bible
"Soliloquy of the Spanish Cloister," Robert Browning
Quality of Mercy speech, *Merchant of Venice*, Shakespeare
Anthony to the Mob, *Julius Caesar*, Shakespeare
Brutus to the Mob, *Julius Caesar*, Shakespeare

   2. Make a selection of your own choice to read to the audience with what you consider to be appropriate physical response.

## Additional Readings

Parrish, W. M., "Concerning Taste," in Johnson, Gertrude E. (ed.), *Studies in the Art of Interpretation.* New York: D. Appleton-Century Co., 1940, pp. 201-206.

Lowrey, Sara, and Gertrude E. Johnson, *Interpretative Reading: Techniques and Selections* (rev. ed.). New York: Appleton-Century-Crofts, Inc., 1953, pp. 46-55.

# Synthesis and Evaluation of Progress

GREEK PLAYS, WRITTEN TO BE ACTED OUT-OF-DOORS IN GREAT amphitheaters before thousands of people, demand clean-cut, well-defined physical responses no longer so necessary on our intimate, well-lighted stages. The prologues and messenger and other long dramatic speeches from the great Greek plays have been used to demonstrate skills learned in the use and control of the body. Indeed they may be used to demonstrate all speaking skills. The Greek plays are great literature. They have rewarded repetition for more than two thousand years. They must have a basic appeal to fundamental truths in people, for they have been translated into most langauges and acted by all mature cultures.

The Greek tragedies deal with the moral struggles of demi-gods—beings who are more than the average man but less than the gods. The comedies, in general, ridicule the heroes and gods by reducing them to the physical, mental, and moral stature of the man in the street. Ancient vase paintings show these themes translated into the costume and bearing of the actors. Tragic actors had their height built up by tall headdresses and special shoes and they held themselves erect, while comic actors appeared stooped and small and ridiculous. Since all actors wore masks, they had to express themselves with their spines and bodies—good training for modern speakers.

Those unacquainted with the Greek plays will probably be surprised to find that the themes are often familiar. The abduction of Helen of Troy and its consequences is particularly well-known.

The most fleeting glance at a Greek play will show that it is composed of dialogue made up of short speeches interspersed with long, highly dramatic speeches. Prologues and messenger's speeches are of the latter kind. The prologue narrates dramatic events that precede the play and provide necessary background, while messenger's speeches narrate violent action that has taken place off-stage. Medea reveals her plotting for vengeance against Jason to the chorus and Hyppolytus rails against women in a long speech to his mother's nurse. All of these speeches encourage the revelation of thought and feeling through movement.

Choose a long, dramatic speech from a Greek play, preferably a tragedy. Study the play. Read as many translations of the speech you have chosen as are available, and select the translation you like best. Study the speech for its fullest meaning. "Feel" through the speech and image the emotions. Study the character speaking for all his strengths, weaknesses, and impulses. Imagine yourself with mask and the added stature of the Greek costume and rehearse the selection to make your body carry all the meaning you have seen in the selection. Check to be sure your posture is good. Repeat the exercises designed to develop good posture. Practice freedom of response in your physical action to the ideas in the selection. Give particular attention to descriptive and emphatic actions which enhance the effectiveness of your communication.

Some speeches suitable for this assignment are the following:

Oedipus the King, Sophocles:

> Messenger's account of the death of Jocasta and the blinding of Oedipus

Hyppolytus, Euripides:

> Hyppolytus' speech on women
>
> Messenger's description of the death of Hyppolytus

Electra, Sophocles:

> Paedagogus' tale of the death of Orestes
>
> Electra's first speech

Medea, Euripides:

> Nurse's first speech
>
> Medea's plotting
>
> Medea's condemnation of Jason
>
> Medea's farewell to her children
>
> Messenger's speech describing death of Jason's intended bride

Agamemnon, Aeschylus:
>Watchman's opening speech
>Clytemnestra's second speech
>Herald's speeches

Electra, Euripides:
>Peasant's opening speech
>Electra's account of her mother's sins
>Messenger's speech on the killing of Aegisthus

Iphigenia in Aulis, Euripides:
>Iphigenia's plea for her life

# 5

PROJECTS IN

# Voice Improvement

# Support of Tone

SO MUCH ATTENTION HAS BEEN DIRECTED TO THE CORRECTION OF defective voice and articulation that it is easy to assume that a voice that is not defective does not need training. The projects that follow as well as those that have preceded are designed for normal speakers who are capable of being excellent or superior speakers. They are directed toward artistic speech. Caruso, at the height of his career, probably practiced more and with more purpose than any beginning singer, and probably saw possibilities of improvement in his greatest performances. However, where the methods used to correct voice and articulation defects can be used to advantage, they will be used, and it will be recognized that each student starts from a different level of proficiency and will, because of his physical mechanism and motivation, have different potentialities. The experience of speakers, as well as of singers, has taught that the normal voice can be improved in quality and responsiveness.

The body is the musical instrument that produces voice, and every part of the torso is active in voice production. The pressure of air against the vocal cords is controlled primarily by the muscles of the lower part of the torso—the diaphragm—which is the chief muscle of *inhalation*, and the abdominal muscles, covering the abdominal cavity and the lower thorax, which are the chief controllers of *exhalation*. (Italics are for the benefit of those who have the functions of these sets of muscles confused.) The lungs hold the breath from which speech is fashioned, but they are passive and are acted upon not only by the muscles which raise the rib arches but chiefly by the diaphragm and abdominal muscles. For this reason, the strength and vitality around the lower torso recommended for good posture become a factor in more sensitive control of exhaled breath from which speech is made. Tone is produced by the pressure of air against the approximated vocal cords, which sets them in vibration. Since there is little, if any, direct control of the muscles governing the vocal cords, the elimination of muscular tensions that might interfere with their functioning is important, and the feeling of ease and flexibility in the neck, shoulders, throat and mouth recommended for good posture is even more important in good voice production. Tone is amplified and modified by the vocal resonators, chief of which are the pharynx, or throat, and the oral and nasal chambers. The nasal chamber is fixed in size and shape, but the oral and pharyngeal chambers are capable of considerable change, and a change in one of the resonators alters the others. For instance, raising of the velum against the back wall of the pharynx in vowel production not only shortens the pharyngeal chamber, but lengthens the oral cavity. The flattening of the tongue narrows the pharynx as compared to the bunching of tongue in the front of the mouth. The back of the tongue forms the front wall of the pharynx. Since we can see the front part of the tongue and have more feeling of control over the front of the mouth, it is generally more rewarding to concentrate on the size and shape of the front of the oral cavity in describing speech sounds and to develop a feeling of ease in the pharynx so that no tensions in that area will interfere with sound formation.

The exercises suggested in this project assume good posture and are directed toward learning a feeling of firm support for tone around the lower torso. Detailed and exact knowledge of the mechanisms that produce speech can be found in several good textbooks and will be of help in learning the feeling of their best functioning. The serious student will take pains to understand his voice-producing mechanism. However, such knowledge does not necessarily result in recognition of the feeling of these mechanisms at work, which is our aim at this stage. Only the student's practice with the help of a teacher with a good ear will accomplish this aim.

## EXERCISES

*1.* When you are lying relaxed and flat on your back, you will expand around the lower ribs when you inhale. Exhalation seems to be a matter of relaxation; the raised structures fall to their rest position. If you put a book on your upper abdomen, you can watch it rise with each inhalation and fall with each exhalation.

2. Voice is produced on exhalation, and the feeling of the abdominal muscles controlling exhalation is the feeling to learn. With the right hand on the upper chest and collar bones and the left hand on the abdomen just below the sternum, cough, sneeze, blow sharply as if blowing out a candle, and laugh. Inhibit any movement under the right hand and note carefully the movement under the left hand.

3. With one hand on the lower abdomen, feel as if you are pushing down on the diaphragm. Notice the feeling of the abdominal muscles and compare it with the feelings during the natural acts described in 2.

4. To become aware of the various ways in which the thorax may be expanded and of the tensions necessary to hold the thorax expanded, hold the breath and (a) raise and lower the shoulders and the upper three ribs only; (b) raise and lower the lower six ribs; (c) move the abdominal wall out and in. Repeat and breathe in and out instead of holding breath. (a) is the only way of expanding the thorax to inhale that is not recommended. Can you see why?

5. Inhale by raising the upper three ribs, shoulders, and collar bones as if to sigh heavily, but do not exhale. Simply hold your breath. Exhale. Now inhale by expanding around your lower ribs and upper abdomen and hold your breath. Which is easier to maintain?

6. In blowing a horn, it is often said that the lips function as the vocal cords do. With fairly loosely closed lips, blow through them so they vibrate. Now, increase the tension of the lips and notice how the pressure of air must increase to make them vibrate evenly. Do not use the larynx at all. With increased tension your lips may produce a rather high-pitched sound. Notice the feeling of the breathing mechanism producing increased breath pressure.

7. Put one hand on the upper chest and one hand on the front abdominal wall to test lack of movement in the upper chest and the sharp movement of the abdominal wall, while you

    a. Blow sharply as if blowing out a candle.

b. Phonate a sharp *Ha!* with the same breath movements and no more throat tension than in blowing.

c. Say, "Hi! How are you!" with the same breath movements as above

1. to an individual in the front of the room.
2. to an individual halfway back in the room.
3. to an individual in the back of the room.
4. to an individual outside the room at a considerable distance.

Keep the throat and mouth as relaxed for *4* as for *1*. The voice will rise somewhat in pitch from *1* to *4*, but considerable change in pitch must be attributed to too much throat tension. Try to keep the pitch the same by "thinking it low" as loudness increases. Note increased action of the abdominal muscles and larger mouth opening with increased loudness.

8. Vary *7b* by using [be-bɑ] instead of [hɑ]. Other vowels may be used, such as [be-bi], [be-boʊ], [be-bu], etc. Consult Chapter 6 for the sounds of phonetic symbols.

9. Use [be-bɑ] in the rhythmical pattern suggested below. Employ a clear 4/4 or 4/8 rhythm except that where (X) is used below accent or stress the syllable. Where (–) is used, pronounce the syllable in a de-emphasized or unstressed manner.

X – – –, X – – –, X – – –, X – – –
X X – –, X X – –, X X – –, X – – –
X X X –, X X X –, X X X –, X – – –
X X X X, X X X X, X X X X, X – – –

Vary the exercise with other vowels and other consonant combinations: [ti-mɑ], [ko-lu], [gɑ-nʌ], etc. Be sure in every instance to form the vowel accurately and at the same time to avoid strain. Begin softly then continue with increasing loudness. Let all sensation of increased work be centered below the sternum.

## Additional Readings

Anderson, Virgil A., *Training the Speaking Voice*. New York: Oxford University Press, Inc., 1942, pp. 11-97.

Crocker, Lionel, and Louis M. Eich, *Oral Reading* (ed. 2). New York: Prentice-Hall, Inc., 1955, pp. 122-127.

Fairbanks, Grant, *Voice and Articulation Drillbook*. New York: Harper & Brothers, 1940, pp. 133-139.

Parrish, Wayland Maxfield, *Reading Aloud* (ed. 3). New York: The Ronald Press Company, 1953, pp. 131-138.

Turner, J. Clifford, *Voice and Speech in the Theatre*. London: Sir Isaac Pitman & Sons, Ltd., 1950, pp. 10-24.

Woolbert, Charles H., and Severina E. Nelson, *The Art of Interpretative Speech* (ed. 4). New York: Appleton-Century-Crofts, Inc., 1956, pp. 243-252.

# Relaxation and Resonance

ANY PERSON WHO HAS FELT HIS THROAT AND THE BACK OF HIS TONGUE so tight that they are almost painful does not need to be told how desirable it would be if he could relax simply by willing to do so. Dr. Edmund Jacobson has developed a theory that a person can develop his sense of relaxation by tensing a muscle and then relaxing it. As he learns the feeling of difference between tension and relaxation, he not only can relax more but he can relax at will. The larnyx, pharynx, and back of the mouth should feel relaxed during speech. The following exercises employ Dr. Jacobson's method of learning this feeling.

## EXERCISES

1. Place your fingertips just inside the angle of the jaw on each side. Bite hard. Feel the muscles of mastication on each side tighten. Now, without opening the lips, let the jaw drop as far as it will of its own weight and the muscles of mastication relax so much you cannot distinguish them. Repeat until you can relax the jaw at will without extreme tension first.

2. With your finger on your "Adam's apple" (larynx), swallow hard, hold the larynx in this raised position, then relax so the larynx slips just a little lower than its original position. Let the jaw relax at the same time.

3. Pucker your lips tensely, then draw the corners of the mouth back in a tense grin. Repeat four times and relax.

4. Draw your shoulders up toward your ears in a tense shrug, then drop them loosely in place.

5. With your two thumbs under your jaw, push the back of the tongue up against the upper back teeth as hard as you can. Relax. Notice the tensions and relaxations under your jaw. Repeat until you can relax the back of the tongue at will.

6. While observing the back of your tongue and your velum in a mirror, inhale as if to yawn. Notice how high the velum is and how low the tongue is. Memorize this feeling. Practice until you can produce this "openness of throat" without thinking of inhaling as if to yawn.

7. Establish the feeling of open throat. Then pronounce each one of the back vowels [ɑ], [ɔ], [oʊ], [u] separately, then blend them into each other by rounding the lips. Think of the lips as a sort of megaphone for the sounds. Feel firm support around the lower ribs and abdomen, relaxation in the back of the throat and tongue, and feel that you are focusing all sounds at the megaphone of the lips.

8. Pronounce an [m] until it hums enough to vibrate in the nose and front of the mouth. Try to make the upper gum ridge vibrate. Then add [i]. Focus the vowel well forward, and make sure it is not unduly nasal by pinching the nostrils closed. Do this for each of the front vowels [i], [eɪ], [ɛ], and [æ].

9. Inhale as if to yawn. With extreme rapidity repeat:

bi-eɪ-beɪ, bi-eɪ-beɪ, bi-eɪ-beɪ, bi-eɪ-beɪ, be-eɪ-beɪ
bi-i-bi, bi-i-bi, bi-i-bi, bi-i-bi, bi-i-bi
bi-aɪ-baɪ, bi-aɪ-baɪ, bi-aɪ-baɪ, bi-aɪ-baɪ, bi-aɪ-baɪ
bi-o-boʊ, bi-o-boʊ, bi-o-boʊ, bi-o-boʊ, bi-o-boʊ
bi-u-bu, bi-u-bu, bi-u-bu, bi-u-bu, bi-u-bu

and all other vowels and diphthongs.

Repeat without pause until the exercise can be run through three times without throat tension or need to pause for breath. Concentrate on the feeling of firm support and open throat and on resonating sounds in the front of the mouth.

10. Read the poem, "Home-Thoughts, from Abroad," by Robert Browning with open throat and resonant tone. Shape the vowels carefully in each of the strong syllables and give them enough time so that you may be sure of good voice quality.

Oh, to be in England
Now that April's there,
And whoever wakes in England
Sees, some morning, unaware,
That the lowest boughs and the brushwood sheaf
Round the elm-tree bole are in tiny leaf,
While the chaffinch sings on the orchard bough
In England—now!
And after April, when May follows,
And the whitethroat builds, and all the swallows!
Hark, where my blossomed pear-tree in the hedge
Leans to the field and scatters on the clover
Blossoms and dewdrops—at the bent spray's edge—
That's the wise thrush; he sings each song twice over,
Lest you should think he never could recapture
The first fine careless rapture!
And though the fields look rough with hoary dew,
All will be gay when noontide wakes anew
The buttercups, the little children's dower—
Far brighter than this gaudy melon-flower!

(1845)

## Additional Readings

Anderson, Virgil A., *Training the Speaking Voice*. New York: Oxford University Press, 1942, pp. 115-160.

Crocker, Lionel, and Louis M. Eich, *Oral Reading* (ed. 2). New York: Prentice-Hall, Inc., 1955, pp. 126-127.

Jacobson, Edmund, *You Must Relax* (ed. 4). New York: McGraw-Hill Book Co., 1957, *passim*.

Parrish, Wayland Maxfield, *Reading Aloud* (ed. 3). New York: The Ronald Press Company, 1953, pp. 138-145.

Turner, J. Clifford, *Voice and Speech in the Theatre*. London: Sir Isaac Pitman & Sons, Ltd., 1950, pp. 25-44; 91-95.

# Synthesis and Evaluation
# of Progress

IN ORDER FOR YOU TO DEMONSTRATE THAT YOU HAVE MASTERED SUPPORT of tone and the production of tones with desirable resonance, this assignment requests you to present a passage of oratory written to be delivered to a large audience, meant to be stirring in its impact, and designed in its style for the use of full and resonant tones.

There is a wealth of such material available. There are political speeches, sermons, speeches to inspire delivered on all sorts of occasions and in many kinds of places. There are speeches imbedded in novels and plays. One of the best sources of contemporary materials is *Vital Speeches of the Day*, volume one of which was published in 1934. Numerous anthologies of famous speeches have been collected, many of which are listed in *Speech Index, an Index of 64 Collections of World Famous Orations and Speeches for Various Occasions*, by Roberta (Briggs) Sutton and published by the H. W. Wilson Company in 1935. Your librarian can assist you in the use of other bibliographical tools. Shakespeare is also a fertile source of shorter selections: battlefield speeches and funeral orations.

The particular problem posed by this kind of material is forceful, even powerful, delivery that never seems to strain. The speaker who yells loses the confidence of his listeners. The speaker who supports his tone with a steady strong stream of breath and who employs his resonators to their best efficiency is usually able to give an impression of reserve power and control which in turn serve to inspire confidence in him.

The room in which you present the speech will no doubt not be so large as a battlefield or the hall in which a political convention is being held. Strive, nevertheless, to fill it with a tone which gives an impression of bigness. Make your voice sound as if you could fill a large hall at any time you needed to do so.

## Additional Readings

Baird, Albert Craig, *American Public Addresses* (1740-1952). New York: McGraw-Hill Book Co., 1956.

Baird, Albert Craig, *Representative American Speeches: 1937/38* (Annual). New York: H. W. Wilson Co., 1938——.

Brigance, William Norwood, *Classified Speech Models of Eighteen Forms of Public Address*. New York: F. S. Crofts & Co., 1928.

Copeland, Lewis, ed., *The World's Great Speeches*. Garden City, New York: Garden City Publishing Co., 1942.

Edgerton, Alice (Craig), *A Speech for Every Occasion, New Speeches*. New York: Noble and Noble, Publishers, Inc., 1949.

Lindgren, Homer Dorr, *Modern Speeches*. New York: F. S. Crofts & Co., 1926.

O'Neill, James Milton, and Floyd K. Riley, *Contemporary Speeches*. New York: The Century Co., 1930.

Parrish, Wayland Maxfield, and Marie Hochmuth, *American Speeches*. New York: Longmans, Green & Co., Inc., 1954.

*Vital Speeches of the Day* (vol. 1, October, 1934, to the present). New York: The City News Publishing Co.

# 6

---

## PROJECTS IN
# *Improving Articulation*

---

# Speech Sounds and the Phonetic Alphabet

FEW OF US SPEAK WITH THE ACCURACY OF SOUND FORMATION THAT WE assume we are using. Most of us can be classified as normal in our pronunciation of the language, but if anyone listens closely to what we say, he is almost sure to discover consonants incompletely formed, vowels slightly distorted from the intended sound or phoneme, sounds missing, and sounds added. The oral interpreter needs better-than-normal speech if he is to be understood easily, if it is to be a pleasure for others to listen to him, and if he is to give the impression of being a disciplined craftsman. Because the speech of nearly all of us can be improved in accuracy of sound formation and because accuracy is essential to the effectiveness of the interpreter, the following projects in articulation have been included for your study.

If you are not already familiar with the phonetic alphabet, learn the symbols for the most commonly used sounds in English. The process of learning them will help you to be more discriminating in the identification of speech sounds. The phonetic alphabet will provide you with an accurate method of making clear to others what sound you are referring to when you have occasion to be talking about sounds, and it will permit you to use several of the pronouncing dictionaries with more intelligence.

The exercises that follow the phonetic alphabet are included as practice material to help you gain control over the formation of any sounds that may need improvement. If your difficulty is one of identifying a sound, it may help you to work across the page in these exercises so that you can hear it in contrast to similar sounds. If your difficulty is in keeping the formation of the sound constant, you may find it helpful to pronounce words down the columns on the page.

The discussions in Projects Two through Six in this chapter are included to provide you with a brief description of each class of sounds. They are intended as an introduction only, to help you to develop, along with some knowledge about the sounds, a more discriminating ear. The act of giving them some study and attention will in itself help you to be a better listener and a more accurate speaker. If you need a fuller treatment of any class of sounds, read further in the recommended sources listed under *Additional Readings*.

## THE MOST COMMON GENERAL AMERICAN SPEECH SOUNDS AND THE PHONETIC ALPHABET

PHONETIC SYMBOLS

FOR

FRONT VOWELS

i        1. flea, reel, even
*Keep me free to see the track meet.*

ɪ        2. sin, if, lit
*Swim to the inn for a fish dinner.*

e        3. hate, cake, ache
*She ate the cake then had a toothache.*

ε        4. set, bet, regret
*We let every net get torn with regret.*

æ        5. cat, fat, and
*He can eat apples after he has had a can of salmon.*

a        6. task, master, chance
*He poured half a glass of milk, then turned down the path toward his aunt.*

MID VOWELS

ɝ        7. churn, her, fern
*If you burn her curl, she will learn to spurn the shop.*

ɚ        8. better, perceive, grammar
*The bachelor tailor was a better singer.*

ʌ        9. done, run, shut
*If you have fun in the sun, come running.*

ə        10. sofa, away, medium
*I am completely aware that Nevada is farther away than Tampa.*

ɜ · 11. (The "dropped" r) bird, word, turn
*In Maine he turned his learned mind to recording words.*

BACK VOWELS

ɑ · 12. father, psalm, tot
*I do not know how far a father should let a child wander.*

ɔ · 13. caught, ought, taught
*He caught me in the hall and said he thought I ought to mow the lawn.*

ʊ · 14. look, nook, foot
*The cook took a look at the book and pushed it away.*

u · 15. school, loot, shoot
*He hid his loot in the boots he wore to school in July.*

DIPHTHONGS

ju · 16. use, cute, you
*You used to be cute when you refused to be amused at my jokes.*

oʊ · 17. go, hello, know
*If you go home, throw a bone to Rover.*

ɑʊ · 18. down, around, how
*The house down the road is brown.*

eɪ · 19. weigh, day, ail
*All the way to the gate he berated his ailments and pains.*

ɑɪ · 20. sigh, I, shy
*Keep to the right and try to keep an eye out for fighters.*

ɔɪ · 21. boil, coy, soil
*He boiled the ointment for the noisy boy.*

NASALS

m · 22. mum, seem, meet
*The music must have met its match in the musicians.*

n          23.  noon, and, done
                *Never go running in the sun when you can rest at
                noon.*

ŋ          24.  think, cling, bringing
                *Bring the thing away from the ink well.*

**PLOSIVES**

p          25.  plop, pup, upper
                *Put the pan up where the pup can have supper in
                peace.*

b          26.  bring, back, tub
                *Bring home some buns and a bit of crab meat,
                Abbie.*

t          27.  toe, toot, into
                *Otto thought the truth was taught by all teachers.*

d          28.  dare, doodle, mad
                *Dad did do the dishes on Monday.*

k          29.  car, lack, acrid
                *Can you take me to the candy counter back of the
                arcade?*

g          30.  glamour, agate, lag
                *Grace got my glasses from the gate leg table an
                hour ago.*

**SEMI-VOWELS
AND GLIDES**

r          31.  rude, rural, roar
                *Ruth rowed over the roaring current.*

l          32.  along, lovely, small
                *Laugh all your troubles away and live happily.*

j          33.  yell, you, yesterday
                *Yesterday the dog yipped and yelled when we used
                his dish.*

hw         34.  wheat, why, what
                *Why did he whisper when the wharf was white
                with frost awhile ago?*

w          35.  with, will, war
                *He went west with a willing heart.*

FRICATIVES

f        36. from, stiff, after
*Far off in the farming country he sought after food.*

v        37. sleeve, very, every
*Even the oven above the stove was very cold.*

θ        38. thunder, oath, thought
*"The very thing," thought Arthur; "Faith in the warmth of humanity."*

ð        39. father, the, another
*The father hid those toys in another room.*

s        40. sell, aspen, mess
*Some footsteps are still to be seen in tall grass.*

z        41. is, trees, zone
*As the breeze fizzled out the capsized boat lay in the muddy ooze.*

ʃ        42. shore, fish, ashen
*She surely fashioned a fresh frock.*

ʒ        43. azure, usual, casual
*In the garage he found the usual collection of casually discarded belongings.*

h        44. hay, height, ha
*He harped happily on the subject in hopes Harry would overhear him.*

AFFRICATES

tʃ        45. church, beach, achieve
*Children change their minds and take a chance on choosing a salad with no spinach.*

dʒ        46. jingle, ledge, object
*The object of jarring the edge is to make the jelly beans jump.*

## EXERCISES FOR FRONT VOWELS

| Consonants | [i] | [ɪ] | [e] | [ɛ] | [æ] | [a] |
|---|---|---|---|---|---|---|
| | ease | in | ate | end | at | aunt |
| LIPS | please | pretty | pate | pen | pat | path |
| | me | mit | make | Mary | mat | master |
| | wheel | will | wait | when | wham | waft |
| LIP-TEETH | feet | vim | vapor | vest | vanish | fast |
| TONGUE-TEETH | three | this | | their | that | path |
| TONGUE-TEETH RIDGE | tea | till | tape | tare | tack | task |
| | lean | lilting | late | let | lattice | last |
| | need | knit | Nate | never | narrow | nasty |
| | see | sit | zany | Sara | sat | Sahara |
| | sheep | ship | shake | shed | shack | shan't |
| | cheap | gypsy | chafe | chess | chat | chance |
| MIDDLE OF TONGUE, HARD PALATE | yield | Yiddish | | yell | Yankee | |
| | read | rip | raid | red | rat | |
| BACK OF TONGUE, SOFT PALATE | key | gingham | gate | care | cranky | glass |
| ASPIRATE | heap | hill | hate | hair | happy | half |

## Sentences for Practice of Front Vowels

1. [i]  Please see me eat the green beans.
2. [ɪ]  He lit a bit of tallow for the prince in his room.
3. [e]  He made a face while he waited for a fast freight.
4. [ɛ]  Seven men rented vests for every party.
5. [æ]  Can't you slap the cat after it has eaten the fish?
6. [a]  The last chance he took to be nasty his aunt sent him home.

## EXERCISES FOR MID-VOWELS

| Consonants | [ɝ] or [ɜ] | [ə] | [ɚ] | [ʌ] |
|---|---|---|---|---|
| | earn | away | wonder | up |
| LIPS | bird<br>Myrtle<br>were | Tampa<br>medium | parade<br><br>westerly | puppy<br>mud<br>won |
| LIP-<br>TEETH | fern | valise | | fudge |
| TONGUE-<br>TEETH | thirty | | thunder | thump |
| TONGUE-<br>TEETH<br>RIDGE | turn<br>learn<br>nerve<br>serve<br>shirk<br>chirp | Nevada<br>Theta<br><br>sofa | tender<br>letter<br>never<br><br>shatter | tongue<br>lump<br>none<br>some<br>such<br>chubby |
| MIDDLE OF<br>TONGUE,<br>HARD PALATE | yearn | relative | youngster | runt<br>young |
| BACK OF<br>TONGUE,<br>SOFT PALATE | girl | complete | | gull |
| ASPIRATE | hurt | | hatter | hunter |

## Sentences for Practice of Mid-vowels

1. [ɝ, ɜ]  *Turn to the first word and learn to chirp when you say it.*
2. [ə]  *Near the sofa but away from the wall sat a medium-sized valise.*
3. [ɚ]  *The thunder of the parade never did frighten the youngster.*
4. [ʌ]  *Such a fuss the old frump made that none was won over.*

## EXERCISES FOR BACK VOWELS

| Consonants | [u] | [ʊ] | [o] | [ɔ] | [ɑ] | [ɑ](r colored) |
|---|---|---|---|---|---|---|
| LIPS | prune<br>moon<br>woo | book<br>woman<br>would | bone<br>moan<br>wove | ball<br>maul<br>walk | bottle<br>mob<br>watch | arm<br>part<br>market<br>far |
| TONGUE-<br>TEETH<br>RIDGE | threw<br>tool<br>loom<br>noon<br>soon<br>shoe<br>juice | took<br>look<br>nook<br>forsook<br>shook<br>jury | throw<br>dough<br>low<br>know<br>soap<br>show<br>choke | thought<br>talk<br>long<br>naught<br>sought<br>shawl<br>jaw | throttle<br>toddy<br>lock<br>not<br>spa<br>shot<br>chop | darling<br>lark<br>narcissus<br>sarcastic<br>sharp<br>charm |
| MIDDLE OF<br>TONGUE,<br>HARD PALATE | you<br><br>roof | you're<br><br>rook | yolk<br><br>row | yawn<br><br>raw | yacht<br><br>rod | yard |
| BACK OF<br>TONGUE,<br>SOFT PALATE | cool | good | go | caught | calm<br>got | garden |
| ASPIRATE | hoop | hook | hope | hall | hop | hark |

## Sentences for Practice of Back Vowels

1. [u]     *The fool soon lost his new shoe in the prune orchard.*
2. [ʊ]     *He looked for the book in every nook he thought would hide it.*
3. [o]     *Hold the opal under your coat when you go over home.*
4. [ɔ]     *He was haunted by the long gawky man in the hall.*
5. [ɑ]     *The mob shot the robber and got a lot of sharp reproof from Arthur.*

## EXERCISES FOR DIPHTHONGS

| Consonants | [eɪ] | [aɪ] | [ou] | [ɔɪ] | [aʊ] |
|---|---|---|---|---|---|
| | | I | oh | oil | out |
| LIPS | pay<br>may<br>weigh | pile<br>mile<br>wide | poke<br>moat<br>woke | point<br>moist | pout<br>mount |
| TONGUE-<br>TEETH<br>RIDGE | they<br>tame<br>lame<br>name<br>same<br>shame<br>jade | thy<br>time<br>light<br>night<br>sight<br>shine<br>jibe | though<br>tow<br>low<br>note<br>so<br>show<br>chose | toil<br><br>loiter<br>noise<br>soil<br><br>joy | thousand<br>town<br>loud<br>noun<br>sound<br>shout<br>joust |
| MIDDLE OF<br>TONGUE,<br>HARD PALATE | Yale<br>rain | yipe<br>right | yolk<br>roll | yoick<br>royal | yowl<br>round |
| BACK OF<br>TONGUE,<br>SOFT PALATE | came | guide | coat | coil | gown |
| ASPIRATE | hale | height | hold | hoist | hound |

## Sentences for Practice of Diphthongs

1. [eɪ]  *They claimed the game was too tame for Yale.*
2. [aɪ]  *I like to try to climb five steps twice a day.*
3. [ou]  *He goes so slowly they chose the rowboat.*
4. [ɔɪ]  *Boys and toys point to noise and joy.*
5. [aʊ]  *Count out loud and shout for a thousand new friends in the town.*

## CONSONANT DRILLS

| Vowels | Two lip consonants | | | | |
|---|---|---|---|---|---|
| | p [p]<br>Voiceless<br>stop-plosive | b [b]<br>Voiced<br>stop-plosive | m [m]<br>Voiced<br>continuant | w [w]<br>Voiced<br>glide | wh [hw]<br>Voiceless<br>fricative |
| FRONT | peep<br>pip<br>pep<br>pare<br>pat<br>path | beet<br>bit<br>bet<br>bare<br>bat<br>bath | meat<br>mit<br>met<br>mare<br>mat<br>master | we<br>wit<br>wet<br>wary<br>wagon<br>waft | whee<br>whip<br>when<br>where<br>whack |
| MID | purple<br>paper<br>puppet | bird<br>better<br>bug | myrtle<br>maroon<br>monk | were<br>westerly<br>won | whirl |
| BACK | plume<br>pudding<br>pony<br>Paul<br>pop<br>part | boom<br>bush<br>bone<br>ball<br>bob<br>bargains | moon<br>Mussolini<br>moat<br>maul<br>mob<br>market | woo<br>woman<br>wore<br>walk<br>water | whoosh<br><br><br>wharf<br>what |
| DIPHTHONG | pay<br>pipe<br>pope<br>point<br>pout | bay<br>bright<br>bone<br>boy<br>about | may<br>might<br>moan<br>moist<br>mountain | way<br>wide<br>wove<br><br>wow | whay<br>white |

## CONSONANT DRILLS

| Vowels | | Tip of tongue-teeth ridge | | |
|---|---|---|---|---|
| | t [t] Voiceless stop-plosive | d [d] Voiced stop-plosive | n [n] Nasal Voiced continuant | l [l] Voiced continuant |
| FRONT | tea | dean | neat | lean |
| | till | did | knit | lit |
| | tell | dell | nest | let |
| | tare | dare | nary | lair |
| | tack | dandy | natty | lamp |
| | task | dance | nasty | last |
| MID | turn | dermal | nerve | learn |
| | tatter | under | manner | letter |
| | untie | dust | nun | luck |
| BACK | toot | doom | noon | loom |
| | took | door | nook | look |
| | tone | daughter | nobody | lone |
| | talked | dot | naught | lost |
| | toddy | dark | Nottingham | lot |
| | target | | narcissus | lark |
| DIPHTHONG | take | date | name | lame |
| | tight | dike | night | light |
| | told | dotage | know | load |
| | toil | doily | noisy | loiter |
| | town | down | now | loud |

## CONSONANT DRILLS

| Vowels | s [s] Voiceless continuant | z [z] Voiced continuant | sh [ʃ] Voiceless continuant | zh [ʒ] Voiced continuant | r [r] Voiced continuant |
|---|---|---|---|---|---|
| | | | *Tip of tongue toward teeth ridge* | | |
| FRONT | seek | zeal | sheep | leisure | reach |
| | sit | zinc | ship | vision | rich |
| | set | zest | shetland | pleasure | wretch |
| | Sarah | Zachary | share | invasion | rare |
| | sap | | shack | jabot | rack |
| | ask | | shaft | | rather |
| MID | concern | zircon | shirt | immersion | earn |
| | setter | zephyr | shaver | decision | return |
| | such | | shut | | runt |
| BACK | soon | zoom | shoot | rouge | rule |
| | forsook | Zurich | shook | | root |
| | soul | zoological | shone | explosion | road |
| | sought | | short | | raw |
| | sot | | shot | garage | rod |
| | sarcasm | | sharp | | |
| DIPHTHONG | same | zany | sheik | invasion | rate |
| | sight | Zion | shine | | ride |
| | so | Zola | show | composure | roll |
| | soil | trapezoid | | | roister |
| | sound | zounds | shroud | | rowdy |

## CONSONANT DRILLS

| Vowels | Tongue-teeth ridge | |
|---|---|---|
| | ch [tʃ]<br>Voiceless<br>*stop-plosive*<br>*plus continuant* | j [dʒ]<br>Voiceless<br>*stop-plosive*<br>*plus continuant* |
| FRONT | cheap<br>chip<br>chess<br>chair<br>chat<br>chance | jeep<br>jitter<br>jelly<br>Jerry<br>jam |
| MID | church<br>chapter<br>chunk | journal<br>jobber<br>jug |
| BACK | chew<br>Chungking<br>chose<br>Chaucer<br>chock<br>charm | June<br>jury<br>joke<br>jaw<br>jot<br>jar |
| DIPHTHONG | chaste<br>child<br>choke<br>choice<br>chow | jail<br>jibe<br>Jonah<br>joy<br>joust |

## CONSONANT DRILLS

| Vowels | Middle of tongue Hard palate | | Back of tongue Soft palate | | |
|---|---|---|---|---|---|
| | y [j] Voiced glide | r [r] Voiced | k [k] Voiceless stop-plosive | g [g] Voiced stop-plosive | ng [ŋ] Nasal continuant |
| FRONT | yield Yiddish yet Yale yank | reed rid red rate ramp | keen kill kept care cat cast | gear give get game glad aghast | peeping pitying getting staring banging asking |
| MID | yearn onion young | rum rung | scurvy command cut | girl gazette glove | earning lung |
| BACK | you you're yoeman York yon yard | root rodent roar rondeau | cute could comb cause cotton card | gloom good gloat gall got garnet | rueing ruining rowing roaring robbing sharpening |
| DIPHTHONG | yea yoke | rail roam | cake kite code coil count | gain guy gauche gargoyle gown | taking chiding loading coiling sounding |

## CONSONANT DRILLS

| Vowels | Aspirate |
|---|---|
| | h [h] <br> Voiceless |
| FRONT | he <br> hip <br> help <br> hair <br> happy |
| MID | rehearse <br> hatter <br> hut |
| BACK | humor <br> hook <br> home <br> haunt <br> hop <br> harp |
| DIPHTHONG | hasty <br> hide <br> hope <br> hoyden <br> hound |

# Forming Vowels

THE VOWELS ARE THE MUSICAL ELEMENTS OF SPEECH. SOME phoneticians like to arrange speech sounds on a continuum from musical to noisy. While some consonants are quite musical there appear to be no vowels that are really noisy. The more open vowels, those made with the jaws wide apart, are generally considered to be more musical than those that are closed. They certainly have more phonetic power. Concentration on the production of musical vowels should be an element in producing pleasant voice. Good posture, firm support, and a feeling of relaxed but energetic forming of all sounds is essential in these projects.

The purpose of this unit is to improve the quality of vowel sounds through ear training and greater consciousness of vowel formation in isolation, in words, and in connected speech. A number of excellent texts describe the formation of the vowel sounds, among them the phonetic section of Gray and Wise's *Bases of Speech*, Fairbanks' *Voice and Articulation Drillbook*, and Hahn, Hargis, Lomas, and Vandraegen's *Training the Voice for Speech*. Kantner and West's *Phonetics* even presents palatograms of the oral chamber in the formation of vowel sounds. All students should know, or learn now, how vowel sounds are formed and the phonetic symbols that represent the sounds.

All of these texts divide the vowel sounds into front vowels [i, ɪ, e, ɛ, æ, a], middle vowels [ʌ, ə, ɝ, ɚ, ɜ], and back vowels [ɑ, ɔ, o, ʊ, u]. There may be some apparent disagreements among phoneticians, but these usually are minimized by scrutiny. For instance, Fairbanks and Hahn et al. consider [eɪ] and [oʊ] as diphthongs and designate them as such, while others point out that all vowels tend to have on- and off-glides in connected speech and that [e] and [o] are not changed enough in sound to warrant their being designated as diphthongs. There is some variation in the formation of the [æ]. Students can settle this matter for themselves by placing a finger over the tongue and pronouncing [æ] and [a]. It will probably be found that the middle of the tongue rises when [æ] is pronounced. However, it should not rise enough to be felt along the upper molars. Not so easily settled is the choice of [aɪ] or [ɑɪ] in the diphthong in *I*. Probably both are used, but it seems evident that [ɑɪ] is more characteristic of mid-western speech. It is usually pointed out that [a], [ɜ], and [ɒ] are not characteristic of General American speech, though they are used in other English dialects. That [ɜ] and [ɒ] are very characteristic of British speech is not usually mentioned. Since we shall do some work on dialects, we shall work on all of the English vowels, and since there is *some* difference between [e] and [eɪ] and [o] and [oʊ], we shall designate these as diphthongs.

# EXERCISES

*1.* Noting that the air channel is comparatively wide for the front vowels and the tongue is bunched toward the front of the mouth, grasp the jaw with thumb and forefinger so you can, at the same time, feel the lip tension as well as jaw movement. Pronounce [i] and [ɪ] alternately, feeling the relaxation of tension for [ɪ] and the closeness of the tongue to the postdental, or alveolar, ridge for [i]. You will probably feel the sides of the front of the tongue against the upper bicuspids.

2. Still grasping your lower jaw, pronounce [i], [e], [ɛ], and [æ]. Try not to diphthongize [e]. Feel the progressively wider mouth opening from vowel to vowel. Try to keep the position of the tongue fairly stable from sound to sound. Reverse the order of these sounds.

3. Pronounce [eɪ] as in *they* and feel the closing of the jaw toward [ɪ].

4. Grasping the jaw as above, pronounce [u] and [ʊ]. Be aware of the closely pursed lips for [u] and the relaxation of lip tension for [ʊ].

5. Still grasping the jaw, pronounce [u], [o], [ɔ], [ɑ]. Try not to diphthongize [o], and be aware of the progressive dropping of the jaw and the enlarging of the mouth opening with each sound. Kelly and Higley, in their x-ray study of tongue position in certain vowels, found that for General American speakers, the back of the tongue was raised farther back for [o] than for [ɔ] or [u]. See if this difference is present in your pronunciation. Reverse the order of these sounds.

6. Add [ɒ] between [ɑ] and [ɔ], and feel that the lips are tenser than for [ɑ] and more open than for [ɔ].

7. Pronounce [oʊ] as in *know* and feel the closing of the lips and jaw on the off-glides.

8. Still grasping the jaw and feeling the movement of the tongue and lips, alternate [ɑ] and [a]. Now add [æ].

9. As before, alternate [ɚ] and [ɜ] feeling, particularly, the movement of the tongue tip. Now alternate [ɜ] and [ʌ].

10. When a feeling of the formation of all the vowel sounds is firmly established, combine the vowel with a consonant, as: [il, ɪl, eɪl, ɛl, æl, ɑl, ɔl, oʊl, ul, ʊl]. It will be harder to feel the forming of the vowel because of the presence of the consonant, but try to make your vowel formations as accurate as possible. Now add a consonant before as well as after the vowel, as [sil, sɪl, seɪl, sɛl, sæl].

11. In the following words and sentences, write the phonetic symbol for each vowel sound as it is pronounced when the word or sentence is read aloud to you. English is not always spelled as it is pronounced—is not a phonetic language—so concentrate on the sounds only and the symbols for the sounds, and forget the spelling.

| word | loose | lost | feel |
|------|-------|------|------|
| kneel | cat | pit | red |
| father | book | rut | above |

*She sells sea shells.*

*The dog fought the cat.*

*This project deals with phonetic symbols.*

*Soon the bell will ring.*

*Practice brings ease in performance.*

12. In the following short sentences, write the phonetic symbol for each vowel sound above the spelling symbol. Read the passage

aloud, noting which vowels are held and stressed and which are barely touched and unstressed. Now, using this same rhythm, pronounce the vowels alone. Be aware of their formation and their quality. Now read the passage again. Do this until the vowels are as clear and good in context as in isolation.

> *Sunset and evening star, and one clear call for me!*
> *The curfew tolls the knell of parting day.*
> *To be, or not to be: that is the question.*
> *Something there is that doesn't love a wall.*
> *Hog Butcher for the World,*
> *Tool Maker, Stacker of Wheat.*

## Additional Readings

Anderson, Virgil A., *Training the Speaking Voice*. New York: Oxford University Press, 1942, pp. 285-307.

Crocker, Lionel, and Louis M. Eich, *Oral Reading* (ed. 2). New York: Prentice-Hall, Inc., 1955, pp. 128-129.

Fairbanks, Grant, *Voice and Articulation Drillbook*. New York: Harper & Brothers, 1940, pp. 21-38.

Gray, Giles W., and Claude M. Wise, *The Bases of Speech*. New York: Harper & Brothers, 1934, pp. 186-247.

Hahn, Elise, Charles W. Lomas, Donald E. Hargis, Daniel Vandraegen, *Basic Voice Training for Speech*. New York: McGraw-Hill Book Company, Inc., 1952, pp. 146-170.

Kantner, Claude E., and Robert West, *Phonetics*. New York: Harper & Brothers, 1941, pp. 66-125.

Kenyon, J. S., *American Pronunciation*. Ann Arbor, Michigan: George Wahr, 1940, pp. 161-203.

Thomas, Charles K., *Phonetics of American English*. New York: The Ronald Press Company, 1947, *passim*.

Wise, Claude M., *Applied Phonetics*. Englewood Cliffs, N. J.: Prentice-Hall, Inc., 1957, pp. 90-120.

# Forming Diphthongs, Glides and Semi-vowels

IN THE PREVIOUS PROJECT IT WAS SUGGESTED THAT A NUMBER OF speech sounds are given their characteristic qualities, not by a stable position of the resonators, but by a gliding movement. [eɪ] and [ou] were the two sounds discussed. There are three other diphthongs in General American speech whose characteristic sounds are very different from the sounds of their components. These sounds are [aɪ] as in *Ike*, [aʊ] as in *out*, and [ɔɪ] as in *boy*. As Fairbanks notes, in General American speech, the diphthongs glide toward either [ɪ] or [ʊ], both relaxed, and relatively high vowels. The mouth is relaxing as it closes. In Southern American speech and often in General American speech, the glide is so short (if it exists at all) that people hear [ɑ] instead of [aɪ]. In Irish speech, on the other hand, the glide starts from a neutral sound and the last sound is the tense one, as in [əi].

A number of consonant sounds are gliding sounds, and these are all quite musical. For [w] the lips move from a pursed to a relaxed position, in [j] the front of the tongue moves toward the front of the hard palate, and then drops, and for the consonant [r] the tip of the tongue flips up toward the alveolar or postdental ridge. [j] serves almost as a glide into a vowel in many words, as in *year, yes, you, yawn, yours, yearn*. Indeed, many who are oriented to spelling rather than to speech sounds make the mistake of pronouncing the phonetic symbol [u] as [ju] and need to take particular notice of the difference between the two.

None of the glide consonants is very noisy. The air channel is obstructed very little. In fact, if the sound could be stopped, so there was no movement, [w] would sound like [ʊ], [j] would sound like [ɪ], and [r] would sound like [ɜ].

**173**

The final consonant of this group, [l], is considered musical enough to be a semi-vowel, but it is very stable in its formation. This is the only lateral sound in the English language—a sound in which the voiced air flows over the sides of the tongue. The tongue tip is placed on the middle of the postdental ridge, and the sides are lowered. If the tip is spread and the tongue is relaxed, we have the light, or initial [l]. If the tip is pointed and the tongue is tensed with a dip in the center, we have the final or dark [l].

It is not uncommon for speakers to omit [l] when it is followed by [j], and [wɪljəm] becomes [wɪjəm], [wɪljəmzbɚg] becomes [wɪjəmzbɚg]. Be sure the tip of the tongue contacts the alveolar ridge for this sound. Americans, generally, are reputed to overuse the dark [l]. This is probably another way of saying the tongue is unduly tensed. If the [l] can be pronounced as initial rather than final in the syllable, as [wɔ-lɪt] instead of [wɔl-ɪt], tension could probably be reduced. Awareness of lack of tension in the tongue tip at any time is probably the best aid.

[w] is the only one of the gliding consonants or semi-vowels that has a voiceless correlative [hw], sometimes written as [ʍ]. Because there is a semantic difference produced by voicing as compared with unvoicing, it is well to become aware of this difference. *Wail* and *whale* are very different because of the unvoicing of the first sound in the second word.

# EXERCISES

1. Grasping the jaw with thumb and forefinger as before, pronounce:

| | | |
|---|---|---|
| [ɑ–ɑ–ɑɪ] | [ɑ–ɑ–ɑɪ] | [ɑ–ɑ–ɑɪ] |
| [a–a–aɪ] | [a–a–aɪ] | [a–a–aɪ] |
| [ɑ–ɑ–ɑʊ] | [ɑ–ɑ–ɑʊ] | [ɑ–ɑ–ɑʊ] |
| [a–a–aʊ] | [a–a–aʊ] | [a–a–aʊ] |
| [ɔ–ɔ–ɔɪ] | [ɔ–ɔ–ɔɪ] | [ɔ–ɔ–ɔɪ] |
| [ɒ–ɒ–ɒɪ] | [ɒ–ɒ–ɒɪ] | [ɒ–ɒ–ɒɪ] |

Be aware of minor differences in tensions and tongue positions for these three pairs of exercises, as well as of the larger movements of the jaw.

2. In the following lists of words, try to determine whether you use [ɑɪ] or [aɪ], [ɑʊ] or [aʊ], [ɔɪ] or [ɒɪ]. Use each word in a sentence. Does your pronunciation vary with the word or its position in context?

| | | |
|---|---|---|
| sight | pound | toiling |
| knife blade | bout | joy |
| fright | town | soil |
| viselike | douse | loiter |
| benign | sauerkraut | bouyant |
| Christlike | yowl | Boyer (actor's name) |
| tiresome | household | Troy |
| guileless | browsing | foist |

3. Place the phonetic symbol for the vowel, diphthong, glide, and semi-vowel sounds you use above the spelling symbol in each word in the above lists.

4. Grasp your throat above your Adam's apple (larynx) while you pronounce the following pairs of words. Feel the vibration of [w] as compared to the lack of vibration of [hw] until you are aware of the difference without feeling your throat.

| | |
|---|---|
| wile – while | wet – whet |
| wail – whale | watt – what |
| wight – white | Y – why |
| weigh – whey | witch – which |
| wit – whit | wen – when |

5. Mark the phonetic symbols for your pronunciation of the italic vowels above the spelling symbol. Then look up the words in a dictionary (Kenyon and Knott have a phonetic dictionary) and see what pronunciations are given there

| | | | |
|---|---|---|---|
| news | newspaper | nuisance | tune |
| few | opportunity | absolutely | use |
| student | soon | plume | revenue |

6. Do you use [r] or [ɝ] stressed, or [ɚ] unstressed in the words in the following sentences? Mark the phonetic symbol for your pronunciation above the spelling symbols. Does rapid or careless pronunciation make a difference in the stability of the sounds?

> You're a thrifty person.
> Rabbits are running around here.
> There were three roads.
> Her verses were widely read.

7. Listen to your favorite actor or actress, preferably on records. Does she (or he) use [ɝ], [ɚ], and [r] as you do? Write down the words in which there are differences and note the pronunciation differences with phonetic symbols. Write the results of your observations in a short paper.

8. In the passages that follow, place the phonetic symbol for the vowel, semi-vowel, diphthong, and glide sounds you think you should use above the spelling symbols. Read each passage aloud to establish its stress and rhythm. Then, grasping the jaw to feel its movement and the movement of your lips, read the vowels and diphthongs with this same stress and rhythm. Pay particular attention to the quality and proper formation of each sound. Still grasping the jaw, read these sounds in their consonant contexts. If jaw or lip movements are curtailed when vowels are in context, practice until the formations are about the same.

### A.

I hear America singing, the varied carols I hear,
Those mechanics, each one singing his as it should be blithe
    and strong,
The carpenter singing his as he measures his plank or beam,
The mason singing his as he makes ready for work, or leaves
    off work,
The boatman singing what belongs to him in his boat, the
    deckhand singing on the steamboat deck,
The shoemaker singing as he sits on his bench, the hatter
    singing as he stands,
The wood-cutter's song, the ploughboy's on his way in the
    morning, or at noon intermission or at sundown,

The delicious singing of the mother, or of the young wife at
    work, or of the girl sewing or washing,
Each singing what belongs to him or her and to none else,
The day what belongs to the day—at night the party of
    young fellows, robust, friendly,
Singing with open mouths their strong melodious songs.

"I Hear America Singing," WALT WHITMAN

## B.

I met a traveller from an antique land
Who said: "Two vast and trunkless legs of stone
Stand in the desert. Near them, on the sand,
Half sunk, a shatter'd visage lies, whose frown,
And wrinkled lip, and sneer of cold command,
Tell that its sculptor well those passions read
Which yet survive, stamp'd on these lifeless things,
The hand that mock'd them, and the heart that fed:
And on the pedestal these words appear:
'My name is Ozymandias, king of kings:
Look on my works, ye Mighty, and despair!'
Nothing beside remains. Round the decay
Of that colossal wreck, boundless and bare
The lone and level sands stretch far away."

"Ozymandias of Egypt," PERCY B. SHELLEY

## C.

A poor Relation—is the most irrelevant thing in nature,—a piece of
impertinent correspondency,—an odious approximation,—a haunting
conscience,—a preposterous shadow, lengthening in the noontide of
our prosperity,—an unwelcome remembrancer,—a perpetually recurring mortification,—a drain on your purse,—a more intolerable dun on
your pride,—a drawback upon success,—a rebuke to your rising,—a
stain in your blood,—a blot on your 'scutcheon,—a rent on your gar-
ment,—a death's head at your banquet,—. . . a lion in your path,—a
frog in your chamber,—a fly in your ointment,—a mote in your eye,—
a triumph to your enemy, an apology to your friends,—the one thing
not needful,—the hail in harvest,—the ounce of sour in a pound of
sweet.

"A Poor Relation," CHARLES LAMB

## Additional Readings

Anderson, Virgil A., *Training the Speaking Voice*. New York: Oxford University Press, 1942, pp. 274-284; 307-313.

Fairbanks, Grant, *Voice and Articulation Drillbook*. New York: Harper & Brothers, 1940, pp. 39-50; 95-104.

Kantner, Claude E., and Robert West, *Phonetics*. New York: Harper & Brothers, 1941, pp. 107-125.

Kenyon, John Samuel, and Thomas Albert Knott, *A Pronouncing Dictionary of American English*. Springfield, Mass.: G. & C. Merriam Co., 1944, *passim*.

Thomas, Charles K., *Phonetics of American English*. New York: The Ronald Press Company, 1947, *passim*.

# Forming Nasal Sounds

THERE ARE ONLY THREE NASAL SOUNDS IN ENGLISH PRONUNCIATION. These are [m], [n], and [ŋ]. For the nasal sounds, the air channel through the mouth is completely blocked by the tongue or lips, and the voiced air flows out through the nose. If the nostrils are pinched shut, there is no sound. For all other speech sounds, the air flows through and is modified in the oral chamber.

[ŋ] is most frequently spelled ng and therefore often proves to be confusing for foreigners learning English, because they tend to pronounce according to the spelling. Some American speakers have trouble with this sound and say [sɪŋgɪŋ] for [sɪŋɪŋ] and [lɔŋgaɪlənd] for [lɔŋaɪlənd].

To some ears, the nasal sounds of women do not have the vibrant hum that they have for most men. According to Curtis' findings and subsequent verification, the characteristic frequency of the nasal sounds and of the nasal cavity is about 300 dv. This is only a little higher in pitch than middle C on the piano. If a woman has a high-pitched voice, it is understandable that her nasal sounds might be different from those of a lower pitched voice. On the other hand, the sounds may not be held long enough to develop vibrancy, or the cavity itself may be at fault.

Voices judged to be nasal can result from a number of different factors, and it is necessary to find the cause for the nasal effect before specific exercises to improve the voice can be prescribed. Kelley's studies in nasality seemed to establish that vowels of superior speakers had a rather large nasal factor at the beginning and the end of the vowel. Apparently the velum rises after the initiation of the vowel and drops before it is finished. Perhaps the British are right in their judgment that American voices are typically a little nasal. This writer observed during x-ray studies that the vela of some superior speakers whose voices had never been judged to be nasal tended to drop during soft speech. However, Kelley observed also that voices judged to be badly nasal had a greater nasal factor than those judged to be superior and that the mouth opening was smaller. Later, Hixon, in his x-ray study of nasality, observed less velar activity in the nasal voices than in the superior, and evidence that, for the open vowels studied, the tongue was raised in the back. Then, too, voices are frequently said to be badly nasal when the nasal passages and nasal pharynx are swollen and inflamed. Thus, it appears that a judgment of unpleasant nasality may be made when (1) there is velar sluggishness and excessive voiced air is passing through the nose, (2) the nasal sounds lack nasality or humming quality, and (3) the tongue is bunched in the back of the mouth for open vowel sounds. Still other causes for the unpleasant quality called nasality may yet be discovered. From Kelley's studies and other observations it appears that exercises at least to maintain the mouth opening of isolated vowels when they are in their consonant contexts as was set forth on page 170 ff. are to the good.

## EXERCISES

1. In a mirror, observe your own velum. You will probably recognize it by the uvula, a fleshy tip hanging down from the middle of the velum at the back. Take a breath as if to yawn and notice how the velum rises and how much. Now breathe through your nose, and notice how it drops. Now say [ɑ] and note the rising of the velum. Does it rise as much as when you took a breath as if to yawn? Now, simply relax and watch the velum fall. Now try to phonate a very unpleasant nasal [ɑ]. What happens? Memorize the feeling of the velum in all these positions so you will know when it is up or down without looking in a mirror. Many people report that when the velum is up it feels as if it were down and vice versa.

2. Pronounce and try to distinguish between the feeling of the tongue rising and the velum rising:

Nasal    Oral
[ŋ — gɑ,  ŋ – gɑ,  ŋ – ɑ]

$$[n — a, \quad n-a, \quad n-a]$$
$$[m — a, \quad m-a, \quad m-a]$$

3. Pinch the nostrils shut and say, quite loudly, and then softly:

*How are you today?*

*This is the house that Jack built.*

*The red roses are spectacular.*

Say the same sentences without pinching the nostrils. Is there any difference in the sound or the feeling? You would feel the air closed up in the nasal chamber and hear the difference in sound if you are nasalizing unduly.

4. Pronounce the following with maximum humming and minimum tension. Do not *make* the sounds vibrate so much as *allow* them to vibrate.

m – m – murmur

n – n – nannie

ŋ – ŋ – singing

5. In the following passages work for singing nasal sounds. If the nasals do not hum sufficiently, practice those words in the same way as in exercise 4.

*This is the forest primeval.*

*The murmuring pines and the hemlocks ...*

Evangeline, LONGFELLOW

*From harmony, from heavenly harmony,*

*This universal frame began:*

*When Nature underneath a heap*

*Of jarring atoms lay,*

*And could not heave her head,*

*The tuneful voice was heard from high:*

*"Arise, ye more than dead."*

"A Song for St. Cecilia's Day," JOHN DRYDEN

*When in disgrace with fortune and men's eyes*

*I all alone beweep my outcast state,*

*And trouble deaf heaven with my bootless cries,*

*And look upon myself, and curse my fate,*

*Wishing me like to one more rich in hope,*

*Featured like him, like him with friends possessed,*

Desiring this man's art, and that man's scope,
With what I most enjoy contented least;
Yet in these thoughts myself almost despising,
Haply I think on Thee,—and then my state,
Like to the lark at break of day arising
From sullen earth, sings hymns at heaven's gate;
     For thy sweet love remember'd such wealth brings
     That then I scorn to change my state with kings.

                        Sonnet XXIX, SHAKESPEARE

I will lift up mine eyes unto the hills, from whence cometh my help.
My help cometh from the Lord, which made heaven and earth.
He will not suffer thy foot to be moved: he that keepeth thee will
    not slumber.
Behold, he that keepeth Israel shall neither slumber nor sleep.
The Lord is thy keeper: the Lord is thy shade upon thy right hand.
The sun shall not smite thee by day, nor the moon by night.
The Lord shall preserve thee from all evil: he shall preserve thy soul.
The Lord shall preserve thy going out and thy coming in from this
    time forth, and even for evermore.

                        Psalm 121

    6. Say [æ] and be sure that the back of the tongue does not touch the upper back molars at all.

    7. Read the passages in Exercise 5, and try to maintain a feeling of openness and lack of tension in the back of the mouth for the sounds that are not nasal.

## Additional Readings

Anderson, Virgil A., *Training the Speaking Voice*. New York: Oxford University Press, 1942, pp. 261-263.

Fairbanks, Grant, *Voice and Articulation Drillbook*. New York: Harper & Brothers, 1940, pp. 51-60.

Kantner, Claude E., and Robert West, *Phonetics*. New York: Harper & Brothers, 1941, pp. 163-170.

Thomas, Charles K., *Phonetics of American English*. New York: The Ronald Press Company, 1947, passim.

# Forming Plosives and Affricates

THERE ARE THREE PAIRS OF PLOSIVE SOUNDS. ONE OF EACH PAIR IS voiced and one is voiceless. The air is stopped in the mouth—at the lips, at the alveolar ridge, and at the velum—just as the air is stopped for the nasal sounds, with the important exception that the velum is raised for the plosive sounds. Pressure builds up and is exploded rather sharply when the stop is released.

Though the sharp "pop" characteristic of plosive sounds is heard almost too clearly when a microphone is used, especially when the microphone is quite close, plosive sounds have rather little phonetic power and do not carry well. It is easy for them to be lost in auditorium speaking. There is a story concerning George Arliss in *The Green Goddess*. Talking to his servant he had the line, "I am weak! I am weak!" However, the final plosives were weak, and what was heard in the auditorium was, "I am wee! I am wee!" Since Arliss was, indeed, wee, the effect was more comic than was intended. So actors who generally perform without a microphone need sufficient stop for a good, sharp explosion, while those who use a microphone should be careful that they do not "blast" it.

Plosives require more energy than nasals. Carelessness and lack of energy result in omission of plosives, weak plosives, and the voicing of plosives, especially when they come between two voiced sounds. [lɪtl] becomes [lɪdl], [bʌtɚ] becomes [bʌdɚ]. On radio, the advertising slogan, "Butter is better" frequently is heard as [bʌdɚ ɪz bɛdɚ]. Sometimes the postdental plosive is omitted altogether and the glottal shock is substituted. The tendency to voice medial plosives may be corrected in part, at least, by dividing words in order that the plosive is initial in the second syllable rather than final in the first, as [bʌ-tɚ], instead of [bʌt-ɚ].

**183**

Even more common in careless speech is a tendency to omit plosives, especially when they are preceded by a similarly formed nasal sound. [wɒntəd] becomes [wɑnəd], [goʋiŋtu] becomes [gʌnə].

In connected speech the plosive is exploded into the following sound. If that sound is another plosive, then the stop is made for the first plosive and then for the second plosive, but only the last one is exploded. In [æpt] the lips close for the [p] while the tongue tip is forming the [t] and the [t] is the plosive that is exploded. *But the stops are always made.* When [l] follows a plosive as in [lɪtl] the sides of the tongue drop for the [l] and what explosion there is is lateral, or when [n] follows a plosive, as in [mɪtn], what explosion there is is nasal. But again the firm closure is necessary for the plosive sound. This same situation exists when certain fricatives of similar formation follow the plosive as in [wɑntðəm] or [meɪkðəm]. [ð] will have a plosive attack.

In a similar way, plosives are exploded into the channels of [s], [z], [ʃ], and [ʒ]. In the case of the last two sounds, [tʃ] as in [tʃɝtʃ] and [dʒ] as in [dʒʌdʒ], the effect of one sound instead of two is so strong that [tʃ] and [dʒ] are often called affricates and listed separately.

Because plosives and the fricative [s] both require considerable precision and energy, many people have difficulty in saying such combinations as [sts]. They simply continue the [s] and have no complete stoppage of breath at all. Such people need special practice on those consonant combinations difficult for them.

The following exercises are designed to encourage precision, lightness, and alacrity in the pronunciation of plosive sounds especially. If there is any stiffness at all in the articulators, it will be almost impossible to do these drills with any speed. Work first for precision and then for speed.

# EXERCISES

1. Hold your hand about an inch away from your lips and say, "Peter Piper picked a peck of pickled peppers." Feel the sharp little

explosions of air on each plosive against your hand. Move your hand farther and farther away until you do not feel the explosions. Now project the tongue twister as if to a person at the back of the room or outside the room. How much farther away can you feel the explosions on your hand?

2. Do the same as above, only use a small flame such as that of a cigarette lighter or candle. Notice how easy it is to blow out the flame with the plosive when it is near the lips. After the flame is far enough away so the plosives do not affect it, change to a vowel, such as [i] or [ɑ]. See how near your lips you can bring the flame without its wavering from the vowel.

3. Practice any consonant, combination of consonants, or combinations of consonants and vowels that need attention in the rhythmic exercise described in Exercise 9, page 145, [t], [d], [bd], [pt], [gn], [tl], [st], [ts], [sts], [eɪp], [teɪpt].

4. This exercise for practice of plosive sounds should be done very slowly and carefully at first, and then with more and more speed without sacrificing accuracy:

    *a.* With stress on first syllable:

        ['pɑ-tɪ-kɑ, 'pɑ-tɪ-kɑ, 'pɑ-tɪ-kɑ, 'pɑ-tɪ-kɑ]

    *b.* With stress on the second syllable:

        [pə-'tɑ-kɑ, pə-'tɑ-kɑ, pə-'tɑ-kɑ, pə-'tɑ-kɑ]

    *c.* With stress on the third syllable:

        [pɑ-tɪ-'kɑ, pɑ-tɪ-'kɑ, pɑ-tɪ-'kɑ, pɑ-tɪ-'kɑ]

    *d.* Change vowels as [pi-tɪ-ki], [poʊ-tɪ-koʊ], [pu-tɪ-ku], etc.

5. Repeat rapidly:  [bə- bə- bə ...........................]

                [də- də- də ...........................]

                [bə- də- bə ...........................]

                [tə- tə- tə ...........................]

                [bə- də- tə ...........................]

    *a.* Stress first syllable of the trio.

    *b.* Stress second syllable of the trio.

    *c.* Stress third syllable of the trio.

Repeat rapidly: [be-de-be, be-de-be, ....................]
a. Stress first syllable of the trio.
b. Stress second syllable of the trio.
c. Stress third syllable of the trio.

Repeat rapidly: [be-be-de, bə-bə-də, ....................]
a. Stress first syllable of the trio.
b. Stress second syllable of the trio.
c. Stress third syllable of the trio.

Practice other variations, using [be, de, te, ke], etc.

6. In a similar way practice the following with various vowels and diphthongs: [bi-dɪ-pɪ-'ti-pi]. The primary stress is on the fourth syllable, and there is secondary stress on the first syllable.

7. Tongue twisters often are good practice for light and firm pronunciation of plosive sounds:

### A.

A tree toad loved a she toad
That lived up in a tree;
She was a three-toed she toad,
But a two-toed tree toad tried to win
The she-toad's friendly nod,
For the tree toad loved the ground
That the three-toed she toad trod.

### B.

If to hoot and to toot a Hottentot tot
Were taught by a Hottentot tutor,
Should the tutor get hot if the Hottentot tot
Should hoot and toot at the tutor?

### C.

Amidst the mists and coldest frosts,
With stoutest wrists and loudest boasts,
He thrusts his fists against the posts,
And still insists he sees the ghosts.

8. The songs of Gilbert and Sullivan provide good practice for rapid and accurate formation of plosive sounds:

### A.

Conceive me if you can,
A crochety cracked young man,
An ultra-poetical,
Super-aesthetical,
Out-of-the-way young man.
Conceive me if you can,
A matter-of-fact young man
An alphabetical, arithmetical,
Everyday young man.

### B.

To sit in solemn silence in a dull, dark dock
In a pestilential prison, with a life-long lock,
Awaiting the sensation of a short, sharp shock,
From a cheap and chippy chopper on a big, black block.

### C.

And I'm a peppery kind of king,
Who's indisposed for parleying
To fit the wit of a bit of a chit,
And that's the long and the short of it!

### D.

You'd find the bread improved, I think,
By getting better flour;
And have you anything to drink
That looks a little less like ink,
And isn't quite so sour?

### E.

The criminal cried, as he dropped him down,
    In a state of wild alarm
With a frightful, frantic, fearful frown,
    I bared my big right arm.
I seized him by his little pig-tail,

And on his knees fell he,
As he squirmed and struggled,
And gurgled and guggled,
I drew my snickersnee!
Oh, never shall I
Forget the cry,
Or the shriek that shrieked he,
As I gnashed my teeth,
When from its sheath
I drew my snickersnee!

9. Difficult consonant combinations that need practice often appear in Shakespearean and Biblical literature:

A.

O, thou didst then ne'er love so heartily!
If thou remember'st not the slightest folly
That ever love did make thee run into,
Thou has not loved:
Or if thou hast not sat as I do now,
Wearying thy hearer in thy mistress' praise,
Thou hast not loved:
Or if thou has not broke from company
Abruptly, as my passion now makes me,
Thou hast not loved.

As You Like It, SHAKESPEARE

B.

Praise waiteth for thee, O god, in Sion; and unto thee shall
    the vow be performed;
O thou that hearest prayer, unto thee shall all flesh come.
Iniquities prevail against me: as for our transgressions, thou
    shalt purge them away.
Blessed is the man whom thou choosest, and causest to
    approach unto thee, that he may dwell in thy courts:
We shall be satisfied with the goodness of thy house, even
    of thy holy temple....

Psalm 65

## Additional Readings

Anderson, Virgil A., *Training the Speaking Voice*. New York: Oxford University Press, 1942, pp. 253-261; 267-274.

Fairbanks, Grant, *Voice and Articulation Drillbook*. New York: Harper & Brothers, 1940, pp. 60-72.

Kantner, Claude E., and Robert West, *Phonetics*. New York: Harper & Brothers, 1941, pp. 139-152.

Thomas, Charles K., *Phonetics of American English*. New York: The Ronald Press Company, 1947, *passim*.

Wise, Claude M., *Applied Phonetics*. Englewood Cliffs, N. J.: Prentice-Hall, Inc., 1957, pp. 123-128.

# Forming Fricatives

Firm support of tone and accurate formation are the requisites for good fricative sounds. They do not carry well, and relaxation of pressure results in omissions as [ɑɪ lɑɪk ə-], for instance, instead of [ɑɪ lɑɪk hə-]. The points where the air channel is narrowed to cause the characteristic sound of friction should be reviewed so that one may reduce or eliminate any extraneous tensions. [f] and [v] are produced by friction between the upper teeth and lower lip, [θ] and [ð] by friction between the tip or front of the tongue and the upper front teeth, and the friction for [h] is between the vocal cords and not in the oral cavity at all. [s] and [z] probably cause more trouble than any other fricatives or any other speech sounds, for that matter. The air is channeled in a narrow stream down the tongue. The pressure of the sides of the tongue against the upper teeth as far forward as the bicuspids can be felt. Contrast this with [ʃ], for which the pressure is not so far forward. If the channel is too broad and air flows over a wider area of the front of the tongue, a slushy [s] that approaches [ʃ] is produced, while this same broadened stream of air making friction too near the backs of the front teeth results in a sound approaching [θ] or lisping.

The chief difficulty that normal speakers encounter with fricatives is a tendency toward careless omissions, as was indicated in the beginning of this project. Not only is [h] omitted, but it is equally common to hear [ð] omitted, as in [hi wɑnts əm] instead of [hi wɑnts ðəm]. Precision of formation is especially essential for [s].

## Additional Readings

Anderson, Virgil A., *Training the Speaking Voice*. New York: Oxford University Press, 1942, pp. 263-267.

Fairbanks, Grant, *Voice and Articulation Drillbook*. New York: Harper
 & Brothers, 1940, pp. 78-95.

Wise, Claude M., *Applied Phonetics*. Englewood Cliffs, N. J.: Prentice-
 Hall, Inc., 1957, pp. 133-138.

# Synthesis and Evaluation
# of Progress

HAMLET'S ADVICE TO THE PLAYERS IS NOT ONLY ADVICE, BUT IS PHRASED in such a way that Hamlet can illustrate what he considers good articulation. The songs of Gilbert and Sullivan are also known for their demands of lingual alacrity. With good support, relaxed throat, and attention directed toward flexibility in the front of the mouth, practice one of the selections suggested below.

A.

Speak the speech, I pray you, as I pronounced it to you, trippingly on the tongue: but if you mouth it, as many of your players do, I had as lief the town-crier spoke my lines. Nor do not saw the air too much with your hand, thus, but use all gently; for in the very torrent, tempest, and, as I may say, the whirlwind of passion, you must acquire and beget a temperance that may give it smoothness. O, it offends me to the soul to hear a robustious periwig-pated fellow tear a passion to tatters, to very rags, to split the ears of the groundlings, who for the most part are capable of nothing but inexplicable dumb-shows and noise: I would have such a fellow whipped for o'erdoing Termagant; it out-herods Herod: pray you, avoid it.

Hamlet, WILLIAM SHAKESPEARE

B.

I am the very pattern of a modern Major-General,
I've information vegetable, animal, and mineral;
I know the kings of England, and I quote the fights historical,
From Marathon to Waterloo, in order categorical;
I'm very well acquainted too with matters mathematical,

I understand equations, both the simple and quadratical,
About binominal theorem I'm teeming with a lot o' news,
With many cheerful facts about the square of the hypotenuse.
I'm very good at integral and differential calculus,
I know the scientific names of beings animalculous,
In short, in matters vegetable, animal and mineral,
I am the very model of a modern Major-General.
I know our mythic history—King Arthur's and Sir Caradoc's,
I answer hard acrostics, I've a pretty taste for paradox,
I quote in elegiacs all the crimes of Heliogabalus,
In conics I can floor peculiarities parabolous.
I can tell undoubted Raphaels from Gerard Dows and Zoffanies,
I know the croaking chorus from the "Frogs" of Aristophanes.
Then I can hum a fugue, of which I've heard the music's din afore,
And whistle all the airs from that confounded nonsense "Pinafore."
Then I can write a washing bill in Babylonic cuneiform,
And tell you every detail of Caractacus's uniform.
In short in matters vegetable, animal and mineral,
I am the very model of a modern Major-General.
In fact when I know what is meant by "mamelon" and "revelin,"
When I can tell at sight a Chassepôt rifle from a javelin,
When such affairs as sorties and surprises I'm more wary at,
And when I know precisely what is meant by Commissariat,
When I have learnt what progress has been made in modern gunnery,
When I know more of tactics than a novice in a nunnery,
In short when I've a smattering of elementary strategy,
You'll say a better Major-General has never sat a gee—
For my military knowledge, though I'm plucky and adventury,
Has only been brought down to the beginning of the century,
But still in learning vegetable, animal and mineral,
I am the very model of a modern Major-General!

Pirates of Penzance, W. S. GILBERT

## C.

When you're lying awake with a dismal headache, and
repose is tabooed by anxiety,
I conceive you may use any language you choose to indulge
in without impropriety,

*For* your brain is on fire—the bedclothes conspire of usual
   slumber to plunder you:
*First* your counterpane goes and uncovers your toes, and
   your sheet slips demurely from under you:
*Then* the blanketing tickles—you feel like mixed pickles,
   so terribly sharp is the pricking;
*And* you're hot and you're cross, and you tumble and toss
   till there's nothing 'twixt you and the ticking;
*Then* your bedclothes all creep to the floor in a heap, and
   you pick 'em all up in a tangle;
*Next* your pillow resigns and politely declines to remain
   at its usual angle.
*Well*, you get some respose in the form of a doze, with hot
   eyeballs and head ever-aching;
*But* your slumber teems with such horrible dreams that
   you'd very much better be waking.
*You*'re a regular wreck, with a crick in your neck,
*And* no wonder you snore, for your head's on the floor,
*And* you're needles and pins from your soles to your shins,
*And* your flesh is a-creep, for your left leg's asleep, . . .
*And* some fluff in your lung, and a feverish tongue,
*And* a thirst that's intense, and a general sense
*That* you haven't been sleeping in clover.
*But* the darkness has past, and it's daylight at last,
*And* the night has been long—ditto, ditto, my song—
*And* thank goodness, they're both of them over!

   *Iolanthe*, W. S. GILBERT

### D.

Out of the hills of Habersham,
   Down the valleys of Hall,
*I* hurry amain to reach the plain,
*Run* the rapid and leap the fall,
*Split* at the rock and together again,
*Accept* my bed, or narrow or wide,
*And* flee from folly on every side
   *With* a lover's pain to attain the plain
      Far from the hills of Habersham,
      Far from the valleys of Hall.

All down the hills of Habersham,
    All through the valleys of Hall,
The rushes cried Abide, abide,
The willful waterweeds held me thrall,
The laving laurel turned my tide,
The fern and the fondling grass said Stay,
The dewberry dipped for to work delay,
And the little reeds sighed Abide, abide,
    Here in the hills of Habersham,
    Here in the valleys of Hall.

    High o'er the hills of Habersham,
    Veiling the valleys of Hall,
The hickory told me manifold
Fair tales of shade, the poplar tall
Wrought me her shadowy self to hold,
The chestnut, the oak, the walnut, the pine,
Overleaning, with flickering meaning and sign,
Said, Pass not, so cold, these manifold
    Deep shades of the hills of Habersham,
    These glades in the valleys of Hall.

    And oft in the hills of Habersham,
    And oft in the valleys of Hall,
The white quartz shone, and the smooth brook-stone
Did bar me of passage with friendly brawl,
And many a luminous jewel lone
—Crystals clear or a-cloud with mist,
Ruby, garnet, and amethyst—
Made lures with the lights of streaming stone
    In the clefts of the hills of Habersham,
    In the beds of the valleys of Hall.

    But oh, not the hills of Habersham,
    And oh, not the valleys of Hall
Avail: I am fain for to water the plain.
Downward the voices of Duty call—
Downward, to toil and be mixed with the main,

The dry fields burn, and the mills are to turn,
And a myriad flowers mortally yearn,
And the lordly main from beyond the plain
    Calls o'er the hills of Habersham,
    Calls through the valleys of Hall.

"Song of the Chattahoochee," SIDNEY LANIER

# 7

# PROJECTS IN
# Control of Articulation

# Speech Standards for
# Public Performance

THERE ARE MANY KINDS OR STYLES OF SPEECH TO BE HEARD FROM THE lips of public performers in America, not only from local people in the school, on the lecture platform, and in the pulpit, but also from national figures who appear on radio, television, the motion picture screen, or the professional stage. We may hear Eastern American speech, Southern American speech, and General American speech all on one program. We hear American dialects strongly flavored with influences from another language.

The problem of setting a standard of speech for public performers in America has long been a subject for lively conversation among teachers of speech, actors, lecturers, ministers, and all others who appear before groups. There are those who would have all performers conform to a single standard, who believe that one standard of speech is more effective, more beautiful, than another. There are others who prefer to permit each performer to speak his native dialect, refined to some extent for use from the public platform. There have been some who would prefer that all speakers adopt a London or South of England dialect as the most desirable speech.

The serious student is often confused as to which way to turn, and well he may be, for there are several aspects of the problem that have no easy or clear answers. One of these is the fact that in America there are three major or regional dialects, each in large part similar to the other, but each with distinguishing characteristics in the use of vowels, consonants, and diphthongs, of elisions and melodic patterns.

What is often even more difficult to assess is the fact that there are hundreds of variations within the dialect of any one region. It is astonishing to the person who has not observed closely that Higgins in Shaw's *Pygmalion* could identify the birthplace of several characters simply by hearing them talk. But Shaw makes these people speak rather sharply differing dialects. The trained ear can often spot the county in the state from which the speaker comes, particularly if that speaker has not been trained to be conscious of dialect or to remove the unique characteristics of his speech. Which area within a region has the "preferred" or the "correct" or the most characteristic version of the general dialect class? No one can say.

A third phenomenon that may confuse the serious student is the fact that each individual usually speaks what amounts to several dialects or variations of a dialect. In some of his conversation we hear a somewhat formal, rather precise speech. At other times his speech is more informal or colloquial, substituting vocabulary and forms of locution as well as pronunciations that have a more relaxed, less guarded, and perhaps less disciplined quality about them. The colloquial more often than not is more colorful and expressive of feeling, more directly revealing of thought than the formal speech. At other times the colloquial speech is observed to be slovenly, undisciplined, and even inaccurate in that the same expression is often used to cover a multitude of situations or ideas. This last is usually the case, however, when the colloquial has degenerated into slang or, worse yet, the vulgar. The subject, the company, the occasion, the place—all seem to have their effect on the speech of an individual.

Many of us who have heard the speech of the trained British actor have come to admire the clarity of articulation, the quality of voice production we usually observe in these people. When we compare their work with that of the American naturalistic school of performers with their attitude that anything is acceptable so long as it is "realistic," we are often so pleased with being able to understand with ease and with finding it a pleasure to listen to the former that we are tempted to assume there is something inherently superior about British (London or South of England) dialect as compared to any of the major American dialects, something of the absolute or "correct" about it in contrast to an American degeneracy of speech.

A fifth phenomenon that may be confusing to the serious student in search of a standard of speech for public performance is the slow but constant change of pronunciation that goes on all the time within a language. If we observe only our own times and the people we hear speak, we may be aware of this phenomenon only as differences of opinion and practice concerning the pronunciation of a few words. It may be a difference over the proper syllable to accent in such words as *advertisement, hospitable, pianist, indisputable,* or *irrefutable.* There is a difference in choice of a sound in all the words listed here too, for the sounds change when the accent changes. The only difference may be in the choice of a sound as in words such as these: *garage, menu, nausea, process, data, scenic.*

Many phenomena of change are constantly going on within a language. Words are being assimilated from foreign languages, often borrowed directly at first, then Americanized in pronunciation. English pronunciations succumb to American patterns of accent and pronunciation. Whole patterns of noun and verb inflections have disappeared and others are in the process of disappearing. We trace great vowel shifts in the language from the time of the Anglo-Saxons, through Middle English, Elizabethan, and modern times. With all these phenomena of change to observe, the student may well wonder where he can look for the "correct," the standard of speech which he can accept and master.

There are two major aspects of this problem which must be considered before principles can be established to guide us in setting a standard of speech for public performance. One of these is the choice of a dialect. The other is the special or unique requirements placed upon the speech by the fact that it is for public performance, in contrast to the speech requirements of conversation.

Settling the question of which dialect to speak is simple if the performer intends to remain in his native area. He would then master the dialect used by cultivated men and women around him. In Cleveland, in Chicago, Denver, Salt Lake City, San Francisco, or in hundreds of other cities and towns of the Middle West and West, the dialect would be General American. In Atlanta, Birmingham, Memphis, or New Orleans the dialect would be Southern American. In Boston, Bar Harbor, or Rutland, Vermont, it would be Eastern American. A definition of correctness or a standard defined as that employed by the cultivated people of the area is a flexible one to be sure, for it depends on knowing how many cultivated users there are —and it is not always possible to know—as well as in making a judgment as to the degree of cultivation in the people who are being considered. Nevertheless, important authorities on the use of the English language support this point of view. The student must learn to listen carefully to those people generally accepted as cultivated people who use language well and who are deferred to in matters of pronunciation, articulation, and even voice usage.

But if the performer expects to appear before audiences from several areas, as would be the case if he performed on television, in the motion pictures, or on the Broadway stage, the problem of choosing a dialect is a little more complex, particularly if he appears along with other performers. The cultivated interpreter who appears alone may use his native dialect anywhere in the country, for the cultivated speaker can be understood with ease almost anywhere English is spoken. The speech of a man from Georgia or Texas or Maine may be regarded as quaint or "interesting" in Iowa or Utah or Oregon, but it is also regarded as quite respectable. The variations from one area to another within a region call attention to themselves and mark the speaker as uncultivated. These peculiarities of diction, of pronunciation, articulation, voice production, and melody pattern which identify a person as a native of Camden, New Jersey or Portland, Maine or Tallahassee, Florida or Columbia, Missouri or Corydon, Iowa or Tucson, Arizona or Brooklyn or any other specific community not only make the speaker difficult to understand when he is away from home and set him aside as quaint and different, but they also usually leave an impression of provincialism, of inexperience and lack of education, if not, which is much worse, an impression of ignorance. The person who speaks the language as it is spoken by the cultivated men and women who speak his dialect is acceptable anywhere.

The performer who appears alongside performers who speak other dialects must sometimes be concerned that the unity of the performance not be destroyed by having people of a single family or town talking in different ways. The tendency on the American stage, in the television industry, and in motion pictures has been in the direction of General American whenever the speech is not intended to characterize by identifying a locale or the native place of a character.

The important choice is not so much which dialect you speak, but what level of accuracy and conformity with the practices of educated and cultivated people you adopt. At all costs the precious, the overprecise, the self-conscious, the too-careful must be avoided. These affectations are far more detrimental to a good reception than any unique but home-grown deviations from the norm of cultivated speech. If you are in doubt about pronunciation, learn how to use and then regularly consult a dictionary. Listen with a discerning ear to the speech of people who are respected and deferred to in matters of taste. Practice. Train your articulators to form sounds fully, clearly, cleanly, vigorously. Master the art of producing easy, strong, resonant tones.

Some special requirements for speech in public performances arise from the fact that the speech is no longer conversational but is intended to reach groups of people. One of these is the increased demand for clarity. Several factors affect this demand. The size of the hall, the acoustical properties of the room, the size of the audience, the distance of the performer from the audience, the ease with which the performer can be seen—all these things affect the degree of energy which must be put into the production of voice and the articulation of sound. The larger the hall and the audience, the more energy must be expended to support tone, to provide air pressure to explode plosives, to sound the fricatives, the aspirates, and all the other consonants and vowels. The rate of syllable production must often be adjusted to the reverberation time in any auditorium with an obvious echo. Clarity of articulation is always affected by the fact that the audience is unfamiliar with you and with your material. Particularly at the beginning of a performance one must take meticulous care to form sounds cleanly and clearly.

Another requirement for speech in public performance is for greater formality of style. The familiar colloquial or conversational style is not usually acceptable for public performance unless the material calls specifically for it. The audience expects a degree of dignity, of formality, a special manner of speech from the public speaker, the reader, the actor, from the pulpit. This is not to imply that the formal style or, more accurately, the formal colloquial, is more nearly correct than the familiar colloquial, any more than long dresses, white ties, and "tails" are any more correct than street dresses, business suits, sports wear, or swim suits. Different occasions call for appropriate speech just as they call for appropriate clothing. The formal style in general is characterized by a more deliberate tempo, fewer elisions, more complete formation of unaccented vowel sounds (where informal speech tends to move all unaccented vowels toward the [ə] or neutral position), a slightly higher pitch, more sustained level of loudness, a more formal vocabulary, and a more formal grammar.

A third requirement of speech for public performance is vigor and strength, with sufficient control to give an impression at all times of reserve power. The articulators must be nimble enough and strong enough to avoid all impressions of strain.

Finally, speech for public performance should be delivered with such accuracy, such ease, such control, and such an air of authority that it creates an impression of fine craftsmanship which, if people become conscious of it at all, causes them to admire as well as take real pleasure from listening.

## EXERCISES

*1.* Listen closely to the speech of actors and announcers over several radio and television stations. Compare their pronunciation with that of your parents or brother or sister. Note particularly differences in the *a* and *r* sounds.

*2.* Make a recording of your own formal colloquial speech as you read a selection as if to an audience. Then have a friend make a recording of your informal conversational speech, preferably at a time when you are in animated conversation and unaware that the recording is being made. Compare them carefully to note the kinds of differences. Then compare both with the recorded speech of any nationally known speaker or actor or minister.

## Additional Readings

Anderson, Virgil A., *Training the Speaking Voice*. New York: Oxford University Press, 1942, pp. 241-250.

Bender, James F., Compiler, *NBC Handbook of Pronunciation* (ed. 2). New York: Thomas Y. Crowell Company, 1951, pp. ix-xii.

Crocker, Lionel, and Louis M. Eich, *Oral Reading* (ed. 2). New York: Prentice-Hall, Inc., 1955, pp. 142-145.

Dolman, John, *The Art of Acting.* New York: Harper & Brothers, 1949, pp. 101-107; 208-237.

Fairbanks, Grant, *Voice and Articulation Drillbook.* New York: Harper & Brothers, 1940, pp. 21-132.

Herman, Lewis, and Marguerite Shalett Herman, *Manual of American Dialects for Radio, Stage, Screen and Television.* Chicago: Ziff-Davis Pub. Co., 1947.

Jones, Daniel, *English Pronouncing Dictionary* (ed. 11). New York: E. P. Dutton & Co., Inc., 1956.

Kenyon, John S., and Thomas A. Knott, *A Pronouncing Dictionary of American English.* Springfield, Mass.: G. & C. Merriam Co., 1944, esp. pp. xv f.

## [PROJECT 7.2]

# *British Dialect*

HEARING AND CONTROLLING THE SOUNDS OF SPEECH, SO NECESSARY TO improve articulation and clarity, is even more obviously necessary in the study of dialects. Everyday speech is so habituated that it is difficult for the ordinary student to realize what sounds he does produce unless he can study a recording of his own speech. Therefore two of the dialects most useful to interpreters and actors will be studied to provide ear training and practice in control of speech sounds. Dozens of other dialects might have been chosen for inclusion in these projects. Many are as common in the world around us as the two we have chosen to include. But South of England dialect is the one often favored whenever educated British dialect is suggested for a selection. It is a dialect quite useful in the interpretation of Shaw, Wilde, Coward, and a score or more of others. It is a dialect the actor finds almost indispensable among his accomplishments. Irish dialect is also a much-used one on the stage and the reading platform. Plays of Dunsany, Synge, Lady Gregory, and others fail to yield up their full charm until they are delivered in the dialect for which they were written.

We have included only these two dialects for your study in part because they prove useful in performance, but also because you probably already have some familiarity with them and will find learning them not so tedious as to discourage you. The most important reason, however, is that they may serve to help you develop a fine ear for sounds and a close control over your articulation.

Some materials are so written that regional or other dialects are almost essential. It would not do for the Dead End kids to use stage speech or for Shaw's cockneys to speak like the upper classes. However, the use of dialects is dangerous and should not be adopted lightly. First of all, there must be the maximum of clarity even though the dialect may be that of a gangster or of an uneducated

**205**

"poor white." The audience must understand what is said at the same time that they get an impression of region, education, or character from the lines and standard of speech used. Secondly, dialects are apt to be unfamiliar to an audience and therefore harder for them to understand than the speech to which they are accustomed. Thirdly, a dialect cannot be an imitation of the speech of one Englishman or Irishman, for instance, but needs to be representative of all Englishmen or Irishmen of a particular class. Indeed, it might be impossible for an American or an American audience to understand many British dialects at all as they are spoken by individuals at home. And, to a certain extent, what an audience considers a dialect should be has considerable influence on the sounds that are used. In her autobiography Eva Le Gallienne speaks of her first tryouts for the American stage. She had been born within the sound of Bow Bells and had made her first great success in England in the role of a cockney maid. Therefore she had considerable hope when she tried out for the role of a cockney maid in an American play. The director, however, considered that her dialect would not do! Apparently it was too accurate for the American stage.

Neither the phonetic nor the nonphonetic characteristics of any dialect may be neglected. As many native speakers and as many recordings of the dialect as possible should be heard. Speech can be analyzed for phonetic differences from General American dialect that are most consistently used, but the most typical nonphonetic differences must be learned by listening and imitation.

A word of warning against overuse of any particular time, pitch, or loudness pattern should be given. Even though an Englishman may say: <sup>A</sup>re <sub>you</sub> g<sub>oin</sub>g? occasionally, this does not mean that he starts and ends every sentence on a high note. Such a pattern can become so monotonous that it obscures meaning.

Compared to American dialects, probably the most important nonphonetic characteristic of standard South of England dialect is its *precision*. As has been mentioned, American democracy extends to American dialects, but the speech of the educated British speaker has none of the gliding carelessness of the cockney speaker. Every sound is accurately formed and there are no careless omissions. There is no phonetic difference in the average American pronunciation of *Mary*, *merry* and *marry*, but the educated British speaker would probably say [meiɪɪ], [mɛɪɪ], and [mæɪɪ]. This precision contributes greatly to what many Americans call "clipped" speech.

All English dialects are characterized by considerable contrast between stressed and unstressed syllables when compared with languages such as Spanish or French. This tendency is seen particularly in words that have secondary stress in General American dialect, such as *secondary*, *secretary*, *stationery*, etc. In the dialect of the South of England there is no secondary stress, but primary stress only. This, combined with precision, adds even more to the "clipped" effect of British speech.

A third characteristic of the dialect of the South of England is a tendency to use inflection rather than time to achieve emphasis. An American speaker might say [hor:əbl] and give the first syllable a great deal of length, but almost level inflection to express his meaning, while the British speaker tends to use a wide, rapid inflection on the first syllable to achieve the same effect. This greater use of pitch rather than time is evidenced in those sentences that begin on a high note, drop in pitch and rise again at the end, as in *Are you going?* or *Do you think so?* mentioned before.

The phonetic differences between British and General American dialects are not many, nor are they very great, but they should be used with consistency and accuracy. The easiest to learn is probably the r-system of British speech. As in Standard Eastern dialect in the United States there is no [ɝ] or [ɚ]. Rather, the tongue tip is kept behind the lower front teeth and [ɜ] and [ə] are produced. There is no diphthongization of [ɜ] and the [ə] is more open and energetic than in American dialects. To many ears [ə] and [ɪ] approach [ɑ]. Practice the differences in the following words:

| | |
|---|---|
| turner | curser |
| murmur | murder |
| burner | purser |
| learner | yearner |
| sterner | earthen |

Consonant r's before consonants and after vowels, either in words or combinations of words, are omitted or an off-glide toward [ə] is substituted. Practice the difference in those above and in the following words and sentences:

form                fearful
barn                card
torture             cord
courtship           bearhug
larger              beer jug

Do you hear the bear growling?
He lingered longer than usual.
He feared for his life.
They formed another ring.
Their dresses were worn shorter than mine.

r between two vowels, whether in a word or combination of words, is pronounced with such a rapid flip of the tongue tip that they are often said to be "topped." To this extent, the sound is produced in a different manner from General American speech. Practice this difference in the following words and combinations of words:

very                bury
for a               merry
worried             carry
hurried             sorry
there are a few     fairy
bear a grudge       hear a story

Probably the difference most difficult to learn between General American and British speech is the use of the so-called "broad a," probably because simply learning the words in which [ɑ] is used instead of [æ] is involved. In the Kenyon and Knott phonetic dictionary, these words are known by the fact that three alternate pronunciations are given, as [pæθ], [paθ] and [pɑθ]. In the *New International Dictionary* these words are indicated by a dot above the printed symbols, as [à]. Vocabulary must be learned, and a list of often-used, though not all, "broad a" words follows:

| behalf | glass | shan't | reprimand |
| telegraph | grass | fast | advance |
| staff | pass | last | chance |

| | | | |
|---|---|---|---|
| after | class | mast | dance |
| laughter | ask | vast | France |
| bath | cask | castle | glance |
| path | task | master | lance |
| wrath | flask | nasty | answer |
| craft | mask | pastor | aunt |
| shaft | clasp | example | can't |
| waft | blast | command | chant |
| rather | cast(e) | demand | grant |
| brass | (re)past | remand | branch |
| grasp | | | |

Can is always pronounced [kæn] but can't is pronounced [kɑnt]. It is easy for the novice to say [ɑi kɑn hi kænt] but when he does, he is not only ridiculous, but incomprehensible. Absolute accuracy is essential and may not be relaxed if the dialect is to be used.

Less difficult to learn is the difference in the formation of the British [ou]. It is made with the high point of the tongue farther forward than in General American pronunciation and with somewhat less diphthongization. American speakers are often helped by thinking of the first element of this diphthong as a tightly rounded [ɛ] and the diphthong as [ɛu]. Practice the British vowel sound in the following words:

| | | |
|---|---|---|
| road | rope | foam |
| no | most | soap |
| though | cold | boast |
| only | sold | toast |
| tone | boat | folder |

In General American pronunciation the [ɑ] and [ɔ] phonemes are each rather large. In British pronunciation the same range of sounds is divided into three phonemes—[ɑ], [ɒ], and [ɔ]—and there is a distinct difference between the semi-rounding for [ɒ] and the more complete rounding of [ɔ]. Indeed, to American ears [ɔ] sounds very much like [ou]. Practice this tight rounding of [ɔ] in the following words:

| | | |
|---|---|---|
| ought | call | fought |
| fall | wrought | ball |
| thought | awful | stall |

In general, [ɒ] is used in words spelled with *wa, wha* and in words spelled with an *o* that is pronounced [ɑ] in General American pronunciation. Practice [ɒ] in the following words. Be sure it can be distinguished from [ɑ].

| | | |
|---|---|---|
| shop | trot | dominate |
| not | borrow | bother |
| wallop | sorrow | |
| what | lot | |
| rot | stolid | |

In the pronunciation of some Americans, as well as in British dialects, [bin] is used for [bɪn], [aɪðə] and [nɑɪðə] for *either* and *neither*, and [əgeɪn] and [əgeɪnst] are used for *again* and *against*. Other typical British pronunciations are [ɪsju] and [tɪsju] for *issue* and *tissue*. [nɛvju] for *nephew*, [lɛftɛnent] for *lieutenant*, [klɑ:k] for *clerk*, and [fɪgə] for *figure*. And whenever there is a choice [ju] is used instead of [u] as in *new, news, newspaper, duty,* etc.

In British dialect, the schwa [ə] is not used as frequently in unstressed syllables as it is in the American dialects. There is a tendency to use [ɪ] in suffixes and unstressed medial syllables, as in the following words: telephone, Alice, boxes, careless, pocket, stolid, minute, ability, syllable, analysis, and dominate. The tendency to use [ɪ] instead of [i] in final syllables ending in y as *awfully, very, horribly, rightly* is probably a result of the heavy syllabic stress mentioned above.

If a dialect is to be used, it is highly desirable that it be learned as lines are learned. The first step, then, is to mark all dialect changes in the script when it is first read and studied. Some students can make all the phonetic changes at once. Others may find it much easier and quicker to mark all r changes first. r's that are silent should be struck out, r's that are topped should be marked with a dot, and [ɜ] and [ə] should be substituted for [ɝ] and [ɚ] respectively. A script so marked is as follows:

> To be, oŕ not to be: that is the question:
> Whetheŕ 'tis nobleŕ in the mind to suffeŕ
> The slings and arrows of outrageous foŕtune,
> Oŕ to take aŕms against a sea of troubles,
> And by opposing, end them?

Some like to mark next the "broad a" words, since some words will need to be checked in a dictionary, while some like to mark all other changes in their second reading of the script. There are no "broad a's" in the above passage. A complete marking of changes would be as follows:

D
*To be, or not to be: that is the question:*

εʊ
*Whether 'tis nobler in a man to suffer*

εʊ
*The slings and arrows of outrageous fortune,*

eɪ
*Or to take arms against a sea of troubles,*

εʊ
*And by opposing, end them?*

In practicing passages aloud, the student must take care not to make any more changes than those marked, and to practice the non-phonetic characteristics of the dialect with the phonetic.

## EXERCISES

1. Mark the phonetic differences between General American and South of England dialect on the following passages:

A.

ANN. *Violet is quite right. You ought to get married.*

TANNER. *(explosively) Ann: I will not marry you. Do you hear? I wont, wont, wont, wont, WONT marry you.*

ANN. *(placidly) Well, nobody axd you, sir she said, sir she said, sir she said. So thats settled.*

TANNER. *Yes, nobody has asked me; but everybody treats the thing as settled. It's in the air. When we meet, the others go away on absurd pretexts to leave us alone together. Ramsden no longer scowls at me; his eye beams, as if he were already giving you away to me in church. Tavy refers me to your mother and gives me his bless-*

ing. Straker openly treats you as his future employer: it was he who first told me of it.

ANN. Was that why you ran away?

TANNER. Yes, only to be stopped by a lovesick brigand and run down like a truant schoolboy.

ANN. Well, if you don't want to be married, you needn't be (she turns away from him and sits down, much at her ease).

TANNER. (following her) Does any man want to be hanged? Yet men let themselves be hanged without a struggle for life, though they could at least give the chaplain a black eye. We do the world's will, not our own. I have a frightful feeling that I shall let myself be married because it is the world's will that you should have a husband.

ANN. I daresay I shall, someday.

TANNER. But why me? me of all men! Marriage is to me apostasy, profanation of the sanctuary of my soul, violation of my manhood, sale of my birthright, shameful surrender, ignominious capitulation, acceptance of defeat. I shall decay like a thing that has served its purpose and is done with; I shall change from a man with a future to a man with a past; I shall see in the greasy eyes of all the other husbands their relief at the arrival of a new prisoner to share their ignominy. The young men will scorn me as one who has sold out: to the women I, who have always been an enigma and a possibility, shall be merely somebody else's property—and damaged goods at that: a secondhand man at best.

Man and Superman, GEORGE BERNARD SHAW

### B.

CANDIDA: Let us sit and talk comfortably over it like three friends. You remember what you told me about yourself, Eugene: how nobody has cared for you since your old nurse died: how those clever, fashionable sisters and successful brothers of yours were your mother's and father's pets: how miserable you were at Eton: how your father is trying to starve you into returning to Oxford: how you have had to live without comfort or welcome or refuge, always lonely, and nearly always disliked and misunderstood, poor boy! Now I want you to look at this other boy here—my boy—spoiled from his cradle. We go once a fortnight to see his parents. You should come with us, Eugene, and see the pictures of the hero of that household. James as a baby!

*the most wonderful of all babies. James holding his first school prize, won at the ripe age of eight! James as the captain of his eleven! James in his first frock coat! James under all sorts of glorious circumstances! You know how strong he is (I hope he didn't hurt you)— how clever he is—how happy! Ask James's mother and his three sisters what it cost to save James the trouble of doing anything but be strong and clever and happy. Ask me what it costs to be James's mother and three sisters and wife and mother to his children all in one. Ask Prossy and Maria how troublesome the house is even when we have no visitors to help us to slice the onions. Ask the tradesmen who want to worry James and spoil his beautiful sermons who it is that puts them off. When there is money to give, he gives it: when there is money to refuse, I refuse it. I build a castle of comfort and indulgence and love for him, and stand sentinel always to keep little vulgar cares out. I make him master here, though he does not know it, and could not tell you a moment ago how it came to be so. And when he thought I might go away with you, his only anxiety was what should become of me! And to tempt me to stay he offered me his strength for my defence, his industry for my livelihood, his dignity for my position, his—ah, I am mixing up your beautiful cadences and spoiling them, am I not, darling?*

Candida, GEORGE BERNARD SHAW

2. Practice aloud the phonetic and nonphonetic characteristics of Southern Standard British dialect of one of the above passages, in preparation for presenting it to the class.

3. Select a passage that should, in your judgment, be read with a British dialect and prepare it for presentation to the class.

## Additional Readings

Herman, Lewis, and Marguerite Shalett Herman, *Manual of Foreign Dialects for Radio, Stage, and Screen.* Chicago: Ziff-Davis Co., 1943, pp. 51-71.

Wise, Claude M., *Applied Phonetics.* Englewood Cliffs: N. J.: Prentice-Hall, Inc., 1957, pp. 239-244.

# Irish Dialect

WE THINK OF IRISH DRAMA AS FOLK DRAMA. THE MOST FAMOUS OF the Irish plays concern themselves with the common people rather than with the educated classes. The educated Irishman tends to sound like the educated Englishman, and it takes a trained ear to hear the Irish characteristics in the speech of a George Bernard Shaw, for instance.

Irish dialect seems to be easier for the General American speaker to master than British dialect, perhaps because every r in the spelling is pronounced. However, these r's in the spelling are pronounced as consonants with loosely flipping tongue tip, and [ɜ] is pronounced as [ʌr] and [ɚ] is pronounced as [ər]. In rapid speech this difference is small but it is distinctive.

The most important of the phonetic differences between Irish and General American dialect are in the pronunciation of the diphthongs and vowels, and some of these differences show tendencies that are diametrically opposed in the two dialects. In General American, for instance, all diphthongs glide from a stressed and definite position to an unstressed, less definite position as in [ɑɪ], or [aɪ]. To make this diphthong sound Irish, one starts from [ə], the most neutral position, and glides to [i], which is tensed and prolonged. It is not the American [ɔɪ] but [əi].

trɑɪŋ ænd trɑɪŋ tu dɑɪ for aɪrlənd

becomes

trəiən ən trəiən tə dɑɪ fər əirlənd

Pronounce the following words with the Irish diphthong [əi]:

| | | |
|---|---|---|
| lie | time | fright |
| sigh | crime | fine |
| I'm | find | mine |
| island | light | rhyme |

General American [ɑʊ] tends, with Irish pronunciation, to be [əʊ], with the first element neutral and the last definite and somewhat prolonged. Practice this diphthong in the following words:

| | | |
|---|---|---|
| now | town | hound |
| how | bound | mound |
| sound | down | round |
| found | gown | wound |

The Irishman's pronunciation of General American [eɪ] shows the same tendency as his [əi] and [əu], but the first element is less rounded. So his sound is [ɒi] or even [əi]. Pronounce the following words with the Irish [ɒi]:

| | | |
|---|---|---|
| boy | oil | voice |
| toy | noise | joint |
| coy | cloister | point |
| joy | toil | enjoy |

In the Irish pronunciation of the General American [eɪ] and [oʊ] these diphthongs tend to become more nearly pure vowels. The first element of [eɪ] is changed to [ɛ] and prolonged to such an extent that the [ɪ] off-glide is hardly heard. For [oʊ] the first element become [ɔ] and the off-glide typical of General American speech is not distinguishable. It is a trait of the folk speech that when [oʊ] is final in such words as *fellow* and *pillow*, it is pronounced as [ə]. Pronounce the Irish [ɛːɪ], and [ɔ] and final [ə] for [oʊ] in the following words:

| | | |
|---|---|---|
| change | road | bellow |
| cake | told | fellow |
| dame | fold | yellow |
| fame | no | mellow |
| game | cold | wallow |
| lame | gold | |
| mate | hold | |
| rate | roll | |
| state | sold | |
| wait | won't | |

One of the noticeable vowel changes that characterize Irish pronunciation is the use of [a] for both the General American [æ] and [ɑ]. General American [faðɚ] is pronounced [faðər] and General American [mæn] is pronounced [man]. Though American speakers often use [a] in so-called "broad a" words such as ask, after, dance, etc., they seem to have considerable difficulty pronouncing the sound in isolation without tension in the back of the tongue. It needs to be relaxed and well forward. The following are words that are pronounced with [a] instead of [æ] or [ɑ] in Irish dialect:

| pass | rather | father |
| ask | after | are |
| and | handsome | hard |
| shadow | alms | heart |
| man | have | calm |

A second conspicuous vowel change from General American pronunciation is the substitution of [ɑ] for [ɔ]. [lɔŋ] becomes [lɑŋ]. [kɔl] becomes [kɑl] and [drɔn] becomes [drɑn]. This together with the tendency to pronounce [ou] as [ɔ] leads to the impression that the Irish do not use much lip rounding for their back vowels. Use the Irish pronunciation of the following words:

| born | ball | small |
| dawn | crawl | drawn |
| all | store | broad |
| talk | for | bought |
| walk | call | gone |

In reading Irish dialect scripts one often sees spellings that indicate a change in the pronunciation of single words, such as tay instead of tea. However, there is no indication that all words pronounced with [i] in General American should be pronounced as [eɪ] or [ɛ:ɪ] in Irish. The best thing to do is to follow the pronunciation indicated in the script for such words, because there is no consistent substitution of [eɪ] for [i].

The short o indicated in the dictionary as [ŏ] is pronounced [ɑ], as it is in General American dialect. However, this is a change from British pronunciation, in which the short o and wa and wha are pronounced as [ɒ]. The only thing to remember, then, is for General American speakers not to change their habitual way of pronouncing such words as not, what, shop, etc.

The last phonetic characteristic of Irish speech is hardly a change from much General American pronunciation. This is a tendency to use the schwa or [ə] in place of a great many unstressed vowels. We have already noted the substitution of [fɛlə] for [fɛlou]; [tə] for [tu], and [ən] instead of the suffix [ɪŋ], as in [wɑkən] and [tɑkən], are even more prevalent.

Nobody hears Irish speech without becoming aware of a singing quality. This is partly due to the characteristic choice and order of words. Sentences often end with *now* or *only*. More probably it is due to a prolongation of the stressed vowels in stressed words and a tendency to shorten unstressed vowels in syllables. For instance, in the following sentence, prolong the italicized vowels and shorten all others:

ə   ɑ      u  ə    ɔ       əu
What *call* have *you* to be *lonesome now?*

In the case of diphthongs, this means a definite prolongation of the final element of the diphthong.

# EXERCISES

*1.* In the following passage from *Playboy of the Western World* by J. M. Synge, phonetic changes as heard on the Irish dialect records of the British Drama League are placed above the spellings. Practice this passage with the Irish pronunciations. If possible, listen to the British Drama League recording and compare it with your reading.

A bit of talk between Pegeen Mike and Christie Mahon from *Playboy of the Western World* by J. M. Synge:

PEGEEN: What *call* have you to be that *lonesome* when there's poor *girls walking* Mayo in their *thousands now?*

CHRISTIE: It's well you *know* what *call I* have. It's well you *know* it's a *lonesome* thing to be *passing small towns* with the *lights shining sideways* when the *night* is *down,* or *going* in *strange places*

      ɑ  ɑi       ɔ   ə        ɑ  ɑi      əi  ɑ  ɑ
with a dog noising before you and a dog noising behind, or drawn to

                       ɑi     n       ɑ  n      ʊ
the cities where you'd hear a voice kissing and talking deep love in

       ɑ  ə                a  n  ɑ
every shadow of the ditch, and you passing on with an empty, hungry

      εi n         a
stomach failing from your heart.

              əi       n        ɑ  a           a
     PEGEEN: I'm thinking you're an odd man, Christy Mahon. The

ɑ    ɑ      ə əi     ɪ əi  ɑ  ə       ə εi
oddest walking fellow I ever set my eyes on to this hour today.

                                ɑ                   n
     CHRISTIE: What would any be but odd men and they living

c          ʌ
lonesome in the world?

              əi  ɑ  ɑ       əi  əi  ɔ  əi      ɪ  a  ər
     PEGEEN: I'm not odd, and I'm my whole life with my father

ɔ
only.

          əu        ʊ     a                   əi
     CHRISTIE: How would a lovely handsome woman the like of you

ɪ  ɔ         ɑ            n  əu  ə
be lonesome when all men should be thronging around to hear the

                    ɒi
sweetness of your voice, and the little infant children should be

n            əi    n       ɑ  n      ɔ
pestering your steps I'm thinking, and you walking the roads.

            ar          əu      εi  ɔ  n   ə
     PEGEEN: I'm hard set to know what way a coaxing fellow the

                ɔ      ər
like of yourself should be lonesome either.

          ɔ  n
     CHRISTIE: Coaxing?

              a                  ɑ
     PEGEEN: Would you have me think a man never talked with

ʌr            ʌr      ɔ     εi    ɔ       n
the girls would have the words you've spoken today? It's only letting

ɑ    ar     ɔ        əi      əu   ɪ  əu
on you are to be lonesome, the way you'd get around me now.

          əi       ɑ əi     n        ɔ
     CHRISTIE: I wish to God I was letting on; but I was lonesome

a    əi        ar   ɔ         əi      n                a
all times, and born lonesome, I'm thinking, as the moon of dawn.

2. In the following selections, disregard the spellings used by the author, Moira O'Neill, but mark above each word any phonetic changes from General American pronunciation that are characteristic of Irish pronunciation, and practice reading the selection, with the Irish prolongation of vowels.

> Dennis was hearty when Dennis was young,
> High was his step in the jig that he sprung,
> He had the looks an' the sootherin tongue,—
>     An' he wanted a girl wid a fortune.
>
> Nannie was gray-eyed an' Nannie was tall,
> Fair was the face hid in-under her shawl,
> Troth! an' he liked her the best o' them all,—
>     But she'd not a traneen to her fortune.
>
> He be to look out for a likelier match,
> So he married a girl that was counted a catch,
> An' as ugly as need be, the dark little patch,—
>     But that was a trifle, he tould her.
>
> She brought him her good-lookin' gold to admire,
> She brought him her good-lookin' cows to his byre,
> But far from good-lookin' she sat by his fire,—
>     An' paid him that "thrifle" he tould her.
>
> He met pretty Nan when a month had gone by,
> An' he thought like a fool to get round her he'd try;
> Wid a smile on her lip an' a spark in her eye,
>     She said, "How is the woman that owns ye?"
>
> Och, never be tellin' the life that he's led!
> Sure many's the night that he'll wish himself dead,
> For the sake o' two eyes in a pretty girl's head,—
>     An' the tongue o' the woman that owns him.
>         "The Grand Match," MOIRA O'NEILL

Sure, he's five months, an' he's two foot long,
        Baby Johneen;

Watch yerself now, for he's terrible sthrong,
> Baby Johneen.

An' his fists 'ill be up if ye make any slips,
He has finger-ends like the daisy-tips,
But he'll have ye attend to the words of his lips,
> Will Johneen.

There's nobody can rightly tell the color of his eyes,
> This Johneen;

For they're partly o' the earth an' still they're partly o' the skies,
> Like Johneen.

So far as he's thraveled he's been laughin' all the way,
For the little soul is quare an' wise, the little heart is gay;
An' he likes the merry daffodils—he thinks they'd do to play
> With Johneen.

He'll sail a boat yet, if he only has his luck,
> Young Johneen;

For he takes to the wather like any little duck,
> Boy Johneen;

Sure, them are the hands now to pull on a rope,
An' nate feet for walkin the deck on a slope,
But the ship she must wait a wee while yet, I hope,
> For Johneen.

For we couldn't do wantin' him, not just yet—
> Och, Johneen,

'T is you that are the daisy, an' you that are the pet,
> Wee Johneen.

Here's to your health, an' we'll dhrink it to-night,
Sláinte gal, avic machree! live an' do right!
Sláinte gal, avourneen! may your days be bright,
> Johneen!

"Johneen," Moira O'Neill

3. Select a passage from the plays of one of the Irish playwrights, such as Lady Gregory, J. M. Synge, or Sean O'Casey. Mark above the lines any phonetic changes from General American pronunciation. Practice reading the passage with these phonetic changes and with the Irish prolongation of stressed vowels.

## Additional Readings

Herman, Lewis, and Marguerite Shalett Herman, *Manual of Foreign Dialects for Radio, Stage and Screen*. Chicago: Ziff-Davis Co., 1943, pp. 77-102.

Johnson, Gertrude E., *Dialects for Oral Interpretation: Selections and Discussion*. New York: The Century Co., 1922, pp. 19-27; 157-200.

Wise, Claude M., *Applied Phonetics*. Englewood Cliffs, N. J.: Prentice-Hall, Inc., 1957, pp. 273-279.

# Synthesis and Evaluation
## of Progress

Accurate reproduction of a dialect which we have not learned to speak while we were children is usually beyond the ability of most of us. People who have lived all their adult lives in a region where the people speak a dialect foreign to that they learned as children normally continue to reveal the fact they are transplants by the way they talk. The speaker—actor, platform reader, orator, announcer—can scarcely expect to present even a reasonably accurate reproduction of a dialect not his own in a few days or weeks of preparation. He must usually be content to make a few alterations in his own dialect which seem, to the ears of those who also speak his dialect, to be most characteristic, to catch the flavor of the dialect he is trying to present. As noted in the foregoing sections, only a few of the differences between his speech and South of England dialect or Irish dialect can be adopted. These must be the ones which give to your listeners the impression of British or Irish speech. If you come from a General American region, you can only suggest Southern or Eastern dialect.

Find a person who speaks a dialect other than your own and record a five-minute portion of his speech. (If everyone in your community is a "native," you may have to use a commercial recording, but in these days of travel and general mobility it is a rare community that doesn't have many people in it who have moved from another part of the country or from abroad.) Study the speech again and again. Write down the characteristics that seem to give it its peculiar "foreign" flavor. Be very careful in your observations not to assume that some kind of change is a universal one. In the British, for instance, not all [æ] sounds of American speech become [ɑ] by any means. Pay attention to melody patterns, timing peculiarities.

When you think you have discovered the elements in the speech which impart its unique flavor, make these types of changes in a short selection of your own choosing. Try to give your listeners an impression that this is the dialect you intend it to be. If there is doubt, play for them your sample so they can compare.

There are two main objectives in this assignment. The first is to sharpen your observation of sounds. The second is to improve your skill in producing at will sounds not always found in your own speech.

# 8

PROJECTS IN

# Control of Voice

# Hearing and Judging Voice in Speech

Desirable as a well-produced voice and well-formed sounds may be for any speaker, they are only the tools of the platform reader. His ultimate goal is to express vocally the precise shades of meaning that his mind is capable of conceiving, and one step toward accomplishing this goal is to become more aware of the attributes of the sound wave and its potentialities for carrying meaning.

It is interesting to contemplate the fact that most of what we can know of each other is carried by light waves and sound waves. Therefore the generation, transmission, and reception of sound waves is extremely important in our lives. The sound wave is generated by a vibrating source of sound—the vibrating vocal cords in the case of speech—and carried through the ear, usually. This sound wave vibrates the ear drum, the vibrations are carried to the inner ear by the bones of the middle ear and received by the nerve endings in the cochlea, which is in the inner ear and which is imbedded in the bones of the skull.

Sound waves have four measurable attributes. The first of these is frequency, or the number of vibrations per second. The ear interprets frequency as pitch, and we are aware that voices are high or low in pitch, and monotonous or varied. The second attribute is intensity, which is the amount of energy in the sound wave, and which is interpreted by the ear as loudness. We are aware that voices are too loud, too soft, or just right. We are aware of variations in the degrees of loudness of various words and syllables, and whether or not these variations are appropriate. We are aware that some sentences are very loud at the onset and that they gradually dwindle to a scarcely heard whisper. On the other hand, we are frequently aware that the change in loudness is most appropriate to the meaning being expressed.

226

Some listeners and writers feel that tones, low tones especially, have a certain bigness, a room-filling characteristic, that they call volume. In order to measure the volume of a sound wave, we can only note measurements of frequency and intensity. Therefore, it seems wise not to use the term *volume*, even though the term is frequently marked on radio and television dials, but to interpret this term as loudness, and to consider that the so-called volume may be altered by altering the level of loudness and the tone control.

The third important characteristic of the sound wave is its composition. The vocal cords and all other musical instruments produce complex waves rather than simple sine waves such as those produced by a tuning fork. Complex waves may be analyzed into a fundamental wave and a series of overtones, and the quality of sound that we hear depends primarily on the number and relating intensities of these component partials. The number and relating intensities of the partials, in turn, are primarily dependent on the size and shape of the resonators. Because the mouth and pharynx assume a different size and shape for each one of the vowels, each of the vowels is characterized by a great deal of energy in one or more characteristic bands of overtones.

Not only does each voiced speech sound have its own characteristic relation of partials, but each individual voice has its characteristic distribution of energy among the partials, because each individual resonating system (mouth, pharynx, etc.) has its peculiar characteristics. To further complicate the picture, human emotions affect the size and shape of the resonators, and consequently the relative distribution of energy in the partials, so that the quality of sound heard is sometimes described as "hard" or "soft," etc.

Complicated as this may seem, we are all familiar with the practical application of these principles. Almost every radio, television, or playback has some tone control dials. These are generally designated as bass or treble, and by adjusting the relative intensities of the treble and bass partials one can produce the quality of tone most pleasing to his ear. The important thing for us to keep in mind now is that the distribution of energy among the partials of the complex sound wave of the human voice determines the quality of sound that we hear.

| ANALYSIS SHEET | | |
| --- | --- | --- |
| | RATING | COMMENTS |
| PITCH | | |
| Level<br>Range<br>Appropriateness | | |
| LOUDNESS | | |
| Level<br>Range<br>Appropriateness | | |
| TIME | | |
| Suitability of rate to<br>  material<br>Suitability of pause<br>  to material<br>Suitability of rate<br>  to articulation<br>Flexibility of rate | | |
| QUALITY | | |
| Suitability of quality<br>  to logical meaning<br>Suitability of quality<br>  to emotional meaning<br>Freedom from defects | | |
| PRONUNCIATION AND<br>ARTICULATION | | |
| Formation of vowels<br>  and diphthongs<br>Formation of conso-<br>  nants and blends<br>Pronunciation | | |
| GENERAL EFFECTIVENESS | | |
| Phrasing<br>Points<br>Characterization<br>Structure and climax | | |

Instructions: Assign a rating from 5 (low) to 1 (high) to each of the six major items. Designate strength or weaknesses of subitems by (+) or (−) and by comments.

Rater_____

The fourth characteristic of the sound wave is that it has duration. It starts and stops, so that the length of time that the vocal cords are in vibration may be measured and compared with the length of time that they are not vibrating. In listening to voices we hear duration as rate and pause, and if unvoiced speech sounds are noted at all, they are usually heard as an aspect of rate.

When we listen to speech, we listen for meaning. If the voice reinforces the meaning of the words being spoken, we tend not to notice the voice at all. We are aware that some speakers move us more than others, but we usually do not know why their speech has such an effect. We are aware that the words sometimes say one thing and the voice another, such as *I am frightened, I am uncertain, I am under nervous tension,* or *I am bored with this.* Then we tend to be uneasy or annoyed with the speaker. Therefore it is necessary for the serious student of speech to learn to become aware of vocal attributes and their potentialities for carrying meaning in his own voice and in the voices of others. One way to awareness is to learn to analyze voices into the four attributes during continuous speech and to make note of such analyses on rating sheets.

There are many schemes for rating voice in connected speech, but most of these rating sheets aim at finding the defects in voices. One of the best sheets, perhaps, is that designed by Fairbanks and printed in his *Voice and Articulation Drillbook,* p. x. Anderson has an outline for voice analysis and diagnosis in the appendix of his *Training the Speaking Voice* that is similar to Fairbanks'. The outline for voice analysis suggested here cannot be very different from the others, but it is designed to be useful in analyzing degrees of excellence as well as areas of inferiority. It is suggested that this chart be used along with that of Fairbanks or Anderson for ear training.

# EXERCISES

1. Listen carefully to Charles Laughton's recordings of readings from the Bible (Decca DL 8031). Then rate his voice on the rating

sheet on page 228. Rate his voice also either on Fairbanks' "Voice and Connected Speech Rating Sheet" or on Anderson's "Outline for Voice Analysis and Diagnosis."

2. Make similar ratings for John Barrymore's reading of Hamlet's Soliloquy (RCA-Victor recording, LCT 1112).

3. Make similar ratings for the readings on the recording of Great Moments from Great Plays (Decca DL 9002).

4. Rate the voices of two radio or television commentator-newsmen (John Daly, John Cameron Swayse, etc.).

5. Rate the voices of your classmates during their reading of a speech of their own choosing. This may be a speech from a play or one that was actually delivered by Lincoln, Churchill, Roosevelt, Patrick Henry, etc.

6. Make a recording of your own voice. Listen to it carefully, and then rate your voice on the sheets given.

## Additional Readings

Anderson, Virgil A., Training the Speaking Voice. New York: Oxford University Press, 1942, pp. 3-10; 365 f.

Fairbanks, Grant, Voice and Articulation Drillbook. New York: Harper & Brothers, 1946, p. x.

Herendeen, Jane, Speech Quality and Interpretation. New York: Harper & Brothers, 1946, pp. 124-139.

Lee, Charlotte I., Oral Interpretation. Boston: Houghton Mifflin Co., 1952, pp. 107-149.

Lowrey, Sara, and Gertrude E. Johnson, Interpretative Reading: Techniques and Selections (rev. ed.). New York: Appleton-Century-Crofts, Inc., 1953, pp. 179-186.

Sarett, Lew, and W. T. Foster, Basic Principles of Speech. Boston: Houghton Mifflin Co., 1936, pp. 192-227.

Turner, J. Clifford, Voice and Speech in the Theatre. London: Sir Isaac Pitman & Sons, Ltd., 1950, pp. 1-9; 129-138.

# Control of Pitch

AFTER ONE HAS DEVELOPED CRITICAL AWARENESS OF THE ATTRIBUTES OF voice, the next step is to develop utmost control of these attributes. A person who can use his high and low pitches, as well as those in the middle of this range, has a tremendous advantage in expressing subtleties of meaning. The interpreter uses pitch to indicate an emotional state; he uses it to convey emotional and logical meanings which the words alone often do not make clear; he uses pitch to help his listeners distinguish one meaning from another when the differences are very slight; he uses pitch to emphasize. Without the melodic line of changing pitch the interpreter would be seriously handicapped. His pitch range serves him better as it increases; his capacity for expressiveness grows as his control of range and variation within the range increase. All of our studies of voice show that the better the speaker, the greater the pitch range he can and does use.[1, 2]

One of the first questions any student of voice asks is, "Is my voice too high or too low in pitch?" Pitch and voice quality are often confused, and we hear of the virtues of a low voice in men as well as in women. At the same time, some of our studies show that trained listeners will express preference for male voices that are high in pitch and excellent in quality as compared with others being judged at the same time that are lower in pitch and of not such good quality.[3] In an effort to determine the pitch level of male speakers who were judged to be superior, it has been found that these speakers did not use their falsetto in factual reading (the passage being tested), but that they used all the pitches in the lower half of their ranges. These pitches fell into a normal distribution on a bell-shaped curve, with the average pitch level one-fourth the way up their total pitch range, including falsetto.[4] For women, it was found that the average pitch

231

level fell one-fifth of the way up the total pitch range and it was reasoned that the women were influenced by social pressures toward a lowered pitch level.[5] If it may be reasoned that superior readers use the best pitch level in reading, then we may say that a point about one-fourth of the way up from the botton of his pitch range (including falsetto) is the best pitch level for readers and that the pitches he uses should be grouped around this point in a normal distribution.

To determine your natural pitch level, follow this procedure:

1. Starting at a pitch in about the middle of your range, sing down the scale to the lowest note your vocal cords will produce. Now, using the tempered scale, sing up through falsetto to the highest note your vocal cords will produce, counting as you go. Record the number of notes sung. Do this several times a day until you can arrive at an average figure. If you have difficulty singing a scale, use a piano or ask a friend to sing along with you. It may even be necessary to locate your lowest and highest notes on a piano.

2. Divide the total number of notes in your singing range by four. Suppose that range is twenty. Twenty divided by four would be five. Starting at a pitch in about the middle of your range, sing down to the lowest note your vocal cords can produce, and then one-fourth of the way up. If your range is twenty notes, this would be five notes up from the bottom. Sustain this tone. Chant "How are you today?" on this note. Now inflect the sentence slightly. Finally, inflect it considerably. Say other sentences, first chanting and then inflecting until it seems easy and natural to inflect around this pitch level.

Finding one's natural pitch level is important chiefly because speaking at that level makes possible wider use of pitches that are both higher and lower. The wide distribution of pitches around this average is the characteristic of superior voices. If one tries to use his lower pitches only, he not only restricts his range, but often introduces strain that may contribute to hoarseness. It would be equivalent to trying to make a bass singer out of a natural tenor. Moreover, research has shown that when a person tries to lower his pitch he becomes more monotonous, while if he tries to raise his pitch level his voice becomes more varied in pitch. Conversely, when he tries to speak monotonously the average pitch level is lowered, and when he tries to speak with great variety the average pitch level is raised.[6] The good speaker should train himself to use all parts of his pitch range with greater and greater facility. The following exercises are designed to accomplish that end.

# EXERCISES

*1.* Starting at your optimum pitch, sing the vowels [eɪ], [i], [ɑɪ], [ou], [ju], blending one into another. Sing one step higher and repeat. Continue to the top of your range. If you feel strain, try to remember the feeling of your resonators at your optimum pitch level and try to keep that feeling when you sing the high pitches. "Think low" when you are singing high. When you have reached the top of your range, sing the vowels on progressively lower pitches until you reach the lowest pitch you can sing. "Think high" when you sing low.

*2.* Repeat the above exercise with these two differences:

a. Chant, rather than sing the vowels.

b. Follow the vowels with this sentence, spoken almost in a monotone, but with as much meaning as you can put into it. "Who did that!"

*3.* Using the sentence, "Oh, I don't know," intone the "Oh" at your natural pitch level, then speak each succeeding word on a progressively higher pitch. Sing up one note on the tempered scale and say "Oh" at this pitch, then speak each word on a progressively higher pitch. Be sure each word is higher in pitch than the word before it. Repeat, intoning "Oh" on the pitches below your natural pitch level.

*4.* Repeat the above exercise, saying each word on a progressively lower pitch.

*5.* In the following sentences, speak the first part on the lowest pitch you can manage without strain, and the second on the highest pitch you can manage without strain.

*I don't care; just stop bothering me.*
*It's time to go, but I don't want to.*
*This can't last, but it's wonderful.*
*How nice it is, but it can't last.*
*Guess what! I got an A.*

6. Repeat the above exercise, speaking the first clause of the sentence on the highest pitch you can use without strain, and the second clause on the lowest pitch you can use without strain.

To be able to use all parts of his range does not necessarily mean that a good reader's voice is continually rising and falling regardless of meaning. Rather, pitch flexibility is desirable in order that the good reader can express, immediately and unmistakably, the meaning he intends so that listeners understand him. The reader with a limited pitch range or a habitual pattern cannot do this. He tends to express all his ideas in the same way, and his vocal pitch does not aid the meaning. It should be self-evident that different meanings are expressed by different voice usage.

In a sense, the reader has greater creative opportunities than the singer. The composer designates the melody the singer shall use and gives instructions for his basic timing and use of loudness as well. The interpreter creates his own melody to suit the precise meaning he has found in the script. The sensitive artist is generally aware that his melody is right or that it does not express his meaning, and he will often experiment until he finds precisely the right melody. How does he know the right one? Many successful interpreters will say that is the talent the interpreter is born with. Let us say, rather, that the successful interpreter has an unusual awareness of word meanings, an unusual empathic responsiveness to the way people express meanings, and an unusual sensitivity to the variations in his own voice and body. The interpreter needs to train himself to be aware of the precise shade of meaning his voice is expressing.

We have already noted the role pitch plays in giving logical emphasis to words. In the following exercise, notice how increasing emphasis may be expressed by increased inflection. Say the sentence, "I am going to work," in a matter-of-fact way with principal emphasis on the word *work*. Now ask yourself, or let somebody else ask, "What are going to do?" and repeat the sentence in order to give greater emphasis and greater inflection to the word *work*. Repeat several times and notice how much greater the inflection on *work* is as the word receives greater emphasis. If you merely give *work* greater loudness, try giving it more and more pitch glide instead.

## EXERCISES

*1.* Make up five sentences similar to the example given. Read them so that the emphasized word in each of the sentences has five degrees of emphasis.

The kind of inflection or pitch given a word can give that single word many meanings. It is interesting to see how many different meanings can be given to one word, such as *Oh!* Notice the pitch and inflection you use when you give the word the following meanings:

a. *Is that really so?*
b. *Now I see what you mean!*
c. *I just don't know.*
d. *Isn't that too bad!*
e. *I acknowledge that I hear you, but I'm not interested.*

*2.* Primarily by means of changing pitch, give five different logical or emotional meanings to each of the following words. Read the words to your class, or listeners, and ask that the meaning they receive be written on a slip of paper. If the listener is uncertain, ask him to put down a question mark. Collect the slips and see how the meaning received corresponds with the meaning intended.

No
Yes
Where
Think!
March

The sounds of some words are imitations of the sounds of nature. Such words are *hiss*, *buzz*, and *thud*. The sounds of many words suggest their sense. This is called onomatopoeia. It is interesting to note how much vocal pitch also helps to suggest the meaning intended.

3. Read the following words aloud so that their sense is communicated by their sound. Notice the pitches and inflections you use. Practice until your expression is precisely what you intend.

| | | |
|---|---|---|
| *smooth* | *murmuring* | *wallow* |
| *sharp* | *tinkling* | *smear* |
| *moaning* | *glide* | *jerk* |
| *squeak* | *leap* | *patter* |
| *crunch* | *skip* | *creamy* |

4. Make up a sentence in which you use each of the above words. Read the sentences aloud until your voice expresses as much meaning for these words in context as it did for them in isolation.

Character and emotion have a definite effect on pitch usage. In a study[7] of the pitch, time, and loudness characteristics of professional actors and actresses, it was found that when one actress portrayed two different characters, she used two different ranges and distributions of pitches. Other studies[1, 8] have shown that emotional reading, even expressions of grief, are, on the average, higher in pitch than factual reading or expressions of indifference. This fact should argue against trying to force one's voice to the bottom of his range, especially in the expression of emotion.

There have been few studies on use of voice in the expression of emotion. In one of the studies that we have,[9] it was found that expressions of emotion by good actors were readily recognized by listeners, and that contempt and grief were expressed on relatively low levels of pitch, while anger and fear were expressed by a relatively high average pitch and wide flexibility. If you remember the feel of your body reacting to these emotions, the pitch characteristics seem entirely reasonable. In contempt, one feels secure and superior. He is relatively relaxed. In grief, one has given up and must accept and react to the inevitable. In anger and fear, on the other hand, the body is tensed and ready for fight or flight. The important point to remember is that each emotion differs from the next in the reaction of the body and consequently in its vocal expression.

As has been pointed out, each thought group differs from the next in meaning and consequently in voice used to express that meaning. A poor reader either does not find these differences in meaning or finds that his anxiety to do well without sufficient preparation is so dominant that his voice will express nothing but anxiety or stage fright—or he finds that his vocal control is not good enough to express differences in meaning. The good interpreter will analyze passages for their over-all meaning, then look for the variety of meanings that will give the over-all idea interest, and then strive for the best way to express each shade of meaning vocally. He needs to *tone* his selection. A general out-pouring of intensity or emotion will not do the job. The voice, and for the time being, the pitch of voice particularly, must be used meaningfully.

## EXERCISES

*1.* The following is a phrasing of the Twenty-third Psalm. Study the Psalm for its over-all meaning and its structure. Now consider how each phrase differs from the next in meaning and in its contribution to the over-all meaning. Then practice reading the Psalm aloud so that the voice, and pitch of voice particularly, produces the precise shade of meaning you have found.

> *The Lord is my shepherd;*
> *I shall not want.*
> *He maketh me to lie down in green pastures;*
> *He leadeth me beside the still waters.*
> *He restoreth my soul;*
> *He leadeth me in the paths of*
>     *righteousness for His name's sake.*
> *Yea, though I walk through the valley of*
>     *The shadow of death, I will fear no evil:*
> *For Thou art with me;*
> *Thy rod and Thy staff they comfort me.*
> *Thou preparest a table before me in the*
>     *presence of mine enemies:*

*Thou anointest my head with oil;*
*My cup runneth over.*
*Surely, goodness and mercy shall follow*
*me all the days of my life;*
*And I will dwell in the house of the*
*Lord forever.*

2. In a manner similar to the above, tone Tennyson's *Crossing the Bar* and practice reading it so the pitch of your voice helps to suggest the various meanings found.

3. Tone a selection of your own choice and practice reading it for your class.

4. Comedy has always made demands for use of all the pitch range the interpreter can muster. The following scene from Sheridan's *The Rivals,* in which Sir Lucius O'Trigger, always ready to defend his honor (even before it is challenged), gives the frightened and reluctant Bob Acres duelling instructions before the latter's adversary arrives on the field, makes particularly heavy demands for expressing meaning by pitch inflection. This is low comedy and energetic. Listen especially for the wide range of pitch usage in Bob Acres.

SIR LUCIUS. *Pray now, how would you receive the gentleman's shot?*

ACRES. *Odds files!—I've practised that—there, Sir Lucius—there.* (Puts himself in an attitude) *A side-front, hey? Odd! I'll make myself small enough: I'll stand edgeways.*

SIR LUCIUS. *Now—you're quite out—for if you stand so when I take my aim—* (Levelling at him.)

ACRES. *Z—ds! Sir Lucius—are you sure it is not cocked?*

SIR LUCIUS. *Never fear.*

ACRES. *But—but—you don't know—it may go off of its own head!*

SIR LUCIUS. *Pho! be easy.—Well, now if I hit you in the body, my bullet has a double chance—for if it misses a vital part of your right side—'twill be very hard if it don't succeed on the left.*

ACRES. *A vital part!*

SIR LUCIUS. *But, there—fix yourself so—* (Placing him)*—let him* see the broad-side of your full front—there!—now a ball or two may pass clean through your body, and never do any harm at all.

ACRES. Clean through me!—a ball or two clean through me!

SIR LUCIUS. Aye—may they—and it is much the genteelest attitude into the bargain.

ACRES. Look'ee! Sir Lucius—I'd just as lieve be shot in an awkward posture as a genteel one; so, by my valor! I will stand edge-ways.

SIR LUCIUS. (Looking at his watch) Sure they don't mean to disappoint us—Hah! no, faith—I think I see them coming.

ACRES. Hey!—what!—coming!—

SIR LUCIUS. Ay—Who are those yonder getting over the stile?

ACRES. There are two of them indeed!—well—let them come— hey, Sir Lucius!—we-we-we-we-won't run.

SIR LUCIUS. Run!

ACRES. No—I say—we won't run, by my valor!

SIR LUCIUS. What the devil's the matter with you?

ACRES. Nothing—nothing—my dear friend—my dear Sir Lucius —but I—I—I don't feel quite so bold, somehow, as I did.

SIR LUCIUS. O fie!—consider your honor.

ACRES. Ay—true—my honor. Do, Sir Lucius, edge in a word or two every now and then about my honor.

SIR LUCIUS. (Looking) Well, here they're coming.

ACRES. Sir Lucius—if I wa'n't with you, I should almost think I was afraid.—If my valor should leave me!—Valor will come and go.

SIR LUCIUS. Then pray keep it fast while you have it.

ACRES. Sir Lucius—I doubt it is going—yes—my valor is certainly going!—it is sneaking off!—I feel it oozing out as it were at the palms of my hands!

SIR LUCIUS. Your honor—your honor!—Here they are.

ACRES. O mercy!—now—that I were safe at Clod-Hall! or could be shot before I was aware!

## References

1. Gladys Lynch, "A Phonophotographic Study of Trained and Untrained Voices Reading Factual and Dramatic Material," *Archives of Speech*, I: 9-25, 1934.

2. E. Murray and J. Tiffin, "An Analysis of Some Basic Aspects of Effective Speech," *Archives of Speech*, I: 61-83, 1934.
3. D. Lewis and J. Tiffin, "A Psychophysical Study of Individual Differences in Speaking Ability," *Archives of Speech*, I: 43-60, 1934.
4. W. Pronovost, "An Experimental Study of Habitual and Natural Pitch Levels of Superior Speakers," Ph. D. dissertation, State University of Iowa, 1939.
5. Eugene Linke, "Pitch Characteristics of Female Voices," Ph. D. dissertation, State University of Iowa, 1953.
6. C. W. McIntosh, "A Study of the Relationship Between Pitch Level and Pitch Variability in the Voices of Superior Speakers," Ph. D. dissertation, State University of Iowa, 1939.
7. M. Cowan, "Pitch and Intensity Characteristics of Stage Speech," *Archives of Speech*, Supplement, 1936.
8. G. Fairbanks and W. Pronovost, "An Experimental Study of the Pitch Characteristics of the Voice During the Expression of Emotion," *Speech Monographs*, 6:87-104, 1939.
9. *Idem.*

## Additional Readings

Aggertt, Otis J., and Elbert R. Bowen, *Communicative Reading.* New York: The Macmillan Co., 1956, pp. 247-301.

Anderson, Virgil A., *Training the Speaking Voice.* New York: Oxford University Press, 1942, pp. 168-174.

Bassett, Lee Emerson, *Handbook of Oral Reading.* Boston: Houghton Mifflin Co., 1917, pp. 51-61; 236-251.

Fairbanks, Grant, *Voice and Articulation Drillbook.* New York: Harper & Brothers, 1940, pp. 165-190.

Fairbanks, Grant, "Recent Experimental Investigations of Vocal Pitch in Speech," *Journal of the Acoustical Society of America*, 11:457-466, 1940.

Fairbanks, Grant, and W. Pronovost, "An Experimental Study of the Pitch Characteristics of Voice During the Expression of Emotion," *Speech Monographs*, 6:87-104, 1939.

Herendeen, Jane, *Speech Quality and Interpretation.* New York: Harper & Brothers, 1946, pp. 90-93.

Lynch, Gladys, "A Phonophotographic Study of Trained and Untrained Voices Reading Factual and Dramatic Material," *Archives of Speech*, 1:9-25, 1934.

Selden, Samuel, *The Stage in Action.* New York: F. S. Crofts and Co., 1946, pp. 120-123.

# Control of Loudness

CONTROL OF LOUDNESS CONTRIBUTES IN SEVERAL WAYS TO THE effectiveness of the interpreter. Unless he can produce enough tone to be heard, everything else he does is weakened if not totally lost. Loudness control contributes to an impression of authority and poise. It is a means to variety and the interest that variety commands. Loudness is one of the means to emphasis. For these reasons the interpreter gives early and constant attention to the control of loudness, recognizing it as an essential tool to his success.

Two principal problems present themselves in learning control of loudness. The first is to produce loudness adequate to the place and occasion without strain and the other is to control degrees of loudness at high and low pitches without changing quality. Solutions for the first problem were given in the projects on support of tone and resonance. Loudness needs to be produced by increased pressure of exhaled breath and by resonance, and not by throat tension. The tendency to become breathy on soft low tones and strident on loud high tones is closely related to the first problem, but needs further attention here.

The fact that "projection" or increase in loudness is usually accompanied by a *slight* rising in pitch level needs to be reiterated. When the rising in pitch is excessive, then you can suspect that there is undue laryngeal tension and the relaxation exercises given in Chapter V, Project 2 need to precede work in control of loudness. You should try to keep the pitch level constant while increasing and decreasing loudness.

# EXERCISES

*1.* Starting at your natural pitch level, intone "Oh" very, very softly. Gradually increase the loudness until you are speaking as loudly as you can at that level. Then decrease the loudness until you are barely vocalizing. Be sure that the tone is always vocalized and not whispered. If your pitch rises and falls like a siren, consider first whether or not you have started at your natural pitch level. Then consider whether or not you are increasing loudness by increasing pressure of exhaled air by use of abdominal muscles. If not, precede this exercise with exercises for control of exhaled air. Work on this exercise until the pitch can be kept relatively constant.

*2.* Repeat this exercise on a pitch 3 tones up from your natural pitch level, then another musical third up and finally an octave above your natural pitch level, keeping the same objectives.

*3.* Repeat Exercise 1 on a pitch a musical third below your natural pitch level, then two more steps below and finally as low as you can, keeping the same objectives as in Exercise 1.

*4.* Imagining that you are speaking to a person at a greater and greater distance from you, practice the following calling exercises. Be careful not to let your throat become tense or your voice strident.

> *Hi! Look out for that car!*
> *Yoo, hoo, John, come back this minute!*
> *Can you hear me out there?*
> *Hello, out there!*

Even more objectionable than stridency in loud voices is stridency in strong emotions. Besides the unpleasant voice quality, the throat tension present is hard on the speaker and suggests to the listener that the emotion is only throat deep. Again, reduction of throat tension and increased control of exhalation are the chief aids in correcting this sort of harshness.

A very famous speech with strong emotion is King Henry's speech to his troops before Harfleur. Here we have problems of loudness as well as of emotion. The speech opens the first scene of Act III of Shakespeare's *Henry V*. Henry is speaking to his army, and his degree of loudness and projection should suggest a considerably larger group than can be accommodated on the usual stage. The first two words, "Once more," suggest that the army has made at least one assault, and has retired. A possible interpretation is that King Henry is attempting to communicate his spirit and vitality to his troops, to pep up a tired or discouraged group. The first sentence is a battle cry and needs to engage the attention of every person. Therefore it must be spoken loudly enough to be heard by every man of the army. The first part of the second sentence is a sharp contrast in loudness as well as subject matter—war and peace. Then follows increasing fierceness and emotion as the actions of a tiger are compared with the actions of the fighting man, ending with increasing loudness and the emotional climax beginning with "bend up every spirit to its full height," and ending with "On, on, you noble English!" This loudness level is somewhat modified by the description of the fathers, and considerably modified by the reference to the mothers. There may be a minor building of loudness, beginning with, "now attest that those whom you called fathers did beget you" through, "And teach them how to war." The pride and affection for the English yeoman could modify the loudness level considerably, but from that point, it could build up steadily to the climax of the speech, "Cry—God for Harry! England! and Saint George!" This, of course, is not the only possible interpretation for the speech, but it serves to illustrate how loudness level can help to express the meanings you see in a selection.

5. Study Henry's speech before Harfleur. Indicate by the musical signs $>$ or $<$ where your meaning calls for decreasing or increasing loudness. Then practice the selection aloud until you are satisfied that you can communicate the emotions desired with the aid of various degrees of loudness produced without throat strain.

> KING HENRY: *Once more unto the breach, dear friends, once more;*
> *Or close the wall up with our English dead!*
> *In peace, there's nothing so becomes a man,*
> *As modest stillness and humility;*

But when the blast of war blows in our ears,
Then imitate the action of the tiger;
Stiffen the sinews, summon up the blood,
Disguise fair nature with hard-favoured rage;
Then lend the eye a terrible aspect;
Let it pry through the portage of the head
Like the brass cannon; let the brow o'erwhelm it
As fearfully as doth a galled rock
O'er hang and jutty his confounded base,
Swilled with the wild and wasteful ocean.
Now set the teeth and stretch the nostril wide;
Hold hard the breath, and bend up every spirit
To his full height!—On, on, you noble English,—
Whose blood is fet from fathers of war-proof!
Fathers, that, like so many Alexanders,
Have, in these parts, from morn till even fought,
And sheathed their swords for lack of argument;
Dishonour not your mothers; now attest,
That those, whom you called fathers, did beget you!
Be copy now to men of grosser blood,
And teach them how to war!—And you, good yeomen,
Whose limbs were made in England, show us here
The mettle of your pasture: let us swear
That you are worth your breeding; which I doubt not;
For there is none of you so mean and base
That hath not noble lustre in your eyes.
I see you stand like greyhounds in the slips,
Straining upon the start. The game's afoot;
Follow your spirit: and, upon this charge,
Cry—God for Harry! England! and Saint George!

Increased use of microphones and loud speaking systems have solved the problem of audibility of quiet emotions for many interpreters who can stay in one place, or who can carry a microphone about with them. Thus, we have the crooners and love scenes in whispers by movie, radio, and television actors. But the good stage actor or interpreter cannot use a microphone successfully, so he needs to learn how to express quiet emotions in quiet tones that will reach to the highest row of the top balcony. He should use a vocalized tone and his resonators rather than more and more breathiness. This takes practice.

6. Inhale easily, and maintain the posture of your breathing muscles (i.e., expansion) so that relaxation in that region does not force air out. Then, using the front of your vocal resonator with a feeling that the tone is focused far forward, speak the following sentences very quietly but with enough tone so it seems that the voice is echoing and building up in the farthest corner of the auditorium or hall:

a.  *How still it is!*
b.  *This is the stillest time of day or night.*
c.  *How sweet the moonlight sleeps upon this bank!*
d.  *Soft stillness and the night become the touches of sweet harmony.* (Remember *become* means are becoming to.)

7. Study the following speeches. Then, working in an auditorium or large room, and using the procedure described in Exercise 5, read the following speeches in the quietest tone you can use and still feel that it is reinforced in the farthest corner of the room.

> *How sweet the moonlight sleeps upon this bank!*
> *Here will we sit, and let the sounds of music*
> *Creep in our ears; soft stillness and the night*
> *Become the touches of sweet harmony.*
> *Sit, Jessica. Look, how the floor of heaven*
> *Is thick inlaid with patines of bright gold.*
> *There's not the smallest orb, which thou behold'st,*
> *But in his motion like an angel sings,*
> *Still quiring to the young-eyed cherubins;*
> *Such harmony is in immortal souls;*
> *But, whilst this muddy vesture of decay*
> *Doth grossly close us in, we cannot hear it.*
> Merchant of Venice, SHAKESPEARE

JULIE: *Sleep, Liliom, sleep—it's no business of hers—I never even told you—but now I'll tell you—now I'll tell you—you bad, quick-*

tempered, rough, unhappy, wicked—dear boy—sleep peacefully, Liliom—they can't understand how I feel—I can't even explain to you —not even to you—how I feel—you'd only laugh at me—but you can't hear me any more. It was wicked of you to beat me—on the breast and on the head and face—but you're gone now.—You treated me badly—that was wicked of you—but sleep peacefully, Liliom—you bad, bad boy, you—I love you—I never told you before—I was ashamed—but now I've told you—I love you. Liliom—sleep—my boy —sleep.

*Liliom*, MOLNAR

Hush! my baby, or soon you will hear
The Sleepy-eye, Weeng-oosh, hovering near;
Out of the timber he will come,
A little round man as small as your thumb.
Swinging his torch of a red fire-fly,
Out of the shadows old Sleepy-eye,
With sound of a ghost, on the wind will creep
To see if a little boy lies asleep;
Over your cheeks old Weeng will go;
With feet as soft as the falling snow—
Tip-toe . . . . . . . tip-toe.
Hush! my little one, close your lids tight,
Before old Sleepy-eye comes to-night;
Yi-yáh! if he finds you are still awake,
He draws from his quiver a thistledown stake;
With an acorn for club he pounds on its butt,
Till Sleepy-eye hammers the open eye shut;
Then from his bundle he pulls out another,
Hops over your nose and closes the other;
Up and down with his club he will rap
On the open lid till he closes the gap—
Tap-tap . . . . . . tap-tap.
If Wéeng-oosh comes at the end of this day,
And finds you asleep he will hurry away . . .
Do you hear him cry on the winds that blow?—
And walk on the earth as soft as a doe?
To-and-fro . . . . . to-and-fro . . .

*Hi-yáh! he has crept away from my lap!*
*For he found my little boy taking a nap.*
*Oh, weep no more and whisper low,*
*I hear the feet of Sleepy-eye go—*
*Tip-toe . . . . . . . . tip-toe.*

"Weeng" (An Indian Slumber-song), LEW SARETT

## Additional Readings

Aggertt, Otis J., and Elbert R. Bowen, *Communicative Reading.* New York: The Macmillan Co., 1956, pp. 247-301.

Anderson, Virgil A., *Training the Speaking Voice.* New York: Oxford University Press, 1942, pp. 167-168.

Bassett, Lee Emerson, *Handbook of Oral Reading.* Boston: Houghton Mifflin Co., 1917, pp. 124-134.

Fairbanks, Grant, *Voice and Articulation Drillbook.* New York: Harper & Brothers, 1940, pp. 191-200.

Herendeen, Jane, *Speech Quality and Interpretation.* New York: Harper & Brothers, 1946, pp. 99-100.

Sarett, Lew, and W. T. Foster, *Basic Principles of Speech.* Boston: Houghton Mifflin Co., 1936, pp. 288-305.

Selden, Samuel, *The Stage in Action.* New York: F. S. Crofts and Co., 1946, pp. 128-130.

Steer, M. D., and J. Tiffin, "A Photographic Study of the Use of Intensity by Superior Speakers," *Speech Monographs*, 1:72-78, 1934.

# Control of Voice Quality

The interpreter depends heavily upon changes in voice quality to convey an impression of his emotional state, for the human voice is highly responsive to the emotional condition of the whole person. At the same time, the interpreter realizes that defects in his own basic voice quality are handicaps in that they call attention to themselves and give others an unpleasant sensation and an undesirable reaction. His training program often calls for practice which helps him cultivate a pleasing quality, helps him eliminate undesirable characteristics of quality, and helps him develop a voice fully flexible in its response to his feelings.

Voice quality has been so frequently identified with personality that it is particularly desirable for each person to learn to use his voice-producing mechanism as well as he possibly can. Most voice quality defects can be eliminated or minimized through proper use of the vocal mechanism. Harshness frequently results from strain in the laryngeal and pharyngeal regions and can be minimized by learning to relax these parts of the vocal mechanism and to improve vowel quality even under emotional stress and conditions that call for loudness. Nasality that results from back mouth tension can be minimized in the same way, while the nasality that results from improper function of the velum is often eliminated as soon as the speaker gains sufficient control of it. Unfortunately, a breathy voice has too often been identified with the desirable soft voice in women or with childishness, and some women have been made to believe that they sound younger and sweeter when they are breathy. As has been pointed out, breathiness has often been a poor substitute for a voice that is soft, yet completely vocalized. One of the best ways to conquer breathiness is to learn more complete control of the breathing mechanism and coordination of breathing with vocal cord approximation. All of these ways to minimize or eliminate voice quality defects have already been pointed out.

Voice quality can often be improved as the speaker learns to control his resonators in such a way that he can produce several voice qualities, none of which is defective. As he learns to project different personalities through voice quality changes, he learns the feeling of his resonators and learns control over them. All of us have imitated others enough so that we can do this. It is probably easiest to start with a well-known nursery rhyme and certain obvious stereotyped personalities.

## EXERCISES

*1.* Using the rhyme,

> *Twinkle, twinkle little star!*
> *How I wonder what you are;*
> *Up above the world so high,*
> *Like a diamond in the sky.*

read the rhyme as it might be done by the following types of persons. Act as much like the individual you imagine as possible.

    a. An old-time political orator
    b. A very precise, "prissy" schoolteacher
    c. An old-time lady elocutionist
    d. A little boy obviously embarrassed to speak such a silly rhyme before an audience
    e. A little girl, very pleased to show herself and her new dress to an audience.

Notice the feeling of your oral and pharyngeal resonators as you make your voice "heavy" or "light" for these characters.

More subtle characteristics show themselves in more subtle voice quality changes, yet it is possible to make these characteristics sharply defined.

2. The following dialogue is between two persons of the same sex with very definite personality characteristics. Try to show these

characteristics in your voice and notice how your resonators achieve these results. The conversation that follows is between a girl scientist and her mother-in-law, who fancies herself as a sweet, self-sacrificing person while she is extremely purposeful underneath. Analyze both characters thoroughly. Read *all* the *lines* they have in Sidney Howard's *Silver Cord* before you attempt to recreate the characters. Decide how they look, how they are dressed, the environment that surrounds them. Notice how other characters react to them. Decide what is the basic urge or motivation for each of them.

MRS. PHLEPS. *You are entitled to your opinions, Christina, just as I am to mine and David is to his. I only hope that he sees the kind of woman he's married. I hope he sees the sordidness, the hardness, the nastiness she offers him for his life.*

CHRISTINA. (An involuntary cry of pain.) *I'm not nasty! I'm not!*

MRS. PHELPS. *What have you to offer David?*

CHRISTINA. *A hard time. A chance to work on his own. A chance to be on his own. Very little money on which to share with me the burden of raising his child. The pleasure of my society. The solace of my love. The enjoyment of my body. To which I have reason to believe he is not indifferent.*

MRS. PHELPS. (Revolted.) *Ugh!*

CHRISTINA. *Can you offer so much?*

MRS. PHELPS. *I offer a mother's love. Or perhaps you scoff at that?*

CHRISTINA. *Not if it's kept within bounds. I hope my baby loves me. I'm practically certain I'm going to love my baby. But within bounds.*

MRS. PHELPS. *And what do you mean by within bounds?*

CHRISTINA. *To love my baby with as much and as deep respect as I hope my baby will feel for me if I deserve its respect. To love my baby unpossessively; above all, unromantically.*

MRS. PHELPS. *I suppose that's biology! You don't know the difference between good and evil!*

CHRISTINA. *As a biologist, though, I do know the difference between life and death. And I know sterility when I see it. I doubt if evil is any more than a fancy name for sterility. And sterility, of*

course, is what you offer Dave. Sterility for his mind as well as for
his body. That's your professional mother's stock in trade.

*The Silver Cord,* SIDNEY HOWARD

3. In order to read the excerpt from the famous wooing scene
from *The Taming of the Shrew* that follows, read the entire play,
then reread all the speeches of these two principal characters. Analyze
both characters. Let the personality characteristics of both characters,
as well as their sex, show in your voice quality. Do not use a high or
falsetto voice for Kate and a low voice for Petruchio. Show the difference through voice quality changes.

PETRUCHIO: Good morrow, Kate; for that's your name, I hear.

KATHERINE: Well have you heard, but something hard of hearing.
They call me—Katherine, that do talk of me.

PETRUCHIO: You lie, in faith; for you are call'd plain Kate,
And bonny Kate, and sometimes Kate the curst;
But Kate, the prettiest Kate in Christendom;
Kate of Kate-Hall, my super-dainty Kate,
For dainties are all cates; and therefore, Kate,
Take this of me, Kate of my consolation;—
Hearing thy mildness praised in every town,
Thy virtues spoke of, and thy beauty sounded,
(Yet not so deeply as to thee belongs,)
Myself am mov'd to woo thee for my wife.

KATHERINE: Moved! in good time; let him that moved you hither,
Remove you hence. I knew you at the first,
You were a movable.

PETRUCHIO: Why, what's a movable?

KATHERINE: A joint stool. . . .

PETRUCHIO: Nay, come, Kate, come; you must not look so sour.

KATHERINE: It is my fashion, when I see a crab.

PETRUCHIO: Why, here's no crab; and therefore look not sour.

KATHERINE: There is, there is.

PETRUCHIO: Then show it me.

KATHERINE: Had I a glass, I would.

PETRUCHIO: What, you mean my face?

KATHERINE: Well aim'd of such a young one. . . .

PETRUCHIO: Nay, hear you, Kate; in sooth you 'scape not so.
KATHERINE: I chafe you, if I tarry. Let me go.

4. The following scene between "De Lawd" and Noah is from Marc Connelly's Green Pastures. Analyze the characters as above and read the passage so there can be no doubt which character is speaking. Notice how you use your resonators.

GOD: You got a fine wife, Brother Noah.

NOAH: She pretty good woman.

GOD: Yes, suh, an' you got a nice little home. Have a ten-cent seegar?

NOAH: Thank you, much obliged.

GOD: Jest what seems to be de main trouble 'mong mankind, Noah?

NOAH: Well, it seems to me de main trouble is dat de whol' distric' is wide open. Now you know dat makes fo' loose livin'. Men folks spen's all dere time fightin', loafin' and gamblin', an' makin' bad likker.

GOD: What about de women?

NOAH: De women is worse dan de men. If dey ain't makin' love powder dey out beg, borrow an' stealin' money for policy tickets. Doggone, I come in de church Sunday fo' las' 'bout an hour befo' de meetin' was to start, and dere was a woman stealin' de altar cloth. She was goin' to hock it. Dey ain't got no moral sense. Now you take dat case las' month, over in East Putney. Case of dat young Willy Roback.

GOD: What about him?

NOAH: Dere is a boy sebenteen years old. Doggone, if he didn't elope with his aunt. Now, you know, dat kin' of goin' on is bad fo' a neighborhood.

GOD: Terrible, terrible.

NOAH: Yes, suh. Dis use' to be a nice, decent community. I been doin' my best to preach de Word, but seems like every time I preach de place jest goes a little mo' to de dogs. De good Lawd only knows what's gonter happen.

GOD: Dat is de truth.

## Additional Readings

Aggertt, Ottis J., and Elbert R. Bowen, *Communicative Reading*. New York: The Macmillan Co., 1956, pp. 302-338.

Anderson, Virgil A., *Training the Speaking Voice*. New York: Oxford University Press, 1942, pp. 174-185.

Bassett, Lee Emerson, *Handbook of Oral Reading*. Boston: Houghton, Mifflin Co., 1917, pp. 203-213.

Selden, Samuel, *The Stage in Action*. New York: F. S. Crofts and Co., 1946, pp. 99-120.

Tresidder, Argus, *Reading to Others*. Chicago: Scott, Foresman & Company, 1940, pp. 197-214.

Woolbert, Charles H., and Severina E. Nelson, *The Art of Interpretative Speech* (ed. 4). New York: Appleton-Century-Crofts, Inc., 1956, pp. 253-301.

# Control of Timing

POPULARLY, THE READER'S PERSONALITY IS OFTEN JUDGED BY HIS VOICE quality. Just as frequently, his skill is judged by his timing. Yet there is very little objective study of timing that goes beyond the number of words spoken per minute. The ear must be the ultimate guide as to how satisfactory the timing is. But the ear can fool us. Southern speech is popularly considered very slow, compared with Eastern Standard or General American speech. Yet studies have shown that the ratio between phonated and total time does not differ significantly among the dialects, particularly not between General American or Southern speech. However, southern speakers tend to prolong stressed vowels significantly longer than either General American or Eastern Standard speakers and hence we probably get the impression of drawling or slowness.

The total time for any passage is accounted for by three elements: the duration of the sounds in the words, pauses, and hesitations. The latter occur, sometimes unvoiced, but too often marred by sounds of "uh" or "mm-m," when the reader is stalling for time to think, to organize his thoughts, or to form the image. If the hesitation is filled with the process of forming the image, it is a useful wait, colored by the developing thought. The voiced hesitation, particularly the empty and meaningless one, is to be avoided. Too often it is the mark of insufficient preparation.

Pauses provide the interpreter with potent means of emphasis, of oral punctuation, of pointing the comic, the poignant, the meaningful. They serve to give a leisurely pace; without them the interpreter can give a feeling of hastening, even while the duration of sounds is prolonged. The pause makes possible a variety difficult to obtain in any other way.

Duration of sound may be varied, particularly as the interpreter prolongs or shortens his vowels, the nasal sounds, the fricatives, diphthongs, glides and semi-vowels. Poetic passages may demand prolongation of sounds to bring out the singing quality of the language, to carry the emotional content of the selection, and to suggest the nature of the imagery.

The combination of duration of sounds, hesitations, and pauses and the variations and changes in their use are what is called timing. The rhythms and the variations of rhythms, the breaks in rate, the sudden sharp changes—all these are part of the interpreter's resources.

The skilled speaker is guided by several factors in determining his timing. The first is the length of time he or the character he is impersonating would need to form the idea, image, or emotion he is about to speak. The second factor is his awareness of how long it will take his audience to grasp and appreciate the idea, image, or emotion he has just spoken. The circular reaction between speaker and audience and audience and speaker is a delightful thing for both to experience. Bennett Cerf in a lecture once spoke of it as a mutual love affair in which the waves of affection flow back and forth from audience to actors. Certainly they are both perfectly attuned to each other.

The skilled speaker's timing is guided by the size and nature of his audience as well as by the nature of the material he is speaking. Political speakers, such as Franklin D. Roosevelt, speaking to large groups as well as to radio and television audiences speak much slower than students reading easily understood factual materials to an audience of twenty-five or so. Material on certain emotions, such as grief, is read much slower than material on other emotions, such as fear or anger. The reader's ability to find the precise rate that is appropriate to the changing ideas and emotions in the material he is communicating is one of his greatest assets. If he does not time his reading well, his voice will be judged as staccato or too prolonged or jerky, and the audience will feel—and quite rightly—that the rate is expressing the reader's personal reactions, such as fear or indifference, and has nothing to do with the material he is supposed to be recreating.

The aims of the interpreter as he tries to improve his timing can be summarized as follows:

1. To know what rates in factual materials will be judged as fast, slow, or medium by the average audience.
2. To be able to gauge audience reaction as closely as possible.
3. To be able to find the right timing for the emotion expressed in each phrase.

Carefully controlled experiments[1, 2] have shown that the average audience will judge that factual materials read to a group of approximately twenty-five people will seem to them to be slow if read at a rate of less than 140 words per minute. Audience interest may be sacrificed if you read too slowly, whereas too rapid a rate may interfere with articulation and hence with audience comprehension. The first step in controlling rate is to get a sense of what is normal rate and how time may be controlled within these limits.

# EXERCISES

*1.* Use the following passage to measure your habitual rate of reading. Use the method described in the passage to calculate your rate in words per minute.

*Your rate of speech will be adequate if it is slow enough to provide for clearness and comprehension, and rapid enough to sustain interest. Your rate is faulty if it is too rapid to accomplish these ends. The easiest way to begin work on the adjustment of your speech to an ideal rate is to measure your present rate in words per minute in a fixed situation which you can keep constant over a number of trials. The best method is to pick a page of simple, factual prose to be read. Read this page in your natural manner, timing yourself in seconds. Count the number of words on the page, divide by the number of seconds, and multiply this result by sixty to calculate the number of words per minute. As you attempt to increase or retard your rate, repeat this procedure from time to time, using the same reading material, to enable you to check your success.*

*A common accompaniment of rapid rate is staccato speech, in which the duration of words and syllables is too short, whereas in slow speech the words and syllables frequently are overprolonged.*

When the person with too rapid rate tries to slow down, he tends to make the error of keeping the duration of his tones short, and of attempting to accomplish the slower rate solely by lengthening the pauses between phrases and by introducing new pauses. On the other hand, the person who is working to speed up his rate tends to do this by shortening the pauses alone and retaining his prolonged tones. It is impossible at the present time to set down in rules the ideal relation between the duration of tones and pauses in speech. Further research is needed before this can be done with any great accuracy.[1]

If your rate is more than 185 words per minute or less than 140 words per minute, practice reading the passage until you bring it within these two limits.

2. Try reading the above passage with a rapid rate within phrases and long pauses between phrases. Keep the over-all rate within the normal limits. What effect do you achieve? Now read the passage with prolonged phonations during phrases and little pauses between phrases. Keep the over-all rate within normal limits. What effect do you achieve?

To judge the time necessary for an audience to react to you and your material requires practice. Not only will your materials vary, but each audience will have different reactions. Most readers like to say a sentence or two to introduce their materials rather than just to announce subject and author. This practice gives the reader a chance to judge audience reaction. Materials in the exercises that follow in this chapter should be memorized to give the reader maximum opportunity to gauge audience reaction. Give particular attention to the timing of final "punch" lines and phrases.

3. The following poems, *Fable* by Ralph Waldo Emerson, and *Height of the Ridiculous* by Oliver Wendell Holmes, should evoke an amused response from any audience. In the first poem it may help you to remember the tempo in which a squirrel moves to get the sauciness of his retort. The timing for the second poem would probably be very different, and will probably vary from reader to reader. Try to get the maximum of good audience response by your introduction and reading of these two poems.

FABLE

The mountain and the squirrel
Had a quarrel,
And the former called the latter 'Little Prig;'
Bun replied,
'You are doubtless very big;
But all sorts of things and weather
Must be taken in together,
To make up a year
And a sphere.
And I think it no disgrace
To occupy my place.
If I'm not so large as you,
You are not so small as I,
And not half so spry.
I'll not deny you make
A very pretty squirrel track;
Talents differ; all is well and wisely put;
If I cannot carry forests on my back,
Neither can you crack a nut.'

## THE HEIGHT OF THE RIDICULOUS

I wrote some lines once on a time
    In wondrous merry mood,
And thought, as usual, men would say
    They were exceeding good.

They were so queer, so very queer,
    I laughed as I would die;
Albeit, in the general way,
    A sober man am I.

I called my servant, and he came;
    How kind it was of him
To mind a slender man like me,
    He of the mighty limb.

"These to the printer," I exclaimed,
    And, in my humorous way,

I added, (as a trifling jest,)
  "There'll be the devil to pay."

He took the paper, and I watched,
  And saw him peep within;
At the first line he read, his face
  Was all upon the grin.

He read the next; the grin grew broad,
  And shot from ear to ear;
He read the third; a chuckling noise
  I now began to hear.

The fourth; he broke into a roar;
  The fifth; his waistband split;
The sixth; he burst five buttons off,
  And tumbled in a fit.

Ten days and nights, with sleepless eye,
  I watched that wretched man,
And since, I never dare to write
  As funny as I can.

4. The following selections should amuse an audience. Introduce and read them in an effort to get maximum response.

Once upon a sunny morning a man who sat in a breakfast nook looked up from his scrambled eggs to see a white unicorn with a gold horn quietly cropping the roses in the garden. The man went up to the bedroom where his wife was still asleep and woke her. "There's a unicorn in the garden," he said. "Eating roses." She opened one unfriendly eye and looked at him. "The unicorn is a mythical beast," she said, and turned her back on him. The man walked slowly downstairs and out into the garden. The unicorn was still there; he was now browsing among the tulips. "Here, unicorn," said the man, and he pulled up a lily and gave it to him. The unicorn ate it gravely. With a high heart, because there was a unicorn in his garden, the man went upstairs and roused his wife again. "The unicorn," he said, "ate a lily." His wife sat up in bed and looked at him coldly. "You are a booby," she said, "and I am going to have you put in the booby-hatch." The man, who had never liked the words "booby" and "booby-hatch," and who liked them even less on a shining morning when there was a unicorn in the garden, thought for a moment. "We'll see about that," he said. He walked over to the door. "He has a golden horn in the middle of his forehead," he told her. Then he went back to the garden to watch the unicorn; but the unicorn had gone away. The man sat down among the roses and went to sleep.

As soon as the husband had gone out of the house, the wife got up and dressed as fast as she could. She was very excited and there was a gloat in her eye. She telephoned the police and she telephoned a psychiatrist; she told them to hurry to her house and bring a strait-jacket. When the police and the psychiatrist arrived they sat down in chairs and looked at her, with great interest. "My husband," she said, "saw a unicorn this morning." The police looked at the psychiatrist and the psychiatrist looked at the police. "He told me it ate a lily," she said. The psychiatrist looked at the police and the police looked at the psychiatrist. "He told me it had a golden horn in the middle of its forehead," she said. At a solemn signal from the psychiatrist, the police leaped from their chairs and seized the wife. They had a hard time subduing her, for she put up a terrific struggle, but they finally subdued her. Just as they got her into the strait-jacket, the husband came back into the house.

"Did you tell your wife you saw a unicorn?" asked the police. "Of course not," said the husband. "The unicorn is a mythical beast." "That's all I wanted to know," said the psychiatrist. "Take her away. I'm sorry, sir, but your wife is as crazy as a jay bird." So they took her away, cursing and screaming, and shut her up in an institution. The husband lived happily ever after.

Moral: Don't count your boobies until they are hatched.

"The Unicorn in the Garden," from *Fables for Our Times*,
JAMES THURBER

Another course that I didn't like, but somehow managed to pass, was economics. I went to that class straight from botany class, which didn't help me in understanding either subject. I used to get them mixed up. But not as mixed up as another student in my economics class who came there direct from a physics laboratory. He was a tackle on the football team, named Bolenciecwcz. At that time

Ohio State University had one of the best football teams in the country, and Bolenciecwcz was one of its outstanding stars. In order to be eligible to play it was necessary for him to keep up in his studies, a very difficult matter, for while he was not dumber than an ox he was not any smarter. Most of his professors were lenient and helped him along. None gave him more hints, in answering questions, or asked him simpler ones than the economics professor, a thin, timid man named Bassum. One day when we were on the subject of transportation and distribution, it came Bolenciecwcz's turn to answer a question. "Name one means of transportation," the professor said to him. No light came into the big tackle's eyes. "Just any means of transportation," said the professor. Bolenciecwcz sat staring at him. "That is," pursued the professor, "any medium, agency, or method of going from one place to another." Bolenciecwcz had the look of a man who is being led into a trap. "You may choose among steam, horse-drawn, or electrically propelled vehicles," said the instructor. "I might suggest the one which we commonly take in making long journeys across land." There was a profound silence in which everybody stirred uneasily, including Bolenciecwcz and Mr. Bassum. Mr. Bassum abruptly broke this silence in an amazing manner. "Choo—choo—choo," he said, in a low voice, and turned instantly scarlet. He glanced appealingly around the room. All of us, of course, shared Mr. Bassum's desire that Bolenciecwcz should stay abreast of the class in economics, for the Illinois game, one of the hardest and most important of the season, was only a week off. "Toot, toot, too-tooooooot!" some student with a deep voice moaned, and we all looked encouragingly at Bolenciecwcz. Somebody else gave a fine imitation of a locomotive letting off steam. Mr. Bassum himself rounded off the show. "Ding, dong, ding, dong," he said, hopefully. Bolenciecwcz was staring at the floor now, trying to think, his great brow furrowed, his huge hands rubbing together, his face red.

"How did you come to college this year, Mr. Bolenciecwcz?" asked the professor. "Chuffa, chuffa, chuffa chuffa."

"M'father sent me," said the football player.

"What on?" asked Bassum.

"I git an 'lowance," said the tackle, in a low, husky voice, obviously embarrassed.

"No, no," said Bassum. "Name a means of transportation. What
did you ride here on?"

"Train," said Bolenciecwcz.

The Illinois game was won.

"University Days," from *My Life and Hard Times*, JAMES THURBER

(With hands together in prayer-like supplication, he walks down
to the footlights and bows to the audience center in solemn ritual.
Then he bows from the waist—to the left and to the right.

Straightening up, he examines the audience seated before him
with open curiosity. The music ceases. At it ceases, Sakini begins
to work his jaws vigorously.)

SAKINI: *Tootie-fruitie.*

(He takes the gum from his mouth and, wrapping it carefully in
a piece of paper, puts it in a matchbox and restores it to a pocket in
his shirt.)

*Most generous gift of American sergeant.*

(He resumes his original posture of dignity.)

*Lovely ladies, kind gentlemen:*

*Please to introduce myself.*

*Sakini by name.*

*Interpreter by profession.*

*Education by ancient dictionary.*

*Okinawan by whim of gods.*

*History of Okinawa reveal distinguished record of conquerors.*

*We have honor to be subjugated in fourteenth century by Chi-
nese pirates.*

*In sixteenth century by English missionaries.*

*In eighteenth century by Japanese war lords.*

*And in twentieth century by American Marines.*

*Okinawa very fortunate.*

*Culture brought to us. . . . Not have to leave home for it.*

*Learn many things.*

*Most important that rest of world not like Okinawa.*

*World filled with delightful variation.*

*Illustration.*

*In Okinawa . . . no locks on doors.*

*Bad manners not to trust neighbors.*

*In America . . . lock and key big industry.*
*Conclusion?*
*Bad manners good business.*
*In Okinawa . . . wash self in public bath with nude lady quite proper.*
*Picture of nude lady in private home . . . quite improper.*
*In America . . . statue of nude lady in park win prize.*
*But nude lady in flesh in park win penalty.*
*Conclusion?*
*Pornography question of geography.*
*But Okinawans most eager to be educated by conquerors.*
*Deep desire to improve friction.*
*Not easy to learn.*
*Sometimes painful.*
*But pain makes man think.*
*Thought makes man wise.*
*Wisdom makes life endurable.*
*So . . .*
*We tell little story to demonstrate splendid example of benevolent assimilation of democracy by Okinawa.*

Teahouse of the August Moon, JOHN PATRICK

5. Not all selections are amusing. Some are inspiring, some impressive, some arouse an audience to anger and some make an audience want to weep. Ingersoll's speech, *At the Tomb of Napoleon,* is impressive, for example. Joan's bell speech in Shaw's *Saint Joan* is inspiring. Select a passage which should evoke a response from the audience other than amusement. Write this desired response on a piece of paper. Time the delivery of your selection for maximum audience response. Ask your listeners to write down their reaction when you have finished, and compare it with the reaction you were trying to get.

# References

1. Darley, F. L., "A Normative Study of Oral Reading Rate," M.A. thesis, State University of Iowa, 1940.

2. Franke, P., "A Preliminary Study Validating the Measurement of Oral Reading Rate in Words per Minute," M.A. thesis, State University of Iowa, 1939.

## Additional Readings

Aggertt, Otis J., and Elbert R. Bowen, *Communicative Reading*. New York The Macmillan Co., 1956, pp. 200-246.

Dolman, John, *The Art of Acting*. New York: Harper & Brothers, 1949, pp. 125-134.

Fairbanks, Grant, *Voice and Articulation Drillbook*. New York: Harper & Brothers, 1940, pp. 140-164.

Herendeen, Jane, *Speech Quality and Interpretation*. New York: Harper & Brothers, 1946, pp. 86-88.

Lowrey, Sara, and Gertrude E. Johnson, *Interpretative Reading: Techniques and Selections* (rev. ed.). New York: Appleton-Century-Crofts, Inc., 1953, pp. 77-123.

Sarett, Lew, and W. T. Foster, *Basic Principles of Speech*. Boston: Houghton Mifflin Co., 1936, pp. 253-287.

# Synthesis and Evaluation
# of Progress

Comic materials make sharp demands on flexibility of voice. Wide ranges and sharp changes of pitch, often very quick, even explosive alterations of loudness, nice adjustments of tempo and pause, and constant variety of quality are all characteristic of comedy materials. The purpose of the assignment in this project is to give the interpreter opportunity to display his skills in the flexible use of voice through the presentation of a scene from a play, a novel, a short story, or a poem which is not only comic, but preferably even hilarious and full of rollicking good spirits.

Literature is full of such materials from the time of Aristophanes to Noel Coward. The comic spirit ranges from the most robust to the very delicate and sly. There can hardly fail to be something to your liking. Besides Aristophanes there are Chaucer and Molière and Shakespeare. There are Alexander Pope; Sheridan and Goldsmith; Thurber, Benchley, and Leacock; Farquhar, Wilde, and Somerset Maugham; Cornelia Otis Skinner, Betty MacDonald, and Margaret Halsey. These writers are only a few who have furnished the world with laughter. From among them or other writers whom you appreciate, choose a passage five minutes or so in length to present.

During preparation particular attention should be given to the vocal means of making the reading more and more spritely, more full of good spirits and, we hope, more funny. Good comic reading is always vital, full of energy, but it must not seem to tax the reader's strength. His use of voice and body must be so well disciplined and so well prepared that his perfomance gives every impression of ease. The interpreter must seem to be having fun, too.

## Additional Readings

Benchley, Robert C., *Benchley Beside Himself.* New York and London: Harper & Brothers, 1943.

Boatright, Mody C., *Folk Laughter on the American Frontier.* New York: The Macmillan Company, 1949.

Day, Clarence, *The Best of Clarence Day.* New York: Alfred A. Knopf, Inc., 1956.

Gilbert, W. S., *The Complete Plays of Gilbert and Sullivan.* New York: Modern Library, Inc., 1936.

Leacock, Stephen B., *The Greatest Pages of American Humor.* Garden City, N. Y.: Doubleday, Doran & Co., Inc., 1936.

Nash, Ogden, *The Moon is Shining Bright as Day: an Anthology of Good-Humored Verse.* Philadelphia: J. B. Lippincott Co., 1953.

Parker, Dorothy, *The Collected Poetry of Dorothy Parker.* New York: Modern Library, Inc., 1936.

Parker, Dorothy, *The Collected Stories of Dorothy Parker.* New York: Modern Library, Inc., 1942.

Skinner, Cornelia Otis, *Soap Behind the Ears.* New York: Dodd, Mead & Co., 1941.

Stewart, Donald Ogden, *A Parody Outline of History.* Garden City, N. Y.: The Sun Dial Press, Inc., 1937.

Untermeyer, Louis, *A Treasury of Laughter.* New York: Simon and Schuster, Inc., 1946.

# 9

## PROJECTS IN
# Emotional Control

# Some Problems in Emotional Expression

FOR PURPOSES OF DRILL AND IMPROVEMENT, WE MAY FOCUS ATTENTION on various characteristics of voice, but we are always aware that pitch, time, loudness, quality, and articulation are parts of a totality. They are so interrelated that improvement in one is quite likely to bring with it improvement in another. The interpreter who is really skilled is most concerned about the behavior of his voice as a totality. If he is not satisfied that his voice is carrying his intended meaning, then he must be concerned whether one or more of the various vocal characteristics is at fault or if the integration of all of them is unsatisfactory. This project presents drills that integrate the skills learned so far. At the same time, special problems presented by some of the more common kinds of emotional expression will be dealt with.

Laughter is often very difficult for interpreters to master. No matter what way of laughing is "natural" to the reader, on the platform he must laugh so that his listeners know what he intends. Achieving such a result means, generally, that his laugh must be vocalized and audible. At the same time, laughter should be individualized. One person will not laugh like another, nor will the same person laugh in the same way under various circumstances. Lastly, while the interpreter has control of his laughter at all times, he should feel genuinely amused. This feeling of amusement is something over which he should have control, because we have all had so much experience with our own laughter or empathic response to laughter of others that having nothing to laugh about is no excuse for not being able to recall the feeling or image of amusement.

The abdominal muscles must control the laugh. If an interpreter simply raises his rib cage and laughs as it falls, the resulting sound is so breathy and wheezy that it will be interpreted by the listener as crying or sighing more often than as laughter. As soon as a feeling of bouncing by the abdominal muscles is achieved, the laugh is usually mastered.

## EXERCISES

1. Take a full breath and hold it a second while neck and shoulders are relaxed. Now vocalize a series of ten *ha*'s. Repeat five times, each time increasing the rate of the *ha*'s. Work until the abdominal bounce is established.

2. Where *Ha* appears in the following exercise, produce the sound with a strong abdominal force. Where *x* appears, remain silent. Maintain an even 1-2-3-4 count throughout. At each repetition vary the tempo. Execute the third and fourth lines with the feeling and sound of robust mirth.

> Ha x x x; Ha x x x; Ha x x x; Ha x x x
> Ha, ha x x; Ha, ha x x; Ha, ha x x; Ha x x x
> Ha, ha, ha x; Ha, ha, ha x; Ha, ha, ha x; Ha x x x
> Ha, ha, ha, ha; ha, ha, ha, ha; ha, ha, ha, ha; ha

Work until there is a feeling of bouncing of the abdominal muscles. Alternate *ha* with *ho, haw, hee,* etc.

3. Start your laugh with an *ah* which slides up an octave from the middle of your range, then follow it with ten *ha*'s, each on a lower pitch than the last.

4. Laugh on various levels of pitch from high to low, changing the syllable you use (*ha, haw, ho, hee*) with each change of pitch.

5. Change the timing of your laugh so that there will be three *ha, ha, ha*'s, for example, followed by six *ha*'s in double time.

6. Select one of the following speeches, and study its back-

ground and the character of the person speaking. Practice until you can laugh in character and as designated by the speeches.

OLIVIA: *Do you mean he's dead?* . . .(laughing hysterically.) *Oh, Mr. Pim, you—oh, what a husband to have—oh, I—*(But that is all she can say for the moment.) (Struggling with her laughter.) *I think you must excuse me, Mr. Pim—I can never thank you enough—a herring—there's something about a herring—morality depends on such little things—George, you—*(Shaking her head at him in a weak state of laughter, she hurries from the room.)

Mr. Pim Passes By, MILNE

WITTIG: (With pretended astonishment, staring open-mouthed at the old weaver.) *Heinerle! you don't mean to tell me that that's you?* (Laughs immoderately.) *O Lord, O Lord! I could laugh myself to death. Old Baumert risin' in rebellion! We'll have the tailors at it next, and then there'll be a rebellion among the baa-lambs, and the rats and the mice. Damn it all, but we'll see some sport.* (He nearly splits with laughter.)

The Weavers, HAUPTMANN

ANNA: *Cape Town? Where's that? Far away?*

BURKE: *'Tis at the end of Africa. That's far for you.*

ANNA: (Forcing a laugh) *You're keeping your word all right, ain't you?* (After a slight pause—curiously.) *What's the boat's name?*

BURKE: *The Londonderry.*

ANNA: (It suddenly comes to her that this is the same ship her father is sailing on.) *The "Londonderry!" It's the same—Oh, this is too much!* (With wild, ironical laughter) *Ha-ha-ha!*

BURKE: *What's up with you now?*

ANNA: *Ha-ha-ha! It's funny, funny! I'll die laughing!*

BURKE: (Irritated) *Laughing at what?*

ANNA: *It's a secret. You'll know soon enough. It's funny.* (Controlling herself—after a pause—cynically) *What kind of a place is this Cape Town? Plenty of dames there, I suppose?*

Anna Christie, EUGENE O'NEILL

Crying is even more individualized than laughter. People may cry because they are happy, or frustrated and angry, or because they are sad. Some people cry more easily than others. It is in most circumstances considered unmanly to cry, so if a man cries, it is generally in spite of every attempt not to and the act is more painful than a woman's crying.

It is not unusual for actors and other interpreters to be so moved that tears run down their cheeks. Many times the audience is not aware that they are crying, but it should be emphasized again that the interpreter is always in control of himself. He can still follow directions, stop the crying, and burst into laughter or ask for clarification of directions. Audiences are very sensitive to this control. A student who once lost control during a class laughing exercise became slightly hysterical. She couldn't stop laughing, and started crying. It was interesting to note that the class enjoyed the exercise until the moment control was lost, and then esthetic distance was broken and every auditor immediately became anxious and concerned for the student.

For crying, the spasmodic inhalation is as important to learn as are the various kinds of exhalation, and this inhalation may be and often is controlled by the muscles that raise the ribs as well as by the diaphragm. The exhalation may range from a shuddering, unvocalized sigh to a loud bawl, and the vocalization is seldom the traditionally written *boo-hoo-hoo*. The vocalization may be aw [ɔ] in the case of the bawling cry or [u] or [o] or a nasal consonant or even a vowel not in General American speech.

## EXERCISES

*1.* Inhale with one catch of the breath, then two, then three, then four. Exhale each time on a long sigh. Do this until the tears begin to start, or at least until you begin to feel like crying.

*2.* Inhale as above; then, instead of the long, shuddering sigh, exhale on one choking, vocalized catch, then two, then three, and then four.

*3.* Cry with as many variations of inhalation, vocalization, and exhalation as you can.

4. Select one of the following speeches, study its background and the character of the person speaking, and practice until you can cry in character and as designated by the speeches:

BURKE: (Shaking Chris off—furiously) *Lave go of me, ye old ape! Marry her, is it? I'd see her roasting in hell first! I'm shipping away out of this, I'm telling you!* (Pointing to Anna—passionately) *And my curse on you and the curse of Almighty God and all the Saints! You've destroyed me this day and may you lie awake in the long nights, tormented with thoughts of Mat Burke and the great wrong you've done him!*

ANNA: (In anguish) *Mat!* (But he turns without another word and strides out of the doorway. Anna looks after him wildly, starts to run after him, then hides her face in her outstretched arms, sobbing. Chris stands in a stupor, staring at the floor.)

CHRIS: (After a pause, dully) *Ay tank Ay go ashore, too.*

ANNA: (Looking up, wildly) *Not after him! Let him go! Don't you dare—*

CHRIS: (Somberly) *Ay go for gat drink.*

ANNA: (with a harsh laugh) *So I'm driving you to drink, too, eh? I s'pose you want to get drunk so's you can forget—like him?*

CHRIS: (Bursting out angrily) *Yes, Ay vant! You tank Ay like hear dem tangs.* (Breaking down—weeping) *Ay tank you vasn't dat kind of gel, Anna.*

ANNA: (Mockingly) *And I s'pose you want me to beat it, don't you? You don't want me here disgracing you, I s'pose?*

CHRIS: *No, you stay here!* (Goes over and pats her on the shoulder, the tears running down his face.) *Ain't your fault, Anna, Ay know dat.* (She looks up at him, softened. . . .)

*Anna Christie,* EUGENE O'NEILL

CHRIS: (He stands hesitatingly—finally blurts out.) *Anna—you forgive me sure?*

ANNA: (Wearily) *Sure I do. You ain't to blame. You're yust— what you are—like me.*

CHRIS: (Pleadingly) *Den—you lat me kiss you again once?*

ANNA: (Raising her face—forcing a wan smile) *Sure. No hard feelings.*

CHRIS: (Kisses her brokenly) *Anna lilla! Ay—*(He fights for words to express himself, but finds none—miserably—with a sob.) *Ay can't say it. Good-night, Anna.*

Anna Christie, EUGENE O'NEILL

ANNA: (Infuriated by his action—stridently) *You will too listen!* (She leans over and pulls his hands from his ears—with hysterical rage.) *You—keeping me safe inland—I wasn't no nurse girl the last two years—I lied when I wrote you—I was in a house, that's what!—yes, that kind of a house—the kind sailors like you and Mat goes to in port—and your nice inland men, too—and all men, God damn 'em! I hate 'em! Hate 'em!* (She breaks into hysterical sobbing, throwing herself into the chair and hiding her face in her hands on the table. The two men have sprung to their feet.)
CHRIS: (Whimpering like a child) *Anna! Anna! It's a lie! It's a lie!* (He stands wringing his hands together and begins to weep.)

Anna Christie, EUGENE O'NEILL

*Hate, anger,* and *fear* are all tense emotions. The problem in reading speeches containing these emotions is to keep the throat and back of the mouth *feeling* relaxed. The characteristic tightness of the emotion may be felt in the abdominal muscles, arms, legs, and even the toes, but if the throat or back of the mouth becomes too tense, then the voice may sound hard and be called nasal, or it may sound throaty. When this happens, the emotion is often said to be "throat deep." A technique for reading these emotions needs to be developed so that they will sound natural.

Characteristically, these emotions are all oxygen-users. Hence, there must always be a plentiful reserve of breath underneath the tone. The breath may be taken slowly or quickly, but it always needs to be taken more often and more deeply than for factual speech.

Studies of anger and fear[1,2,3] have shown that they are expressed on a relatively high pitch, with fear expressed on a somewhat higher median pitch level than anger. These higher pitches are to be expected because of the degree of tension in the emotions. Both emotions are expressed by a wide range of pitches, with the widest inflections used to express anger. We are all aware, when we express these emotions, of a tendency to try to control them, alternating with bursts that seem almost uncontrollable. Some tones are prolonged and others are almost staccato, with fear showing the fastest rate.

## EXERCISES

1. In reading the following selections, work especially to feel the emotion in any part of the body except the throat. Keep the throat feeling as relaxed as you can. Always keep a large reserve of breath under the tone and work for a wide variety of pitch and time, especially for the emotions of anger and hate.

### HATE.

Gr-r-r——there go, my heart's abhorrence!
　　Water your damned flower-pots, do!
If hate killed men, Brother Lawrence,
　　God's blood, would not mine kill you!
What? your myrtle-bush wants trimming?
　　Oh, that rose has prior claims—
Needs its leaden vase filled brimming?
　　Hell dry you up with its flames!
"Soliloquy of the Spanish Cloister," BROWNING

Now that I, tying the glass mask tightly,
May gaze through these faint smokes curling whitely,
As thou pliest thy trade in this devil's-smithy—
Which is the poison to poison her, prithee?
He is with her, and they know that I know
Where they are, what they do: they believe my tears flow
While they laugh, laugh at me, at me fled to the drear
Empty church, to pray God in, for them!—I am here.
"The Laboratory," BROWNING

### FEAR.

What's dat odder queer clickety sound I heah? Dere it is! Sound close! Sound like—sound like— Fo' God sake, sound like some nigger was shootin' crap! (Frightenedly) I better beat it quick when I gits dem notions. (He walks quickly into the clear space—then stands transfixed as he sees Jeff—in a terrified gasp.) *Who dar? Who dat? Is dat you, Jeff?* (Starting toward the other, forgetful for a moment of his surroundings and really believing it is a living man that he sees—in a tone of happy relief.) *Jeff! I'se sho' mighty glad to see you! Dey tol' me you done died from dat razor cut I gives you!* (Stopping suddenly, bewilderedly.) *But how you come to be heah, nigger?* (He stares fascinatedly at the other who continues his mechanical play with the dice. Jones' eyes begin to roll wildly. He stutters.) *Ain't you gwine—look up—can't you speak to me? Is you— is you—a ha'nt?*

The Emperor Jones, EUGENE O'NEILL

*Oh Lawd, Lawd! Oh Lawd, Lawd!* (Suddenly he throws himself on his knees and raises his clasped hands to the sky—in a voice of agonized pleading.) *Lawd Jesus, heah my prayer! I'se a po' sinner, a po' sinner! I knows I done wrong, I knows it! When I cotches Jeff cheatin' wid loaded dice my anger overcomes me and I kills him dead! Lawd, I done wrong! When dat guard hits me wid de whip, my anger overcomes me, and I kills him dead. Lawd, I done wrong! And down heah whar dese fool bush niggers raises me up to the seat o' de mighty, I steals all I could grab. Lawd, I done wrong! I knows it! I'se sorry! Forgive dis po' sinner!* (Then beseeching terrifiedly.) *And keep dem away, Lawd! Keep dem away from me! And stop dat drum soundin' in my ears! Dat begin to sound ha'nted, too.*

The Emperor Jones, EUGENE O'NEILL

### ANGER.

But if it does come to that, I know who I've got to thank for it, who it is that's blabbed to the manufacturers an' all the gentlemen round an' blackened my character to that extent that they never give me a hand's turn of work to do—an' set the peasants an' the millers against me, so that I'm often a whole week without a horse to shoe or a wheel to put a tire on. I know who's done it. I once pulled the damned brute off his horse, because he was givin' a little stupid boy the most awful flogging for stealin' a few unripe pears. But I tell you this, Kutsche, and you know me—if you get me put into prison, you may make your own will. If I hear as much as a whisper of it, I'll take the first thing as comes handy, whether it's a horse-shoe or a hammer, a wheelspoke or a pail; I'll get hold of you, if I've to drag you out of bed from beside your wife, and I'll beat in your brains, as sure as my name's Wittig.

The Weavers, GERHART HAUPTMANN

## References

1. Fairbanks, G., and Pronovost, W., "An Experimental Study of the Pitch Characteristics of the Voice During the Expression of Emotion," *Speech Monographs*, 6:87-104, 1939.
2. Hoaglin, L. W., "The Durational Aspects of Emotional Speech," M.A. thesis, State University of Iowa, 1937.
3. Lynch, G., "A Phonophotographic Study of Trained and Untrained Voices Reading Factual and Dramatic Material," *Archives of Speech*, 1:9-25, 1934.

## Additional Readings

Franklin, Miriam, *Rehearsal* (ed. 3). New York: Prentice-Hall, Inc., 1950, pp. 285-320.
Lee, Charlotte I., *Oral Interpretation*. Boston: Houghton Mifflin Co., 1952, pp. 380-381.
Parrish, Wayland Maxfield, *Reading Aloud* (ed. 3). New York: The Ronald Press Company, 1953, pp. 366-387.

# Variation of Emotional Tone

A THOROUGH ANALYSIS OF ANY SELECTION REVEALS THAT IT IS MADE UP not only of many ideas woven together to make a total impression, but also of many different kinds and degrees of emotion. In the play or the novel this rise and fall and shift of emotional content is obvious from one large section, act, or chapter to another. Closer inspection reveals smaller sections, episodes, scenes, each with its own emotional tone. But point by point, sentence by sentence, the thorough analysis reveals an ebb and flow, a shift and change of emotional content, sometimes subtle, sometimes obvious. It is difficult to find even a short passage with only one emotion expressed in it.

The writer has taken great care to vary the emotional content of his material, just as he has taken care that his thought moves forward and that his work is developed into a structural pattern. This development is part of the artistic principle of unity in variety which gives a richness of texture to the writing and which we find adds considerably to our interest in it.

We have already noted in the sections on analysis that there is an over-all mood or style, heavy or light, formal or informal, sad or gay, which colors the whole selection. Milton's "Lycidas," Shelley's "Adonais," Tennyson's "In Memoriam," and Arnold's "Thyrsis" all have a solemn, thoughtful, dignified mood fitting an elegy for a dead friend, but each has its lighter moments of remembered times and places, each its concern that such a friend should be lost, each its moment of looking forward. Galsworthy's The Apple Tree has hanging over it a mood of nostalgia, but there are moments of laughter, of love, of fear, of longing which come and go in the novel. James Thurber's Fables, although they do have a general air of ironical satire, are at moments serious, at others gay, at others matter of fact.

It is the task of the sensitive interpreter to find these various emotions and the different tones to express them in every selection he reads, and to unify them through his feeling for the structure of the selection and his sense of the limits imposed by the mood which permeates the whole piece. The variations of mood must not be permitted to seem out of place with or to get out of the bounds of the mood that frames the whole piece like a picture frame. It would not do, in the brawling "Chicago" of Carl Sandburg, to allow the voice to change to soft, melting tones for the passage about the women. Nor would it be in keeping to read the famous scene in Congreve's *The Way of the World* where Millament and Mirabel agree to marry (with certain provisos!) with the same rowdy abandon one would read the wooing scene in Shakespeare's *Taming of the Shrew*. There are limits of control and simulated good breeding imposed by the former which do not apply in the latter.

The reader does not often need to be warned, however, about overstepping the bounds of the "picture frame" by using too much variation in mood. We are all familiar with two kinds of bad reading which result from not having used enough or even any variation at all. In one, the interpreter sees no shades of meaning and emotion. Everything is read with a tone of indifference or boredom. In the other, the interpreter sees that there is strong emotion, but he expresses no shades of ideas or emotions. Everything is panted or gasped. The interpreter has caught the pervading mood and reads everything in his selection in this one emotional key. It is as if he had gone off and left his motor running, with the governor set, giving it no attention as the emotional load increases or decreases, and permitting the governor to keep the motor at a steady pace. Inexperienced readers often fall into this pattern, lulled into believing they are doing well because the general key is right. Actors often take their key from another (and stronger) actor and make the same error. To be sure you do not fall into any of these categories, learn to tone each selection and then to find different shades of emotion and meaning within it.

At first it may prove helpful to mark each emotion that is found and to consider the vocal and physical means of expressing it. Note, as you build the emotional pattern, its close relation to the thought structure. Note that sometimes emotional quality changes but little, at other times it seems to change considerably. But rarely does any feeling repeat itself exactly.

## EXERCISES

*1.* Mark the different emotions in the following speech and consider the toning that will best express each emotion. In practicing, with or without a recorder, be sure you are not expressing different emotions in the same way.

*You don't wan't to hear me, then? You'll listen to Rous and to that old man, but not to me. You'll listen to Sim Harness of the Union that's treated you so fair; maybe you'll listen to those men from London? Ah! You groan! What for? You love their feet on your necks, don't you? . . . Am I a liar, a coward, a traitor? If only I were, ye'd listen to me, I'm sure. Is there a man of you here that has less to gain by striking? Is there a man of you that had more to lose? Is there a man of you that has given up eight hundred pounds since this trouble began? Come now, is there? How much has Thomas given up—ten pounds or five, or what? You listened to him, and what had he to say? "None can pretend," he said, "that I'm not a believer in principle—but when Nature says: 'No further, 'tes going agenst Nature!'" I tell you if a man cannot say to Nature: "Budge me from this if ye can!"—his principles are but his belly. "Oh, but," Thomas says, "a man may be pure and honest, just and merciful, and take off his hat to Nature!" I tell you Nature's neither pure nor honest, just nor merciful. You chaps that live over the hill, an' go home dead beat in the dark on a snowy night—don't ye fight your way every inch of it? Do ye go lyin' down an' trustin' to the tender mercies of this merciful Nature? Try it and you'll soon know with what ye've got to deal. 'Tes only by that—(he strikes a blow with his clenched fist)— in Nature's face that a man can be a man.*

Strife, GALSWORTHY

*2.* Since the lyrical poem is often very nearly one piece of emotional fabric and since its changes are often very subtle, you may sharpen your sensitivity to emotional change by analysis of its emotional content. The following poem by Andrew Marvel ("To His Coy Mistress") is an especially interesting problem. Permeating the whole poem is a mood of frustration. Look carefully for the variety of feeling within this general framework. There is expectation, philosophic consideration, impatient, sad realization, fear, love, admiration, desire, even ironic humor. Label the moods in the margin and practice with voice and body to make them clear to your audience.

> Had we but world enough, and time,
> This coyness, Lady, were no crime,
> We would sit down and think which way
> To walk and pass our long love's day.
> Thou by the Indian Ganges' side
> Shouldst rubies find; I by the tide
> Of Humber would complain. I would
> Love you ten years before the Flood,
> And you should, if you please, refuse
> Till the conversion of the Jews;
> My vegetable love should grow
> Vaster than empires, and more slow;
> And hundred years should go to praise
> Thine eyes and on thy forehead gaze;
> Two hundred to adore each breast,
> But thirty thousand to the rest;
> An age at least to every part,
> And the last age should show your heart.
> For, Lady, you deserve this state,
> Nor would I love at lower rate.
> But at my back I always hear
> Time's wingèd chariot hurrying near;
> And yonder all before us lie
> Deserts of vast eternity.
> Thy beauty shall no more be found,
> Nor, in thy marble vault, shall sound
> My echoing song; then worms shall try
> That long preserved virginity,

And your quaint honor turn to dust,
And into ashes all my lust:
The grave's a fine and private place,
But none, I think, do there embrace.

Now therefore, while the youthful hue
Sits on thy skin like morning dew,
And while thy willing soul transpires
At every pore with instant fires,
Now let us sport us while we may,
And now, like amorous birds of prey,
Rather at once our time devour
Than languish in his slow-chappt power.
Let us roll all our strength and all
Our sweetness up into one ball,
And tear our pleasures with rough strife
Thorough the iron gates of life:
Thus, though we cannot make our sun
Stand still, yet we will make him run.

"To His Coy Mistress," ANDREW MARVELL

3. In a selection of your own choosing, but again in a tightly unified passage such as a lyrical poem, a long single speech from a novel or play, or a paragraph from an essay, find the changes of mood and through as much exaggeration in presentation as the key mood will permit make it more than usually clear to your audience how the moods in the selection change. Think of this as more of a trial run or rehearsal than a performance. The purpose of this exercise is to give you further opportunity to increase your variety of expression.

## Additional Readings

Bassett, Lee Emerson, *Handbook of Oral Reading.* Boston: Houghton Mifflin Co., 1917, pp. 105-115.

Clark, S. H., and Maud May Babcock, *Interpretation of the Printed Page.* New York: Prentice-Hall, Inc., 1940, pp. 245-278.

Cunningham, Cornelius C., *Literature as a Fine Art*. New York: Thomas Nelson & Sons, 1941, pp. 133-158.

Dolman, John, *The Art of Acting*. New York: Harper & Brothers, 1949, pp. 40-53.

Lowrey, Sara, and Gertrude E. Johnson, *Interpretative Reading: Techniques and Selections* (rev. ed.). New York: Appleton-Century-Crofts, Inc., 1953, pp. 146-151.

# Climax and Transition

THE INTERPRETER WHO HAS THE ABILITY TO IDENTIFY THE PLACE where a climax belongs in a selection and the skill to build a controlled climax in his presentation exhibits one of the important marks of artistry and self-discipline. The ability to identify the place where a climax should come is a sign of skillful and careful analysis, appreciation of the significance of structure, and sensitivity to relationships within the selection. The ability to build a controlled climax in presenting the selection is evidence that the interpreter has mastered the techniques of pitch, loudness, quality, and timing control in voice as well as physical control of the body.

Climax is a progressive increase in force throughout a passage culminating, at the close, in a peak or acme. The force may be the force of loudness, pitch, tempo, quality, or any combination of these, an increase in force of ideas, an increase in force of emotion, force of contrasts—anything that gives a feeling of rising toward a peak. It is as if one moved up a hill and over the hump at the top. Normally there is a build-up of tension, a sort of expectancy, which is released as the peak is reached. Some climaxes build slowly, some very quickly; some build to great heights of intensity, some are very mild. But all effective climaxes usually gather momentum as they proceed toward their culmination.

The most common type of climax builds through a paragraph or stanza or speech to the end, where the peak is reached and the tension falls away quickly. This rise, peaking, and fall of tension is easily observed in the following stanza from Sir Walter Scott's "Lochinvar."

> One touch to her hand and one word in her ear,
> When they reached the hall-door, and the charger stood near;
> So light to the croupe the fair lady he swung,

So light to the saddle before her he sprung!
'She is won! we are gone, over bank, bush, and scaur;
They'll have fleet steeds that follow," quoth young Lochinvar.

The force of excitement increases steadily and quickly until it peaks in the next to the last line, then falls away in the last line. Study of the whole poem will reveal that this stanza is the peak of a series of mounting tensions in the poem, which are released in the final stanza which follows the one above.

Sometimes the climax appears in the middle of the passage with a more leisurely letting down of tension from the peak. The following paragraph from the opening chapter of John Steinbeck's The Grapes of Wrath peaks just past the middle in the sentence beginning "After a while the face of the watching men . . ." and slowly relaxes to the end:

The people came out of their houses and smelled the hot stinging air and covered their noses from it. And the children came out of the houses, but they did not run or shout as they would have done after a rain. Men stood by their fences and looked at the ruined corn, drying fast now, only a little green showing through the film of dust. The men were silent and they did not move often. And the women came out of the houses to stand beside their men—to feel whether this time the men would break. The women studied the men's faces secretly, for the corn could go, as long as something else remained. The children stood near by, drawing figures in the dust with bare toes, and the children sent exploring senses out to see whether men and women would break. The children peeked at the faces of the men and women, and then drew careful lines in the dust with their toes. Horses came to the watering troughs and nuzzled the water to clear the surface dust. After a while the faces of the watching men lost their bemused perplexity and became hard and angry and resistant. Then the women knew that they were safe and that there was no break. Then they asked, What'll we do? And the men replied, I don't know. But it was all right. The women knew it was all right, and the watching children knew it was all right. Women and children knew deep in themselves that no misfortune was too great to bear if their men were whole. The women went into the houses to their work, and the children began to play, but cautiously at first. As the day went forward the sun became less red. It flared down on the dust-blanketed land. The men sat in the doorways of their houses; their hands were busy with sticks and little rocks. The men sat still— thinking—figuring.

Rarely the writer begins at a peak and works away from it. Note A. E. Housman's use of this technique:

> Shot? so quick, so clean an ending?
> Oh that was right, lad, that was brave:
> Yours was not an ill for mending,
> 'Twas best to take it to the grave.
>
> Oh you had forethought, you could reason
> And saw your road and where it led,
> And early wise and brave in season
> Put the pistol to your head. . . .

Five more stanzas explore the implications of the suicide, but the peak was reached in the first word. All that follows is a falling away.

It is clear, then, that the climax may appear anywhere in the passage, but that there is always the characteristic rhythm of rise, peak, and fall. Long passages or selections usually have several climaxes, often related, and building to a major climax for the selection. A full-length play may have twenty or more such peaks. A motion picture is often built with a peak of tension every ten minutes or so. The novel can afford to be more leisurely in building climaxes.

The interpreter will choose his technique for each climax in accordance with his material. Sometimes he will steadily increase loudness, sometimes he will raise his pitch from step to step toward the peak. Some materials call for steadily increasing emotional energy. Quite frequently the tempo becomes faster as the reader approaches the point of highest excitement, then slows down as the tension decreases. Many selections do not demand a steady increase of force, but dictate climaxes built from level to level with a holding steady for periods of time. It is as if you climbed a step then took a few steps forward on a level floor, then up another step and the few steps forward, repeated until the top is reached. The possibilities for technique are numerous and the materials will suggest the right technique or combination of techniques to the alert interpreter.

Artistry in the employment of climax comes from judgment and control. Judgment is involved both in choosing the technique to be used and in selecting the degree of change to be used. Control is exhibited when the interpreter so disciplines his vocal and physical mechanism that he accomplishes what he set out to do with ease and does not go beyond his mark. The climax that is too weak, that fails to build to a peak commensurate with the demands of the materials, is a disappointment. The climax that rises too high, particularly if it results in vocal or physical strain, is an embarrassment to the audience. The interpreter who reaches the end of his pitch range, the maximum of his loudness, the top of his speed, the limit of his emotional power disappoints his audience and is often an object of laughter as well. The building of climaxes needs considerable rehearsal.

Another technique which if handled successfully leaves an impression of artistry with an audience is the technique of transitions, the process of changing from one idea or part to another. Dozens of devices are employed to indicate change—words of time such as *then, when, later, in a little while,* etc.; words of direction, such as *up, down, farther, left, on the north,* etc.; words of order, such as *first, second, in the beginning, later,* etc. Sometimes whole sentences indicate transitions. Sometimes ideas change by association: some stimulus in the earlier passage sets off a train of thought in the following passage. Sometimes there is a break of stanza, paragraph, scene, or chapter. Again there may be no word or visible sign to mark the place of transition.

But the interpreter must never leave the audience in doubt as to the place of transition. The need for clarity has already been discussed. If there is a word or phrase it must be sufficiently stressed to call attention to it. If there is an association of ideas, stress may again serve to mark the change. When there is no word, the interpreter must use other techniques. One of these is the pause. Long or short, the pause indicates a break, but a more extended pause than usual normally signals a transition into a new idea to an audience. Strong transitions are indicated on occasion by combining the pause with some change of bodily position. Any marked change of pace, change of emotional quality, change of loudness level, or even change of pitch warns the listener to expect a change of idea or structure or feeling in the selection. The important principle to be grasped is that the change must be sufficiently marked that the audience does not miss it. The inexperienced performer more often leaves his transitions insufficiently marked than not. It is well, then, in rehearsal to pay them particular attention.

## EXERCISES

1. Turn back to the poem by Andrew Marvel in the previous project. Note what transitional material the poet supplies. Note also where there are important transitions for which no words are provided. Plan your means of making clear to an audience where the changes in thought and feeling occur.

At the same time, locate the climax of the poem, the course the poet pursues in building toward it and his means of releasing tension after the peak has been reached.

Practice to read the poem in such a way that the transitions are unmistakable and the climax develops sufficient power to have its emotional impact.

2. Choose a favorite ballad or narrative poem to present with special emphasis on building to a climax. Remember, neither too little nor too much, but all under control.

## Additional Readings

Bassett, Lee Emerson, *Handbook of Oral Reading*. Boston: Houghton Mifflin Co., 1917, pp. 83-88.

Henneke, Ben Graf, *Reading Aloud Effectively*. New York: Rinehart & Company, Inc., 1954, pp. 25-27.

Lowrey, Sara, and Gertrude E. Johnson, *Interpretative Reading: Techniques and Selections* (rev. ed.). New York: Appleton-Century-Crofts, Inc., 1953, pp. 134-146.

Woolbert, Charles H., and Severina E. Nelson, *The Art of Interpretative Speech* (ed. 4). New York: Appleton-Century-Crofts, Inc., 1956, pp. 325-326.

# Synthesis and Evaluation of Progress

FOR THIS ASSIGNMENT SELECT AN ACTION SCENE OF EIGHT TO TWELVE minutes in length from a short story or novel which builds to or sustains a high level of emotional intensity. Choose a passage that is for the most part self-contained—that is, it should need little advance explanation, and it should not be broken by expository and descriptive passages of such length that they dissipate the emotional tensions of the passage. You may discover that some sentences, even paragraphs, can be omitted for your purposes. The action of the selected material should move to some sort of climax and solution which will give it a feeling of being at least momentarily complete.

Prepare to present this material as a demonstration of your skill in controlling emotional materials. Build to a moving climax, show a knowledge of the principles of variety within unity. Make your transitions clear. You will need all your skill in assimilation, analysis, and physical and vocal expressiveness to move your audience emotionally.

You will have in mind a favorite story. If you do not, perhaps one of the following which other interpreters have enjoyed presenting would be acceptable to you.

| | |
|---|---|
| Jane Austin | *Pride and Prejudice* |
| Stephen Vincent Benét | "The Devil and Daniel Webster," from *Thirteen O'Clock* |
| Willa Cather | "Paul's Case," from *Youth and the Bright Medusa* |
| Charles Dickens | *Christmas Carol; Tale of Two Cities* |
| George Elliot | *Adam Bede; Silas Marner* |
| F. Scott Fitzgerald | "May Day," from *Tales of the Jazz Age* |

| | |
|---|---|
| John Galsworthy | *The Apple Tree* |
| Ernest Hemingway | "The Killers," from *Men Without Women* |
| Katherine Mansfield | "Life of Ma Parker," from *The Garden Party* |
| William March | "Nine Prisoners," from *Company K* |
| Leonard Q. Ross | "Mr. Kaplan and the Magi," from *The Education of Hyman Kaplan* |
| William Saroyan | "Where I Come From People Are Polite," from *Little Children* |
| Edith Wharton | *Ethan Frome* |

# 10

# PROJECTS IN

# Selecting and Arranging Material

[PROJECT 10.1]
*Selecting Material to Present*

[PROJECT 10.2]
**Arranging the Program**

[PROJECT 10.3]
*Synthesis and Evaluation of Progress*

# [PROJECT 10.1]

# Selecting Material to Present

ONE OF THE MAJOR CONCERNS OF EVERY PERFORMER IN THE ENTER-tainment field is the selection of his material, for he knows that no matter how skillful he is, he cannot long survive in such a competitive field if his material is poor. Thus the famous star must spend long hours in search of new material, reading many bad plays hoping to find a good one or working laboriously through magazines, newspapers, and books in the search of ideas and copy for sketches, readings, stories, or poetry adaptable or usable as they are. The interpreter who is just beginning is faced with the same problem, and sometimes uses more time wondering what to present than on any other aspect of his preparation.

There is, of course, no easy road to material selection, and no one can put down a set of rules to follow, much less provide a list of sure-fire poems, plays, and stories. So many factors must be considered and so many variables in the situation must be weighed one against the other that in the end someone has to make a judgment. It is very much like buying a house, a car, a suit of clothes, or draperies for your window. You must weigh so many factors—cost, durability, styling, use, personal peculiarities of your taste, tastes of friends and neighbors, etc.—that there is rarely a clear-cut answer to your question of which is better.

But selecting material to interpret can be based on a studied judgment of all factors involved. One rarely makes a serious error in selection if he has considered his choice in relation to the occasion on which it is to be presented, the audience that is to hear it, the interests and qualifications of the person who is to present it, the quality of the material itself, and the availability of the material for public performance.

292

The nature of the occasion at which the interpretation is to be presented often limits and sometimes suggests the kind of material that would be suitable. Is this a dinner meeting with a program to follow? Is it a regular meeting of a study club or a special meeting called to do honor to a retiring member? Is it a class meeting of people studying interpretation? Is it a public affair for which tickets have been sold for the express purpose of presenting you or a group of readers? Is it a worship service in which you have been invited to participate? Your knowledge of what goes on at such meetings (gained from experience or from inquiry) will help you in judging the length of selection desirable, may suggest a suitable type of subject matter, and may even suggest an acceptable kind of mood for the material. Light, humorous material usually goes well at the after-dinner meeting, but it would be in bad taste at the worship service. The audience that has paid to hear you would no doubt welcome an intellectual challenge in at least some portion of your program, as well as material with some emotional impact, for it probably expects the performer on such an occasion to "show his wares."

The place of the meeting (another aspect of the occasion) has its influence on the selection of material, too. Small living rooms or tiny club rooms are somewhat strained with a presentation of *Tamburlaine the Great* or the brawling quality of Sandburg's "Chicago." Intimate materials which would be at home in these small places, however, would be lost in the large auditorium where much of the audience is so far away as to be unable to discern subtle changes of facial expression and bodily muscular adjustment. In addition, the habitual uses of the meeting room will affect choice of material. A room used regularly for religious purposes is probably not the place to present lusty and even irreverent materials. A room dedicated to performances in the arts invites a wide range of materials. A night club would not be the place to present seriously philosophical or religious poetry.

The purpose of including interpretation on the program bears examination, too. Has it been included for the sake of variety, something to lighten up an otherwise monotonous program? Is it there as an inconspicuous element? Or is it to be made the focus of attention, the *pièce de résistance*? If it is the former, it would be in bad taste to choose an overlong or taxing selection. If the latter, the reader would be expected to choose a somewhat ambitious selection. Usually a word with the program chairman is sufficient to settle the matter. He will be glad to explain his purpose in including your part of the program.

The audience must unquestionably be given a careful scrutiny before one can have confidence that the materials he chooses are suitable. Scholars in the field of rhetoric and public address, long aware of the audience's importance in the speaking situation, have reported the results of much observation and research in audience analysis useful to the interpreter. They have shown the importance of recognizing that the experience and the attitudes of the audience will color its reactions to the speaker and his material. One must seek the answers to questions about average age and age range, educational background, reading habits, travel, and occupational and outside interests as indexes to the store of knowledge, breadth of thought, and general sophistication one may encounter. If the audience has had no experience with a subject, then the treatment of that subject must be especially clear and easy to follow. If it has had experience with the subject, then the audience will have much to contribute. One must be particularly careful in gauging the tastes of the audience, its special likes and dislikes, the kind of material it may find offensive and the kind it finds notably admirable or pleasing. One should never offend an audience by presenting material with subjects or vocabulary that are taboo in that group. Some audiences are pleased with fantasy and romantically imaginative materials. Others think they are a silly waste of time and prefer "meaty" psychological explorations of character, philosophical considerations and implications in the material, or sociological or historical studies. Others are sophisticated enough to enjoy lyrical poetry, Greek and Elizabethan drama, or the experimental writings of Gertrude Stein and James Joyce. Nearly all audiences, however, can be held by a story, particularly if it is devised with some suspense and has in it one or more characters who appeal.

The experience of the audience with interpreters—be they readers, actors, or announcers—makes some difference, too. They may have grown to expect certain forms of platform behavior; they may have learned to expect a pleasant experience; and they may have learned to recognize and appreciate fine technique when it is before them. The broader their experience with interpretation the greater the range of materials and manners of presentation that are likely to please.

There may even be a preformed attitude toward the performer. Almost never will he encounter hostile feelings. If the audience has never heard him before, he is usually accorded the courtesy of a friendly, expectant attitude. If he is relatively inexperienced, the attitude is usually one of encouragement and a willingness to overlook the fact that the interpreter's art has not yet been perfected. After all, the audience is as eager for the interpreter to succeed as he is. They want to enjoy this experience. Sometimes, of course, an interpreter gains a reputation for a particular kind of performance. If he is known as a comedian, it is difficult for him to be taken seriously on serious material. If he is well known for skillful reading of Dickens' novels, an audience will probably be disappointed if he does not include something of Dickens in the program.

Judging the thoughts and feelings of an audience accurately demands time and ingenuity, particularly if it is a group of which the interpreter is not or has not been a part. Aspects of the audience's thought and feeling which make the most difference are not ordinarily reported on in most studies. This unwritten climate of feeling and opinion must be sensed, sampled, and probed by questions to available members of the group (the program chairman will assist the interpreter). Conversation, patterns of social behavior such as church attendance, lecture attendance, library usage, and other manifestations of their interests and prejudices provide useful information. Their habits of entertainment and recreation can reveal their real interests, very often more accurately than their activities which they look on as proper and dutiful.

The relationship between the performer and the selection of his material is largely influenced by two considerations: What is he interested in? What do his skills best fit him to present? It is assumed that the interpreter has some kind of interest in literature or he would never have become an interpreter. It is also assumed that like most people he has his preferences. Through continued reading and study the range of his interests will broaden and new preferences will develop as he matures further as a person and as an artist. But the interpreter will do well to choose materials that interest him at the moment because he finds them moving or intellectually challenging or particularly apropos of the times and the occasion, or because they are especially well written, or because they appeal in any way that strikes his fancy. Material that is not interesting or stimulating to the interpreter can rarely be made very absorbing to the audience.

A narrow range of interest can usually be attributed, however, to a limited acquaintance with literature. The poems, stories, and plays we have read and studied closely often, if not usually, become interesting to us. They are like old friends to whom we turn. We observe, too, that the "authority" on a given kind of literature is not only the most enthusiastic or interested person in that kind of literature, but he also seems to reap the most pleasure and satisfaction from it. The best course, then, for the person who has few interests in literature is to study some of it intensively.

Related to the subject of interest in the material, therefore, is the interpreter's understanding of it. Nearly all materials will yield to close study, but it does seem to be a fact that interpreters (and people who do not interpret) understand in a total way some materials better than others. There is less sensitivity, less response to, and less ability to project or communicate some emotional material than others. We recognize the fact that some materials are "wrong" for certain readers, "right" for others. Being right for a reading or a role is not simply a matter of physical suitability; there is also an aspect of emotional and intellectual understanding to be considered. The actor or reader or announcer or storyteller should seek to find the kind of material he understands best. Usually he can sense when the material is right for him, and a discerning friend or teacher can often help to point out the kind of material he seems to understand best.

The wise performer always asks whether he is equipped in performance skill and natural gifts to present the selections he is considering for a program. The seasoned reader has learned to refuse to perform certain selections because he cannot perform them well: the sonority demanded in the reading of the lines is more than his voice can produce, the emotional intensity in the material is too great for him, the need for emphatic action is so great that his physical resources will be strained. If he has never studied phonetics and dialects, the performer will beware the selection which depends upon accuracy of dialect for its successful presentation.

On the other hand, the prospective interpreter should be careful not to underrate his abilities. Few performers ever believe they have perfected their skills, but an objective and dispassionate evaluation of them made in reference to the demands of a selection being considered for inclusion on a program can be an important guide. There is almost always adequate skill for presenting some kind of material.

Perhaps the subtlest consideration of all in the inventory of the interpreter's skills and assets is that of the empathic response others normally have to him as a person. Each of us is put together physically in a unique way and each of us has a pattern of muscular tensions characteristic of our persons and personalities. These affect our associates—all who see us—with an impact which leaves an impression of our emotional quality upon them. In some people the effect is so strong that they are limited to gangly, gawky comic materials. In others the effect is always that of sensitivity, warmth, and affection. The latter kind of person never can play the villain. This effect upon others does not seem to be a trustworthy index of what is inside the person, but it should always be an important element in considering material he can present. The casting director recognizes this aspect of the actor to be of primary importance. It is not the sort of problem people will find easy to discuss with him, but the interpreter should watch closely the kind of roles (in or out of plays) directors cast him in, the kind of assumptions people tend to make about his feelings. He should ask what kind of material he is most successful in performing. All of these considerations should provide clues.

One other consideration in regard to the interpreter is the time available for preparation. Be realistic in recognizing the difficulty of a selection and the number of hours that will be required for an adequate preparation. Audiences will excuse much but they do not easily forgive the interpreter who has not prepared sufficiently.

Judging the quality of literature is the particular profession of the literary critic, but it is also the prerogative of every individual who reads or hears literature, and the material presented will be judged by everyone, not simply for its subject matter appeal but for the quality of its writing, too. As long as the subject matter is also interesting, audiences prefer to hear material that is artistically written. The interpreter who has read much has developed taste and judgment, but many are not sure enough to be confident in their choices without other checks. Therefore, they turn to critical reviews for expert opinions. They check to see whether anthologists have thought well enough of the piece to include it in their collections. They give the selection a time and usage test of their own to discover whether repetition of reading and close study bring out more and more values and pleasure in the piece, or whether it then seems empty or false or boring. Selections that reveal their full meaning and significance at a first or second reading are rarely satisfactory as materials for the interpreter's art.

There is, of course, a wealth of good material all around us. The biggest problem is to make time to search for and read it. A regular program of browsing in the library, even for a few minutes every other day, soon turns up far more material than there is ever time to work up for presentation. There is usually a backlog of materials "to do some day."

A few generalizations may be made about the kind of material to choose, however. For instance, it should have clarity. If the material is not so written that its meaning is clear, an audience can hardly be expected to grasp it at one sitting. This is not to say that its meaning must be simple, for many difficult concepts and interrelationships have been stated clearly. Nor should one rule out the subtle, for there is much delight to be had in finely drawn discriminations of idea or impression. But muddy expression, only half-realized expression, is rarely worth the effort of preparation.

Another quality of desirable materials is vividness and vitality of expression. Palely expressed imagery rarely moves an audience. The vivid picture, the vigorous dialogue, the movement of well-written action prove stimulating and satisfying to interpreter and audience alike.

Material with a narrative or story threaded into it is almost always interesting to an audience, particularly if there is a vivid character or two involved. We are drawn to Robert Browning's character studies in large part because there is the suggestion of a story to carry us along. The epic, the ballad, the short story, the novel, and the play have long been popular with the interpreter because of their narrative nature.

One warning to the inexperienced person is necessary at this point. Read carefully all statements of rights, copyrights, and restrictions before you present materials in public. Plays are usually restricted for public performance and the payment of a royalty is required. Many other materials are restricted in much the same way. Written permission from the author or the publisher may be required before performance is permitted. Do not assume that permission will always be forthcoming and proceed to prepare for performance. Sometimes bitter disappointment is the result.

There will always be factors too subtle to be judged and factors unknown to the interpreter as he builds his program, but not very often will he make a grievous error if he considers the nature of the occasion on which he is to appear, the special attitudes, backgrounds, and interests of his audience, his own capacities and interests, and the quality of his material.

# EXERCISES

*1.* Using the next meeting of your class as the occasion and audience, choose a selection to present. Outline your analysis of occasion, audience, yourself, and the material. Evaluate your choice of material in the light of your analysis.

*2.* Choose material for the program of some club or organization in the community. Present an analysis of what made you think the material chosen would be suitable.

## Additional Readings

Aggertt, Otis J., and Elbert R. Bowen, *Communicative Reading.* New York: The Macmillan Co., 1956, pp. 18-39.

Henneke, Ben Graf, *Reading Aloud Effectively*. New York: Rinehart & Company, Inc., pp. 53-59.

Johnson, Gertrude E., ed., *Studies in the Art of Interpretation*. New York: D. Appleton-Century Co., 1940, pp. 196-200.

Lee, Charlotte I., *Oral Interpretation*. Boston: Houghton Mifflin Co., 1952, pp. 13-16.

Lowrey, Sara, and Gertrude E. Johnson, *Interpretative Reading* (rev. ed.). New York: Appleton-Century-Crofts, Inc., 1953, pp. 243-253.

# Arranging the Program

SELECTING PROGRAM CONTENT AND ARRANGING IT FOR PRESENTATION
are processes which many times challenge the ingenuity and creative
powers of the reader. Even though individual selections may be well
made, their effect is often vitiated if not spoiled by poor arrangement
or a poor sense of what needs to be left out. Almost as many kinds
of programs are possible as there are combinations of interpreters,
audiences, and occasions. But whether they are long or short, certain
principles of selection and arrangement must be followed to give the
program unity and focus, coherence and clarity, artistic purpose and
impact. Some performances may be as brief as a four-line poem,
others may last for a full evening, but each should have a discernible
character which comes from theme, thought, form, or some one
aspect of the material. This focus is easy to manage when the program is brief. The longer program, particularly the lecture recital and
the cutting from a novel, play, or long poem needs special study.

The lecture recital is a reading program. Lecture recitals are of
many kinds, but they are always made up of selections of related
materials organized around an idea, theme, technique, specific content, or quality which helps to give the program unity. The good
lecture recital is never a hodge-podge of selections; a specific purpose
always binds them together. This is in principle the same kind of
specific purpose that is to be found in a single selection: a subject,
an idea, a thesis to be made clear, an emotional experience to be had,
an esthetic experience to be lived through.

The lecture recital may be built in many ways. One of these is to
so select materials that they reveal some particular aspect of an author
—a favorite theme, a recurring character, his "best" story, his humor,
his use of unusual rhythm patterns, anything which appeals to the

reader and he believes he can make into an interesting program for an audience. The possibilities here are almost endless. A program on Thomas Hardy might take any one of dozens of turns: characters in *Satires of Circumstance*, a cutting from the novel, *Tess of the D'Urbervilles* or *The Mayor of Casterbridge*, the recurring theme of chance and change, etc., etc. A program of F. Scott Fitzgerald might be a long cutting from any one of his works of fiction (*The Beautiful and Damned, The Great Gatsby, All the Sad Young Men*); it might be a selection of passages which reveals the Paris of America's expatriates in the twenties; or New York City and Long Island society in the postwar and predepression years could serve as a topic for a lecture recital. The point is that the interpreter selects a unified body of material which will illustrate or present something about or of an author and which will give an audience some feeling that it grasps or understands the specific purpose the interpreter had in mind.

The lecture recital may develop a single theme as it is treated by several authors. One could make many interesting programs from the love poetry of Edna St. Vincent Millay, Elinor Wylie, John Crowe Ransom, Emily Dickinson, Amy Lowell, A. E. Housman, and Elizabeth Barrett Browning. Their attitudes toward their own feelings while in love could be compared or contrasted. Their attitudes toward faithfulness, the abiding quality of love, sacrifices of one lover for another, or the transforming powers of love—there are many possibilities—could be set side by side to illustrate a theme. The success of such a lecture recital depends in part on the sharpness with which the interpreter focuses on a theme, how painstakingly he has selected his material so that nothing in it is off-theme, and how skillfully, through his own remarks and through his manner of presentation, he keeps clear to his audience what the theme is.

Other ways of selecting material for a lecture recital will occur to the thoughtful student. Many of them require considerable research in the collection of materials for reading and in backgrounds which illuminate them. The person who has had very little experience ought to begin very simply by preparing a ten- to fifteen-minute performance which presents the handling of a single theme by one author. The presentation need not, probably should not, be exhaustive, but it should range over at least two or three works of the author. One could present a lecture recital on Robert Frost's treatment of the taciturn New Englander by reading parts of "Death of the Hired Man," "The Fear," and "Home Burial." One could give a good sampling of Carl Sandburg's attitude toward the American people by reading a few passages from "The People, Yes," "Chicago," and "Prairie" (from *Cornhuskers*).

For one who has a good literary background, choosing an author to study and present will not be difficult, but if one has little literary background, the following suggestions may be helpful. First of all, consider your own tastes: Do you like humor? Then investigate the humorists. If nature and rural life holds particular appeal for you, then investigate those who like to write about nature or rural living. Some writers are sophisticated, some are more philosophic than others, some write about city life. Or perhaps you may want to investigate an author because you have heard a great deal about him and would like to know more.

Second, select a writer whose works will reward the time you put on them and choose selections that will bear repetition. Some works that seem interesting and clever at first reading do not stand repetition. If you do not feel able to judge what selections will bear repeating, then consider whether or not the author has been read and studied through a generation or two and still continues to be read and studied. If so, his works will probably reward your study.

Third, select an author who has a variety of moods or facets in his writing. A little humor is sometimes a welcome relief from intense feeling and serious philosophy, for instance.

Last, seek works that have universal appeal to what is fundamental in all people, works that show the author's originality and individuality of expression and are not trite, and works that set your imagination to working after you have put down the text. Such works are appreciated more and more as one becomes better and better acquainted with them.

In preparing the lecture recital, read enough about the author to feel that you know him well. Then look for the selections that best reveal the traits you see in him, the theme you desire to present, or any other aspect of his writing that you have chosen. Study and appreciate his language, the organization of his ideas, the purposes he has in each selection, the audience to which each selection is addressed. See how each part of each selection is related to and reveals the purpose.

When you have completed your study of the author's background, his writings and their contexts, it is time to arrange your program. Determine the order of presentation you believe will be most effective. You will not only have a general purpose (to entertain or inform or persuade or inspire), but you should have a specific purpose as well. It is to be hoped you can arrange and select your materials so effectively that you have an esthetic experience to offer your audience. Failing that, surely you can manage to move them emotionally—even a smile or a chuckle is evidence of emotion—or to give them some kind of intellectual understanding: "One of ———'s most charming themes is to be found in his recurring treatment of nostalgia for a lost love," or "The tender love for children plays hide and seek among the lines of all of ———'s nonsense verse."

When you are sure of your purpose and have arranged your selections in the best possible order, plan how much explanation you will need for your audience. Introductions are always useful even if they are as brief as an announcement of the author's name and the selection's title, but for the lecture recital of materials from several sources something more is usually needed: a few sentences that announce the subject (author and particular aspect of the author you expect to treat), a few words about the author (if the audience is unfamiliar with him and these facts are useful in getting the kind of understanding and sympathetic hearing you want), whatever background or explanation or introduction of characters or résumé of material you are omitting, and any other remarks you believe are necessary. You may decide that all your remarks can be included in an introduction; you may decide that some need to precede each selection. But wherever they come, keep them as brief as possible. Your function is not that of literary critic or literary historian. Be very careful not to say things the selections say for themselves. The chances are that your author will say them better; the audience will probably need to hear them only once; and the audience will doubtless prefer to "discover" these things for itself.

The lecture recital made up of several selections or parts of selections is not always the kind of program most desirable for a particular occasion. Nor does that kind of program always challenge the performer. One of the best tests of the talents and skills of the interpreter is his reading of a novel or play. These readings, frequently called play or novel reviews, are very popular and in great demand as entertainment for organized groups and clubs where plays cannot be produced successfully because of inadequate space and equipment. However, neither the play nor the novel can be read in its entirety in the time usually allotted for such programs, so they must both be shortened.

To cut a play or novel demands full understanding of the author and a sensitive appreciation of what he is trying to do. Otherwise the cutting may be a mutilation. Understanding of what the author is trying to do involves sensitive appreciation of the structure of the piece. Before a reader is ready to read a play or novel he must have become acquainted with his own peculiar interests, skills, and limitations, and this knowledge should lead him to the material he wants to work with and should use. The fact that a reading has been very successful with one reader does not mean that it will necessarily be successful with another.

Several warnings need to be made at this point. First, and most important to the pocketbook, the reader is again reminded to give the copyright a careful study.

A second warning is that the reading of a play or novel demands more than acting a role in a play. Aside from the sheer vitality and energy necessary to hold the attention of an audience for forty-five minutes to an hour, the reader must remember that attention is on him and what he is doing without relief or respite. Most novices do not realize how much strength it takes to present an entire evening's program and do not rehearse a program from start to finish often enough to build up their strength. It goes without saying that such a performance demands all the interpreter's vocal and physical skills.

Making cuttings has often been compared to making gravy. Almost everybody does it—some better than others—but almost nobody uses a recipe. It is suggested to those who are not used to making cuttings that they do not think in terms of cutting, but consider, and frankly state, that they are reading those portions of the play or novel that seem most impressive and interesting to them. Then a rather definite procedure may be established.

First, select a play or novel that centers around rather few characters. Though we can all suggest a number of characters, trying to characterize more than five invites superficial treatment, which we do not want, because everybody has vocal limitations which he should not forget. Second, select a play or novel that will exploit your particular skills and abilities and background of understanding. If you enjoy and understand humorous more than dramatic selections, then select a whimsical or humorous play or novel. Third, select a play or novel that has relatively few climactic scenes. And last, but by no means least, select a play or novel that will reward the many hours that must be spent with it. No cutting should be made until after several readings of the work. Too many interpreters read a selection hastily, spend a great deal of time cutting it, and then, when they start serious practice, find they are tired of their material.

After about the third reading of the play or novel, close the book and write down the sections or scenes that are most vivid, interesting, and climactic to you. From these, select from one to five, depending on the length of reading time at your disposal. Now return to the script and put marks around the scenes you have selected. Depending on the reading time at your disposal, cut each scene to not less than five minutes. Then, if possible, find bridging parts between scenes. If this is not possible, narrate the connecting bits quite frankly and openly. Lastly, lay the background for your first scene, in the words of the author if possible. If not, describe the opening events in your own words. Be brief and to the point. You will not need to include all the details the author has furnished you. The audience will be able to fill in much of the background by inference from the scenes you read. Other details may not be necessary to their enjoyment and understanding.

It is always painful to dispense with choice bits and expressions. What, then, can be omitted from the scenes you do choose to read? A good general rule is to omit anything that can be shown by the vocal and physical behavior of the reader. Both novelists and play-

wrights must include material that is essentially stage directions—
how something is said, or the nature and mood of the speaker. This
can be suggested by the reader. If an interpreter is skilled in charac-
terization and there are not too many characters, it is not necessary
to state who is speaking, and the *he said's* and *she said's* that so
frequently break the mood of what is being said can be cut. Finally,
in the reading of favorite scenes, the entrances and exits of characters that give variety to long scenes when a work is performed in
its entirety can be omitted.

In general it is well to include the passages full of action, omitting where possible long descriptions, incidents from the past, and
lengthy philosophizings. Action and suspense command attention;
use them as powerful allies in controlling your audience. If the
material is well written the meaning of the action should be clear
without further exposition.

A little experience with selecting and cutting short stories will
prepare one for the selection and cutting of longer works. A good
rule to consider is that short stories should not exceed twenty minutes
in length, and cuttings of longer prose or poetic selections should not
exceed an hour.

# EXERCISES

1. Select a magazine that is available to all members of the group
and has a number of short stories, such as the *Saturday Evening Post*,
read all the stories, and choose the one you feel will be the best for
cutting. Be ready to defend your choice.

2. Following the suggestions for cutting that have been made,
make a cutting of the short story you have selected.

3. Read *John Brown's Body* by Stephen Vincent Benét and be
ready to suggest methods for cutting this long narrative poem.

4. From among the many themes that have caught your interest
as you have browsed in the library and from the works of three or four

authors who deal with one of these themes build a program of about twenty minutes in length. Focus your selection of materials and your introductory remarks on a specific purpose that is simple and clear.

## Additional Readings

Aggertt, Otis J., and Elbert R. Bowen, *Communicative Reading.* New York: The Macmillan Co., 1956, pp. 369-370.

Boardman, Gail, *Oral Communication of Literature.* New York: Prentice-Hall, Inc., 1952, pp. 289-309.

Crocker, Lionel, and Louis M. Eich, *Oral Reading* (ed. 2). New York: Prentice-Hall, Inc., 1955, pp. 195-209.

Henneke, Ben Graf, *Reading Aloud Effectively.* New York: Rinehart & Company, Inc., 1954, pp. 59-62.

Lowrey, Sara, and Gertrude E. Johnson, *Interpretative Reading: Techniques and Selections* (rev. ed.). New York: Appleton-Century-Crofts, Inc., 1953, pp. 243-253.

# Synthesis and Evaluation
# of Progress

THE ULTIMATE PURPOSE OF THE INTERPRETER IS TO BRING THE experience of a piece of literature to an audience with such authority of technique, such insights into the meaning of the piece, and such emotional and intellectual impact that the experience becomes a memorable one for everyone present. Accomplishing so satisfying an objective is no mere accident. Nor is it simply the result of inspiration at the moment of performance. Experienced performers know full well that these memorable occasions result from careful selection of material, intense study of it to the point where the material is fully understood and assimilated, and a presentation marked by control of articulation, voice, and body skills. The student who has mastered the techniques and processes described in the projects of this book should be ready to appear before an audience and entertain it with a thoroughly effective program.

The satisfaction derived from the experience of a longer selection is usually greater than from that of several shorter selections. One long play usually gives more pleasure than three one-act plays. Assuming that all are of approximately even merit, a novel usually gives more pleasure than several short stories.

Prepare a full program, of forty-five minutes to an hour in duration, that is a cutting from a novel or a play. Since the presentation will prove a very taxing experience, be sure to train for it by rehearsing the entire performance several times. Gauge your strength and endurance carefully and do not let the excitement of an audience stimulate you to pitch the performance too intensely at the beginning for you to reach the climaxes as they arrive further along in the selection. The result would be a flat and disappointing performance without the contrasts you had planned.

Invite an audience or get yourself invited to appear before an audience other than the class before which you have been accustomed to appear. Analyze your audience to be sure your selection is right.

Dress simply, but dress up. Your audience will be pleased, and they will be alerted that this is to be an *occasion*. Their anticipation will be whetted, and your battle is well on the way to being won. Keep your dress simple so that it does not vie with you for attention.

Look to the physical arrangements, being sure there is sufficient light on your face and body, that you have some suitable place to rest your book, and that you are in full view of the audience. The program chairman will be glad to help you with these arrangements— will usually attend to them for you—if you will make your needs clear. Remember that program chairmen err not willfully nor from laziness, but because they, not being performers, do not *know* what is needed.

Keep calm. If you are prepared, there is nothing to worry about. And do not mistake the excitement (even to trembling) of the anticipated experience for stage fright. Performers are almost invariably keyed up before they go on stage. Within limits that feeling is good, for it usually means they are physically and mentally and emotionally poised and awake, ready to respond sensitively to their material, to themselves, and to the audience. Enjoy yourself. The audience is enjoying you.

# Indexes

*Index of Selections*

*Index of Topics*

# Index of Selections

# Index of Topics

Actor, 3, 4, 5, 8
Affricates, 158
    see also Consonants
Allusion, 66
Alphabet, phonetic, 154 ff.
Analogy, 66 f.
Analyses of meaning, 8
Anger, 255, 273 f.
Anthologies, use of, 8
Appearance, 104 f.
Art, growth in, 7
Articulation, 7
Artistic performance, 10
Art of interpretation, 7
Aspirate, 168
    see also Consonants
Assimilation
    defined, 14
    exercises in, 17 ff.
    and feeling, 15 f.
    fundamental process in interpreta-
        tion, 6
    necessity for, 48
    not automatic, 8
Audience
    embarrassment of, 55
    as listener, 53 ff.
    role of, 54 f., 57
Author, 49 ff., 304

Background
    of author, 49 f.
    of selection, 50
Behavior, see Physical behavior
Believability, 14
Biographical details, 49 f.
Breathiness, 248
Breathing, exercises in, 144
"Building," 87

Cause and effect, see Organization
Clarity, necessary in interpreter's mate-
    rials, 298

Climactic order, see Organization
Climax
    control of technique, 286
    definition, 283
    judgment in choosing technique, 286
    major, 285
    rhythm of, 283, 285
    and transition, 286
    types of, 283 ff.
Colloquial speech, see Dialects
Communication
    functions of body in, 105 f.
    interacting process of, 2 f.
    skill in, 9
    through physical behavior, 105
Communicative arts, 1 ff.
Comparison, see Analogy and Simile
Concentration, 119 f.
Conclusion, 76
Condensation, 77 f.
Connotation, 62 f.
Consonants, 163 ff.
    affricates, 158, 184
    aspirate, 168
    continuant, 163, ff., 166
    fricatives, 158, 163, 190
    nasal, 156 f., 164, 167, 176 ff., 179
        ff.
    plosives, 157, 163, 164, 166, 167,
        183 f., 185 f.
Context, 50 f.
Continuant, 166
    see also Consonants
Continuity in phrasing, 40 ff., 44
Copyrights, 299, 305
Crying, 270 f.
Cutting, 305 f.

Deemphasis, 91
    see also Emphasis
Denotation, 61 f.
Dialects
    colloquial, 199, 202

316